Prescribed by the University of Delhi
for the B.A. (Pass) Stream B Course in English
I year

Developing Language Skills I

Oral Communication and Reading Comprehension, Writing Skills, and Workbook

Board of Editors

S C SOOD (Coordinator)
MITA BOSE
NARESH JAIN
GOPAL KRISHAN
SUDESH SAWHNEY
MANJIT S SINGH
SHEELA SRIVASTAVA
VINOD SRIVASTAVA
PROMODINI VARMA

MANOHAR
2016

First published 1991 by
Spantech Publishers Pvt Ltd
Second impression 1991

Third impression by
Ajay Kumar Jain for
Manohar Publishers & Distributors
4753/23 Ansari Road, Daryaganj
New Delhi 110 002

Twelfth impression 2016

ISBN 81-7304-185-7

Cover design and illustrations by Ajit Edwin

Designed and set by Spantech Publishers Pvt Ltd
Printed at Salasar Imaging Systems

Contents

Book III: Workbook

Editors' Note

The aim of this book is to help students develop some basic language skills. It concentrates on giving them proficiency in three major areas: oral communication, reading comprehension and written communication. It is also meant to enable students to acquire study skills.
The materials have been chosen keeping in view the needs of the average learner. They have also been graded. But teachers should feel free to adapt them or devise their own materials to suit the requirements of their students.

This being a learner-centred course, there is little scope in it for lecture-type teaching. Most of the work is required to be done by learners themselves rather than by the teacher, whose essential task would be to facilitate learning. A great deal of emphasis has been laid on pair/group work, role playing, problem solving exercises and simulation activities. This will involve rearranging the traditional classroom, with the teacher moving freely among the pairs/groups and acting as moderator and supervisor. The primary aim is to provide a meaningful and interesting context in which language learning can take placc

This volume consists of three books:

Book I: Oral Communication and Reading Comprehension
Book II: Writing Skills
Book III: Workbook

Book I consists of three parts. The first two are devoted to oral communication and the third to reading comprehension. The emphasis in this book is on fluency rather than accuracy, i.e. students are encouraged to speak in English, no matter how broken, to boost their confidence. At this stage it would not be desirable to correct their grammatical mistakes unless communication is seriously impaired. The first part of this book, 'Games', is meant to provide the teacher ideas and suggestions for fluency exercises and no testing will take place based on this section of the book.

The second part, 'Speech Patterns', deals with the functional use of language. At the beginning of each unit are listed a set of formulas that can be used in certain social situations to perform definite functions. They are grouped under three headings: 'Formal', 'Informal' and 'Anytime/Anywhere'. Under 'Formal' are listed formulas used in speaking to people older than us in age or superior in position or even strangers, in official or semiofficial circumstances on matters that are important or serious in a business-like manner. 'Informal' lists formulas used in speaking to friends, colleagues and equals on everyday matters in everyday situations in an informal manner. 'Anytime/Anywhere' lists formulas that can safely be used in either formal or informal situations as well as intermediate situations. To be able to select which formulas to use where, students should be made aware of the social parameters that govern the use of language. For instance, though in English thanks and regrets are expressed far more frequently than in Indian languages, a formal pattern of speech is no longer necessary when speaking to parents or older people who are close to us, as it is in the Indian languages. The difference between talking to friends and talking to parents, etc., is conveyed more through tone rather than words.

The formulas, in which no internal correspondence between the list of functions and the list of responses is maintained, is followed by sample usages which show how the functional phrases can be used. Teachers and students should feel free to add to, and write their own samples. The tasks that follow the samples should be done orally and in pairs/groups unless otherwise stated. In longer conversations students can be given roles, allowed to discuss them with their partner/group and then asked to act out the situation. However, since testing on this section will necessarily have to take a written form, teachers are advised to give adequate practice to their students by asking them to write down their responses after the oral work is done. This holds true for the third part, 'Reading Comprehension', as well, where also all exercises should be done in pairs/groups and responses written down after the oral work is done. However, it should be pointed out here that testing will be of the skills taught and not based on the contents of the lessons.

The materials used in the third part are authentic and uncorrected. Teachers should point this out to students as and when necessary. Improvements and corrections of these materials can be another exercise, depending on the ability and the level of the class. To make the learning process more meaningful, we suggest that teachers hold tutorials or occasional classes in which students can bring letters, notices, newspaper reports or any other materials which they have come across in their reading outside the classroom and which they have not understood. Groups can be formed to deal with the problem with the teacher acting as moderator and guide.

Book II teaches written communication. Writing is a skill like any other and can be systematically taught and learnt. A writing task involves both language proficiency and writing skills. This book lays emphasis on the *process* of writing rather than on the final product. Accordingly, the wide variety of activities provided aim at training learners in handling the different stages involved in this process.

The units are graded from simple activities to more difficult ones. The attempt has been mainly to avoid giving a model. Students are instead expected to work on their own, or more frequently, with the help of their peers. All units are based on the following sequence of activities:

1 Getting ideas by brainstorming and discussion.
2 Writing ideas down in note form.
3 Organizing ideas.
4 Preparing a first draft.
5 Improving the draft.
6 Writing the final draft.
7 Exchanging the writing with a partner and commenting on it.

Book III is a workbook which has been designed to complement and supplement the work of the first two books. It contains activities and exercises that are meant to provide further practice in oral communication and the skills and subskills needed for language learning. Hence, exercises have been designed to give students practise in:

1 Vocabulary building.
2 Use of lexical and grammatical cohesion.
3 Discourse markers and linking devices.
4 Skimming, scanning and predicting.
5 Understanding the nature of written communication.

In the final section some attempt has been made to teach grammar in context through tasks and activities, although much of it is also traditional. This section is meant to provide practise in problem areas in language usage where students need special remedial help.

Acknowledgements

The editors and publishers are grateful to the following copyright owners for permission to reproduce texts, photographs and illustrations. Every endeavour has been made to contact copyright owners and apologies are expressed for any omissions.

p. 46: Cartoon by Ajit from *Target*, Living Media India Ltd, July 1987
p. 47: *Times of India*, Bennett, Coleman & Co Ltd, 16 Aug 1987
pp. 49–51: *Destination India*, Cross Section Publications Pvt Ltd, April 1987
p. 52: Petroleum Conservation Research Association for their advertisement
pp. 58–9: *Oxford Advanced Dictionary of Current English* by A S Hornby, OUP, ELBS edn of 3rd edn, 1974
p. 60: *Target*, Living Media India Ltd, Sept 1986
p. 61: *Times of India*, Bennett, Coleman & Co Ltd, 15 Aug 1947
p. 63: *Times of India*, Bennett, Coleman & Co Ltd, 26 July 1987
p. 66: *The Select Nonsense of Sukumar Ray*, trans Sukanta Chaudhury, OUP, 1987
p. 68: Ramesh Kapoor
p. 86: 'The Portrait of a Lady' from *The Collected Short Stories* by Khushwant Singh, Ravi Dayal Publisher, 1990
p. 112: National Literacy Mission for their advertisement
p. 113: Times Eye Research Foundation for their advertisement
p. 134: Himachal Pradesh Tourism Development Corporation Ltd, The Spastics Society of Northern India and New Delhi YMCA for their advertisements
p. 149–50: 'The Electronics Revolution' by Philip H Abelson & Allen L Hammond, *Span*, July 1979
p. 150–1: *Aesop's Fables*, Ward Lock and Co Ltd, 1962
p. 152: *The Wisdom Stories* by J Maurus, St Paul Publications, 1976
p. 154: 'King Gold' from *Target*, Living Media India Ltd, 11 Nov 1990
p. 155: *Aesop's Fables*, Ward Lock and Co Ltd, 1962
p. 156: *Challenge to Think* by Christine Frank, Mario Rinvolucri and Marge Berer, OUP, 1982
p. 157: *The Wisdom Stories* by J Maurus, St Paul Publications, 1976
p. 158: 'A Living Museum Needs to Grow' by Manini Chatterjee, *Span*, Nov 1983
pp. 162–4: Photographs by Sondeep Shankar
p. 165: *Aesop's Fables*, Ward Lock and Co Ltd, 1962
pp. 167–9: 'My Greatest Olympic Prize' by Jesse Owens
pp. 170–2: 'My Financial Career' from *Literary Lapses* by Stephen Leacock, Penguin, rpt 1939
pp. 173–4: *Times of India*, Bennett, Coleman & Co Ltd, 9 July 1987
pp. 176–7: *Hindustan Times*, The Hindustan Times Ltd, 19 Feb 1987
pp. 178–9: 'The Priest and the Mulberry Tree' by T L Peacock
pp. 179–80: 'The Atheist and the Acorn' by Anne, Countess of Winchilsea

Till the final proof stage the copyright permission for some of the above had not arrived. However, payments will be made as soon as the copyright owners respond.

BOOK I

Oral Communication and Reading Comprehension

Sudesh Sawhney
Manjit S Singh
Promodini Varma

Oral Communication: Games

UNIT 1 CONFIDENCE BUILDING EXERCISES

1 The teacher begins by introducing himself: 'My name is Sudesh. I'm Sudesh Sawhney.' He then asks one of the students, 'What's your name?' The teacher then writes on the blackboard: 'My name is .... What's yours?'

He subsequently asks a student in the first row to introduce herself to the student next to her by saying either, 'My name is ....' or 'I'm ....' and then asking for her neighbour's name by saying, 'What's yours?' The second student then introduces himself to his neighbour on the other side and asks her for her name. This may be allowed to go on till each one in the class has introduced herself/himself and has asked for her/his neighbour's name.

2 The teacher calls one of the students to the dais. He then says, 'I'm Sudesh' and, pointing to the student, says 'This is Divya.' He then turns towards the class and asks one of the students, 'What's your name?' After he gets the answer, he writes on the blackboard, 'I'm .... This is .... What's your name?'

Students can be asked to practice this in a chain drill. The first student on the first bench introduces the third student on the bench to the second student and asks her for the third's name. Next the second student introduces the fourth student to the third and asks for the fourth's name. In this way the drill goes on:

Student 1 (ANURAG) : Salma, this is Supriya. Who is she?
Student 2 (SALMA) : She is Supriya. Supriya, this is Philip. Who is he?
Student 3 (SUPRIYA) : He is Philip. Philip, this is Harpreet. Who is he?
Student 4 (PHILIP) : He is Harpreet. . . .

How this drill proceeds is shown in Exercises 3, 4 and 5.*

3 Student 1 to 2 : My name is Anurag Kumar. I live in Janakpuri. Where do you live?
Student 2 to 1 : I'm Salma. I live in Greater Kailash.
Student 2 to 3 : I'm Salma. I live in Greater Kailash. Where do you live?

*The teacher can think of many items which he can use as material for chain drilling. The idea is to build up the learners' confidence so that they begin to speak in English.

4 Student 1 to 3 : (Pointing to student 2)
This is Salma. She lives in Greater Kailash.

Student 2 to 4 : (Pointing to student 3)
This is .... She lives in ....

5 Student 1 : I have two brothers and one sister. How many do you have?
Student 2 : I have one brother and no sister. How many do you have?
Student 3 : I have one brother and two sisters. He has two brothers and one sister. How many do you have?

6 The teacher tells the class that he will whisper a message to the first student on the first bench. That student will whisper the same message to the next one and that one to the next and so on till the message reaches the last student who then speaks it out loud. The message has to be passed on quickly and under no circumstances is the message to be repeated to the same student. S/he simply passes on what s/he hears. If s/he has not been able to catch the message s/he must invent her/his own. Finally, the class can try and discover where and how the distortions in the original message took place.

UNIT 2 INTERVIEWING AND QUESTIONING

1 Arrange the students into pairs. Each student has to interview her/his partner and find out her/his name, age, hobbies, favourite subject, where s/he lives and how many brothers and sisters s/he has. Then, each student comes up in turn and speaks at least five sentences on the person he has interviewed. The teacher could write out sentences like, 'Her name is .... She lives in .... She has .... She likes ....' on the blackboard before the class starts.

2 Each student finds out from her/his partner three things that could not be guessed about that person simply by looking at him/her.

3 Divide students into groups of seven or eight. Let each group prepare a set of five questions that they would like to ask the teacher (e.g. 'How long have you been teaching? Are you married? How many children do you have? Where did you get your education?' etc.). The leader of the group stands up and asks the questions. All group leaders that come later must see to it that they do not repeat questions that have already been asked. The teacher may or may not answer all the questions just as s/he may have done in real life.

4 Form students into groups of six or seven. Let them prepare a set of ten questions that they would ask Sunil Gavaskar (or Amrita Pritam or J R D Tata) if they could interview him.

UNIT 3 GUESSING GAMES

1 The teacher thinks of a person, place or thing. The class has to guess what it is by asking questions that can be answered only with a 'Yes' or a 'No'. One student comes up as a moderator. Students put up their hands to ask questions, the moderator

decides who will speak. Only 20 questions are allowed. The teacher puts questions like the following on the blackboard before the class begins:

Is it living?	Is it dead?
Is it male?	Is it female?
Is s/he an Indian?	Is it an animal?

After the first 20 questions a student can replace the teacher and the game goes on.

2 The students could be divided into groups and a map given to each group. In each group one person is asked to think of a river or a mountain or a city or a lake or a desert, etc. The other members of the group are asked to guess what the first student has thought of by asking her/him not more than ten questions. The questions have to be Yes/No type questions, i.e. questions which can be answered only with a 'Yes' or 'No'.

3 This game can be played by the whole class or by small groups in a large class. One student is asked to come and mime some everyday actions in front of the group or class. The other students have to guess what the first student has mimed. The students are allowed not more than three guesses for each item. This sort of game could be made more interesting by dividing the class or group into teams and awarding points for correct guesses. If the correct guess is made in the first attempt three points are awarded, if the correct guess is made in the second attempt two points are given and if the correct guess is made in the third attempt only one point is given. Whichever team gets the highest number of points wins the game.

4 The teacher can prepare slips of paper each having the name of a famous person on it, like Kapil Dev, Indira Gandhi, P T Usha, etc. He pins one slip on the back of each student. The student then has to find out who s/he is. S/he goes around asking the others simple Yes/No questions to help her/him find out who s/he is. Once a student finds out who s/he is s/he can ask for another slip. Each student is allowed to ask one question per student in large groups and two or three questions in small groups or as decided by the teacher.

UNIT 4 CHOOSING AND JUSTIFYING

1 The teacher lists the following items on the blackboard: a match box, a newspaper, a transistor, a small tent, a road map of the Kumaon hills, a packet of biscuits, a sleeping bag, a piece of jewellery, a pair of binoculars, an extra pair of socks, a camera, a picture of a goddess, a 20 metre roll of nylon rope, a jungle knife, a pack of playing cards, a first-aid kit, a compass, a badminton racket, a plastic bucket, etc.

The teacher tells the class that they are going trekking from Nainital to Ranikhet. The class is divided into groups for this purpose. Each group can select only ten items from the above list to take on the trek. The group has to discuss and arrive at a consensus on the items it would like to carry.

The list of each group is put on the board and the items common to all groups are scored out. The group leaders then have to explain why they wanted to take the other items included in their lists.

2 There is a devastating fire in your area. Your house too is in serious danger of being burnt down. You cannot carry more than five items out of your house before it catches fire. Which items would you like to carry out? Justify your choice.

The class may be divided into groups and each group may imagine itself to be a family. They can then discuss which five items the family considers most important to be taken out before the fire spreads to the house. Remember that it is easier for the family together to take out heavier items than for an individual to do so.

UNIT 5 EXERCISING THE IMAGINATION

1 The teacher puts up two lists on the blackboard. List 1 consists of persons/living beings and List 2 consists of things. For example:

List 1	*List 2*
dog teacher postman cat	safety pin hanky pen scooter

The class is divided into two or four teams. The teams face each other. Then a member from Team A picks one item from List 1 and one item from List 2 and puts a question to the other team, e.g. 'What can a dog do with a hanky?' Team B has to suggest three things that can be done (plausible or fantastic) and it gets three points for actually doing so. Then Team B can take its turn and Team A has to suggest three things within two minutes. After each team has had five turns the scores are compared and the team that has the highest score wins. No item can be used more than two times and the same combination cannot be repeated.

UNIT 6 TELLING A STORY

1 The teacher tells a short story to the class. The class makes notes on the story. But before s/he tells the story to the class the teacher sends three to five students out of the class. When s/he finishes telling the story (twice if the class so desires) the teacher calls in one of the students sent out earlier. This student can ask anyone of the students to tell her/him the story told by the teacher to the class. In turn, this student can call in anyone of the other students, still outside, and tell her/him the story. In turn s/he calls in yet another student and tells the story and so on till all the students have come in.

The students in the class are asked by the teacher now to comment on the retelling of the story by the various students and to point out what (if any) changes took place in the story and who (i.e. which student) brought in the change/changes. This activity can be repeated or preceded by jokes, short poems, etc., as material to be retold.

2 The teacher tells the class that they will write a story together. Each student can contribute only one line but s/he can do it when they like. The teacher writes the first sentence on the blackboard: 'Once upon a time there was a king.' After that the students continue. Each student must take into account or build on what the others before her/him have said. When the story is ready, students can copy it down and rewrite or edit it for homework.

3 This activity is meant for a small group. The teacher writes a story—each sentence on a separate strip of paper. Each student receives one strip. The students must memorize their sentences in two minutes and then return the slips to the teacher. No one is to look at the others' sentences. After the strips have been collected, the students get together as a group and decide upon the correct sequence of the sentences. The teacher refuses to answer any questions till the sequence is decided upon. Afterwards a discussion can be held on how easy or difficult the task was or how the story could be changed by changing the sequence of the sentences.

UNIT 7 ROLE PLAYING

1 One of the members of a group is asked to play the role of a dietician who is gathering information about the eating habits of people in her/his neighbourhood. The other members of the group act as neighbours. The teacher tells the surveyor that s/he must introduce herself/himself to the neighbour, apologize for bothering her/him, tell him/her why s/he has come and then seek information on her/his eating habits. S/he then must thank the neighbour and go on to the next person. Students can take turns. Each student must visit at least three neighbours.

Each surveyor must take down notes on a survey sheet that s/he carries with her/him. The questions asked could take into account food items, drinks, fruits, etc.

Other subjects to be surveyed could be: what people read in their leisure time; what language people speak at home; what other languages they would like to learn; what they would like to do when they grow up; their attitude towards the different subjects they study; their attitude towards working women, etc.

Here is an example of a survey sheet:

Sl. No.	*Name*	*Breakfast*	*Lunch*	*Dinner*	*Snacks*
(*i*)	Yasmin	Bread Butter Egg Milk	Dal Rice Vegetable Curds	Chapati Vegetable Salad Fruits	Tea Biscuits
(*ii*)					
(*iii*)					

2 The teacher describes a problem situation to the class. A young housewife, Maya, wants to take up a job. Her husband does not mind, but he himself has a demanding job and cannot help with the housework. The couple's little son does not want his mother to start working because he feels he will be neglected. Maya's mother-in-law, a working woman, encourages Maya also to take up a job. Maya's mother is a conservative housewife and feels that her daughter's first duty is towards her husband and family.

The teacher assigns to four students the roles of husband, mother, mother-in-law and child. Each of these can pick three or four other students to discuss their role with. After five minutes of discussion each role-player comes up and talks about the way s/he feels about the situation. The rest of the class can then decide what Maya should do.

Oral Communication: Speech Patterns

UNIT 1 STARTING A CONVERSATION: GREETINGS AND ASKING AFTER

Starting a conversation—even if brief and meant only to establish contact—normally involves two steps: greeting others and asking after their well-being. The formulas for these are fixed and usually carry no literal meaning. We say 'Good morning' even if it is not a good morning, and the answer to 'How are you?' is normally 'Fine, thanks' even if we are not feeling all that fine. Greetings are generally returned in the same form with a slightly different intonation. It is well to remember that questions of well-being are not genuine questions and require a fixed response: no one, except close friends *really* wants to know all about our troubles.

1 Greetings

Informal	*Anytime/Anywhere*	*Formal*
Hello!	Morning/Afternoon/ Evening!	Good morning!
Hi (everybody/ everyone/Bulbul)!	Good to see you (again)! How (very) nice to see you (again)!	Good afternoon (sir/ma'am)! (from 12 noon to end of working day)
Hi there (everybody/ everyone/Bulbul)!	What a pleasure to see you!	Good evening (gentlemen)! (6 p.m. onwards)
Long time no see!		
What a pleasant surprise!		

2 Responses

Informal	*Anytime/Anywhere*	*Formal*
Hi!	Morning/Afternoon/ Evening!	Good morning/afternoon/ evening, (sir/ma'am)!
Hello!		
Yes, long time no see!		

3 Asking after

Informal	*Anytime/Anywhere*	*Formal*
How's life (treating you)?	How are you?	I trust you're keeping well.
What's new/ the latest?	How are you keeping?	I hope all goes well with you.

Informal	*Anytime/Anywhere*	*Formal*
How's things?	Ah, Mr Anand! Are you well?	
How are things with you?	Are you better now? (after someone has been ill)	
How're you doing?		
How's it going?		

4 Responses

Informal	*Anytime/Anywhere*	*Formal*
OK, thanks.	Fine, thanks.	(I'm) Very well, thank you.
So-so, thanks.	I'm fine, thank you. And how are you?	(I'm) Very well indeed, thank you.
Nothing much.	Quite well, thank you.	I'm in excellent health, thank you.
Not (too) bad.	All right, thanks.	
Fine. How about you?		
Fine. And you?		

Samples

1 **A** : Hello, Imran! How are you?
B : Fine, thanks.

2 **A** : What a pleasure to see you Mr Wagle! How are you keeping?
B : Not bad. How about you? How's life treating you these days?

3 **A** : Hi, Vikram! Coming to the English class?
B : Oh, hello! Yeah.

4 **A** : Hello, Anju! Just the person I was looking for.
B : Hello, Sushil! What can I do for you?

5 **A** : Good morning, sir!
B : Good morning, Vikram! I didn't see you in class yesterday. Are you keeping well?
A : Yes sir, thank you very much.

6 **A** : Hello, Mrs Sharma! How are you?
B : I'm well, thank you doctor.

7 **A** : Good morning, Mr Singh! I trust you're keeping well?
B : I'm very well indeed, thank you Mr Chairman.

8 **A** : Hello, Rani! How're you doing?
B : Fine. And you?

Tasks

1 One morning in college you meet the following people at the following times and places. How will you greet them? How would they greet you and what would be your response?

Place	*Time*	*Person*
College compound	10 a.m.	Your friend Rakesh
Staff-room	10.30 a.m.	Your English teacher
Principal's room	12.00 noon	Your college principal
Verandah	2.30 p.m.	Your classmate's mother
Cafeteria	3.00 p.m.	An old schoolmate
College gate	6.00 p.m.	Your sports teacher
Sports field	6.15 p.m.	Your team-mates

2 A young employee greets the managing director of his company, whom he is meeting for the second time, saying:

'Hi, Rahul! Long time no see.'

The managing director is not at all pleased. Why?

3 You have gone to see your uncle who has been admitted to a hospital. Your uncle introduces you to Mr Wagle, the patient on the next bed. You wish to enquire politely after Mr Wagle's health. Which of the following will you say to him:

(*a*) In good shape, are you?
(*b*) How are you feeling now?
(*c*) How's life?
(*d*) I hope you're keeping well.
(*e*) Hey! How are you?
(*f*) Are you OK?

4 Match the response to the greeting in the following table:

Greeting	*Response*
(*i*) Hi, Kiran! Long time no see.	(*a*) Very well, thank you, sir.
(*ii*) Good morning, Mr Basu! I hope everything goes well with you.	(*b*) I'm very well indeed, thank you.
(*iii*) Its great to see you again. So, how's life?	(*c*) Hello, Rani! Everything all right, I hope?
(*iv*) Hello, Mala! Just the person I was looking for.	(*d*) Hello, Geeta! I've been staying at my aunt's for the last couple of weeks.
(*v*) Hello, Mr Gupta! And how are you keeping?	(*e*) Fine, thanks. And how are you doing?

5 Given below is a list of persons and their roles/relationships to others in the list. If these persons were to greet each other, what greeting would they use and what response would they get?

(*a*) Mr L D Bhatia, principal of the college.
(*b*) Mr I K Mohanty, chairman of the college.
(*c*) Mrs Fatima Ahmed, English teacher.
(*d*) Mr Imtiaz Ahmed, Mrs Ahmed's husband, and Mr Bhatia's neighbour.
(*e*) Rakesh Rai, clerk in the college.
(*f*) Gita, student.
(*g*) Sheila, Gita's friend.

UNIT 2 INTRODUCING ONESELF AND OTHERS

It is always good to introduce people who do not or may not know each other, so that misunderstandings may be avoided. Sometimes, when we are with strangers or want to start a conversation with someone we don't know, we may also need to introduce ourselves. When introducing others, we must also provide information about the person being introduced so that a conversation can be started. In more formal situations, it is always the younger person who is presented to the older, the man to the woman and the junior to the senior or superior. Men usually shake hands on being introduced; women may or may not, the choice is theirs. The standard greetings on introduction, 'How do you do', or 'Pleased to meet you', usually accompanied by a handshake, are *always* answered with 'How do you do', and 'Pleased to meet you', respectively. When addressing people by their first names we do not use a title (Miss, Ms, Mrs, Mr). If you do want to add the title always use the surname. So Girish Wagle will either be addressed as 'Girish' or 'Mr Wagle', but *never* as 'Mr Girish'.

1 Introducing yourself

Informal	*Anywhere/Anytime*	*Formal*
Hi! I'm Mukul Ray.	Hello, I'm Mukul Ray.	Good morning. I'm Mukul Ray.
Hello, you must be Kiran. I'm Mukul.	How do you do? (shaking hands) My name is Mukul.	May I introduce myself? I'm Mukul Ray, Regional Sales Manager, Vishal Enterprises.
Excuse me, you're Kiran, aren't you? I'm Mukul.	Excuse me, my name is Mukul Ray.	I'd like to introduce myself. I'm Mukul Ray.
Aren't you Mukul? I'm Kiran. Remember me?	Excuse me. I don't think we've met before. My name is Mukul.	Allow me to introduce myself. I'm Mukul Ray.
	I'm afraid I don't know/remember your name. I'm Mukul.	
	Good morning. This is/I'm Mukul speaking (on phone).	

2 Introducing others

Informal	*Anywhere/Anytime*	*Formal*
Kiran, meet Mukul.	This is Mukul. I'd like you to meet Mukul.	Good morning Mr Sahni. May I introduce Mr Lal, our new Marketing Manager?
Kiran, this is Mukul,	Have you met/ Do you know Mukul?	Let me introduce our new Marketing Manager, Mr Lal.
By the way, do you know each other?	Kiran, Mukul. Mukul, Kiran.	It gives me great pleasure to introduce (to you) this evening's guest/speaker, Mr Lal.

3 Responding to introductions

Informal	*Anywhere/Anytime*	*Formal*
Hi/Hello!	How do you do?	It's a great pleasure to meet you.
Hello, how do you do?	Nice meeting you.	Delighted to meet you.
Hi/Hello, I'm Kiran.	Pleased to meet you.	I'm very glad to meet you.
Yes, I'm/It is.	I've been eager to meet you.	
Yes, I am. I'm Kiran. Nice meeting you.		
I'm not Kiran. I'm Kavita.		
I'm Meena. Good to meet you.		

Samples

1 **A** : Hi, I'm Meera. Are you also in the first year?
  B : Hello, I'm Kiran. Yes I am. I'm doing Economics Honours.

2 **A** : Pardon me, your name is Meera, isn't it?
  B : Yes it is. Have we met before?

3 **A** : Excuse me. I don't think we've met before. I'm Meera.
  B : No, we haven't. I'm Kiran. Glad to meet you.

4 **A** : Hello. Is that Meera speaking? I'm Kiran. How are you? Haven't heard from you for ages.

5 **A** : Hello. Is that the Maya Book Depot? May I speak to Mr Natarajan, please? I'm Meera Lal speaking.

6 **A** : Good morning, class. Let me introduce myself. I'm Mrs Varma, the new English teacher and I shall meet you four times a week.

7 **A** : Ladies and gentlemen, this evening I would like to introduce to you the

Chairman of Vishal Enterprises, Mr S C Shukla. Mr Shukla will talk to us about marketing strategies.

Tasks

1 On the first day of college, how will you introduce yourself to:

(*a*) your fellow students in the class?
(*b*) your English teacher?
(*c*) an old schoolmate whom you have seen often but have never been very friendly with?

2 How will you introduce your new friend Meera, who has come to your house for the first time, to:

(*a*) your mother?
(*b*) your brother/sister?
(*c*) your aunt who is visiting you?

3 Complete this dialogue.

Mukul : Hey, Sumit. Have you met Manik before?
Sumit : ....
Manik : How do you do?

4 **Kiran** : Meera, this is Divya. Divya, Meera.
Meera : Hello, how are you?
Divya : Fine, thanks. How are you?

Is Kiran's introduction formal or informal? Say why.

5 On your way to the market with your parents, you run into your teacher. They have not met before. How will you introduce them?

6 Your friend Susheel, a senior, is standing for election to the post of college president. He comes to address your class. Introduce him to the class before he starts his election speech.

7 On college day, you are introduced to the chief guest, Mr Naresh Kumar Pandey. Which of the following would you choose to address him with:

(*a*) Hello, Naresh!
(*b*) Hi, Mr Pandey!
(*c*) How do you do, Mr Pandey?
(*d*) Pleased to meet you, Mr Pandey.
(*e*) It's an honour to meet you, Mr Pandey.

Give reasons why you would reject the other responses.

8 When would you say this:

'Allow me to introduce Mr Abid Ali, President, Rotary Club.'

(*a*) to your friend at a party in his house?
(*b*) to another member of the Rotary Club who is attending the Rotary Club meeting for the first time?
(*c*) to a friend you meet at the airport where you have gone to receive Mr Ali?

9 Outside the college staff-room you overhear a conversation between Mr Bhatia, Mrs Ahmed and Mr Takahashi, a professor from Japan. Mr Takahashi is saying, 'Pleased to meet you, Mrs Ahmed'. What had Mr Bhatia said to Mr Takahashi and what will Mrs Ahmed say to him?

UNIT 3 THANKING, WISHING WELL, APOLOGIZING AND EXCUSING

In English, we express gratitude and apologies far more frequently than we do in the Indian languages. We thank people not only for gifts and favours but also for offers of help, compliments, wishes of good luck and success and when others ask after us. More formally, when leaving a party or formal gathering, we thank the hostess and host for having invited us. We express our thanks for services that others may have done us.

Apologies are offered when we have done something socially unacceptable or when we have caused annoyance or inconvenience to others. The more serious the offence, the more formal is the apology. In English, we also use the phrases of regret 'I'm afraid' or 'I'm sorry' before giving bad news or before refusing to do something others expected or asked us to do. When in the middle of a conversation or gathering we have suddenly to attend to something or someone else, or when we interrupt others we must excuse ourselves so that others are not offended.

1 Thanking

Informal	*Anytime/Anywhere*	*Formal*
Thanks.	Thank you (very much/ indeed).	You've been so/very kind.
Many thanks.	You're most kind.	I'm most/extremely grateful to you.
Thanks a lot (for ....).	It's very good of you.	I'm much/extremely obliged to you.
That was/It's really nice of you.	It's most kind of you.	I really don't know how to thank you.
	I'm obliged (to you)./ I'm really obliged to you for	I really can't thank you enough.
		I should like to express my gratitude for ....

2 Responding to thanks

Informal	*Anytime/Anywhere*	*Formal*
(You're) Welcome.	Not at all.	Delighted to help.
It's OK.	It's a pleasure.	Glad to be of (some) service.
That's all right.	(It was) My pleasure.	It was the least I could do.
Anytime.	(Please) Don't mention it.	The pleasure was mine.
	It's no trouble at all.	
	Thank you.	

3 Wishing good luck and wishing well

Informal	*Anytime/Anywhere*	*Formal*
Good luck.	Best of luck.	Let me wish you good luck/all the best.
Enjoy yourself/ yourselves.	All the best.	May you do well/ succeed/prosper.
Have fun.	I hope you have a good journey.	I wish you success (in ....).
	Have a nice time/holiday/ journey.	Have a good day.
	(I) Wish you all the best.	
Hope things go well.	I wish you luck.	

4 Responding to good wishes

Informal	*Anytime/Anywhere*	*Formal*
Thanks.	Thank you.	It's very kind of you.
Many thanks.	Thank you very much.	It's very nice of you to wish me so.
Same to you.	Good luck to you too.	
And you.		

5 Apologizing

Informal	*Anytime/Anywhere*	*Formal*
Sorry about that, my fault.	Sorry/Very sorry.	I beg your pardon (for ....).
	I'm sorry to/to be/ to have	I (do/must) apologize (for ....).
	I'm really very/terribly/ awfully sorry.	Please forgive me (for ....).
		Please (do) accept my apologies (for ....).
		I'm sorry, it was entirely my fault.

6 Responses to apologies

Informal	*Anytime/Anywhere*	*Formal*
It's/That's OK.	That's (quite) all right.	It's/That's perfectly all right.
Forget it.	Not at all.	There's no reason/need to.
No problem.	Please don't worry.	

Informal	Anytime/Anywhere	Formal
What for!	It really doesn't matter (at all).	It's really not necessary.
Let's forget it.		
It's not your fault.		

7 Excusing oneself

Informal	Anytime/Anywhere	Formal
Sorry.	(Please) Excuse me.*	Pardon me.*
I'm sorry.	Excuse me. Could I ....?	I beg your pardon.
	Will you excuse me for a minute please.	May I be excused for/from ....

8 Responses to excuses

Informal	Anytime/Anywhere	Formal
That's OK.	Of course.	You're excused.
It's all right.		You may be excused.

Samples

1 **A** : May I borrow your book for the weekend, please?
B : Yes, of course.
A : Thanks a lot. It's very nice of you.

2 **A** : Many thanks for the lovely birthday present.
B : Not at all. I hope you liked it.

3 **A** : Here's some tea for you, Rani.
B : Thanks a lot. That's just what I needed.

4 **A** : Congratulations, Kiran. You've done very well in the exams.
B : Thank you very much, sir. I'm grateful to you for having taken so much trouble with me.
A : Oh, that was nothing. It was your hard work, really, that has paid off.

5 **A** : Can I help carry your books Mrs Singh?
B : Oh that's very kind of you. Thank you very much.

6 **A** : We are extremely grateful to you, sir, for having taken time off your busy schedule to address our students this afternoon. We would also like to express our gratitude for the assurances that you have given us.
B : Thank you very much for the warm welcome you have given me. I am delighted to be here and to have been of some service to you. Thank you very much indeed.

* Also said immediately after acts like sneezing, yawning, hiccuping, etc.

7 **A** : Bye, Mom. I'm off to my friend's party.
B : Bye, Kapil. Enjoy yourself but be home by eleven o'clock.
A : Thanks Mom, I will.

8 **A** : Good luck with the exams, Neeta. Do well.
B : Thanks! I need the good wishes.

9 **A** : Hello, Neha! All the best to you in your new life.
B : Thank you very much. Meet my husband Jayant.
A : Hello! Congratulations.

10 **A** : Good luck, Kiran.
B : And to you too.

11 **A** : I wish you success in your new venture. May you do well and prosper in life.
B : Thank you very much, Mr Singh. It's very nice of you to wish me so.

12 **A** : Off for the vacations?
B : Yes, but I don't know if it'll be much of a vacation. I'm taking the kids on a trek to Pindari.
A : Well, good luck. I hope everything goes well.

13 **A** : I'm sorry we couldn't make it to your party. Our car broke down just as we were leaving.
B : What a pity. We did miss you a lot.

14 **A** : Oops, my fault! I didn't see you.
B : That's OK. I hope you aren't hurt.

15 **A** : Just a routine check, sir. We're sorry for the inconvenience.
B : That's all right.

16 **A** : I'm sorry about what I said. I didn't mean to hurt you.
B : Let's forget it, shall we?

17 **A** : I must apologize for my son's behaviour yesterday.
B : There's no need to, really.

Tasks

1 Supply the missing lines in the following dialogue:

A : Happy birthday Jasleen. Here's a small gift for you

....

B : Well, I hope it's of some use to you.

A : ....

2 By mistake you took your friend's book home. How will you apologize to her/him the next day?

3 You are late for your class by ten minutes because your bus broke down. How will you apologize to your teacher on entering class?

4 How will you thank your mother for the beautiful birthday gift you have received from her?

5 You promised to pick up your mother's clothes from the dry-cleaners but forgot. How will you apologize to her?

6 Which one of the following five expressions of gratitude would you use for your classmate and good friend as you leave her/his house after a dinner you have enjoyed very much? Explain your choice and state your reasons for rejecting the other four options:

(*a*) That was a lovely meal.
(*b*) It was really nice of you to have asked me.
(*c*) I am obliged to you for the dinner.
(*d*) I should like to express my gratitude for the excellent meal.
(*e*) Hey! That was great. Thanks a lot. I really enjoyed myself.

7 You have qualified to participate in an inter-college quiz competition and are leaving to take part in it. Your college principal, class teacher, best friend and a classmate whom you don't know very well wish you good luck. What would they say to you and how would you respond to each of them?

8 You are in a hurry and as you come round the corner you bump into someone and knock him down. What will you say to him?

9 'Thanks for everything. Take care of yourself, won't you?' Which of the following would be the correct response to the above?

(*a*) The pleasure was entirely mine.
(*b*) Why?
(*c*) Yes, of course. And you too.

10 You're not feeling well and don't want to take part in the NCC parade. How will you excuse yourself?

11 **A** : Mrs Wagle?
B : Yes?
A : Good morning, ma'am. I'm from ABC TV Ltd. I've come in response to your complaint about your TV set.
B : Please come in. I'm really dissatisfied with the set. It's broken down for the third time in two months.
A : I'm sorry to hear that. I'll see what I can do about it.

Read the above conversation and answer the following questions:

(*a*) Have A and B met before? How do you know?
(*b*) What is the relationship between A and B?
(*c*) Is A really sorry?
(*d*) What is the attitude of B towards A—friendly, angry or neutral?

Write a short dialogue between A and B after the TV set has been repaired.

UNIT 4 ASKING FOR AND GIVING INFORMATION

It is important to know how to ask for information politely and to thank people for it afterwards. 'Excuse me . . .' and 'please' are the two most important phrases in this unit. Informal questions can be asked directly, but in formal situations a longer 'preamble' to the question is used: 'I was wondering if you could tell me . . .' or 'I hope you don't mind my asking . . .'.

1 Asking for information

Informal	*Anytime/Anywhere*	*Formal*
Could anyone tell me ....?	Can/Could you tell me please, ...?	Sorry to trouble you, but ....?
Know (anything about) ....?	Excuse me. D'you know if/when/where/why/anything about ....?	Would you be kind enough to please ....?
Have you (got) any idea about ....?/ (Got) Any idea	D'you happen to know if/why/where/when/what/anything about ....?	I hope you don't mind my asking ....?
Any clue (to/about) ....?	I'd like to know ...., please.	I wonder if you could please tell me ....?
		Could you please give me any information about ....?

2 Responding to queries about information

Informal	*Anytime/Anywhere*	*Formal*
Yeah! Sure	Yes/Of course.	Definitely/Certainly/Gladly.
Er, yes/A bit.	Sure.	I shall be delighted to.
Why not?	I'm not sure, but	I'm afraid I don't have that information.
Sorry, I don't know.	I'm sorry, I don't know.	
Sorry, no idea.	I'm afraid I don't know anything/much about	
	I've no idea.	

Samples

1 **A** : Excuse me. Could you tell me the way to the library, please?
B : Sure. Go straight ahead and then turn left. There will be a large notice on the door.
A : Thanks.

2 **A** : Would you mind telling me when the next bus for Chandigarh leaves?
B : I'm sorry, I don't know. You'd better ask at the information counter.

3 **A** : Would you be kind enough to tell me where I could get my watch repaired?
B : Yes, certainly, sir. Here's a list of all our authorized dealers who will accept your watch for servicing and repair.

4 **A** : D'you happen to know where I left the car keys, Sheila?
B : I've no idea, dear.

5 **A** : I'd like to see the latest models you've got in television sets, please.
B : Definitely, sir. Please come this way.

6 **A** : Know anything about gems? I want to buy my wife a bracelet for her birthday.
B : I'm afraid I don't know much about precious stones. We could ask at the Government Emporium, though. They have a reliable jewellery shop.

7 **A** : Sorry to trouble you, but could you tell me if Mr Kapoor has vacated this flat?
B : I'm sorry, I don't know. Perhaps you could ask the lady upstairs. I'm new here.

Tasks

1 You are a new student in college and wish to apply for a change of subjects. You want to find out what you have to do. You ask different people such as:

(*a*) a senior student—in the canteen.
(*b*) your English teacher—at his home.
(*c*) the college clerk—in the office.
(*d*) the principal—in his office.

What will you say to each one?

2 You are new in Delhi and want to find the way from the New Delhi Railway Station to the ISBT by car. How will you ask the following people for directions:

(*a*) a stranger on the road.
(*b*) a woman at the bus-stop.
(*c*) a traffic policeman.

3 To whom would you say this:

'I wonder if you could tell me the principal's telephone number.'

(*a*) to your English teacher?
(*b*) to a fellow-student?
(*c*) to the president of the student's union?

Could you use it with the others as well? If not how would you reword the question in the two other contexts?

4 You are visiting Jaipur for the first time and want to find a good place to stay for a few days. How will you ask for this information from:

(*a*) your fellow passenger on the train to Jaipur?
(*b*) a stranger at the station?
(*c*) the Tourist Information Officer in Jaipur?

5 To whom would you say this:

'Didn't you know I was going to Bombay next Monday?'

(*a*) to your English teacher who wants to take an extra class on Monday?
(*b*) to a friend who has invited you and some other friends to dinner at his house next Monday?
(*c*) to the manager of a firm who has called you for an interview the following Monday?
(*d*) to your secretary who has fixed an appointment for you on Monday morning at eleven o'clock.

Why can't you say it to the others?

6 You have just bought a new VCR and don't know how to operate it. You go over to your neighbour's house to seek his help. He is not at home. You talk to his mother. Complete the conversation below:

You	:	Good morning, Mrs Sharma.
Mrs Sharma	:	Hello, Rahul! No, I'm afraid Sudhir isn't home.
You	:	....?
Mrs Sharma	:	He said he was going to visit Pradeep and then they would both sit and work in the library.
You	:	....?
Mrs Sharma	:	I couldn't say for sure, but he's usually home by six o'clock. Can I do anything to help?
You	:	I was wondering if Sudhir could take a look at my new VCR. I don't know how to operate it.
Mrs Sharma	:	....
You	:	....

7 You don't know where the local post office is. When a stranger asks you for directions to the post office, what will you say?

8 You have been rehearsing the annual play for sometime. One day, in the corridor, the college principal asks you when the play will be put up. Which of the following responses would you make and why:

(*a*) Don't know.
(*b*) I'm sorry sir, but, I don't know.
(*c*) Sorry, no idea.
(*d*) I wish I knew.
(*e*) Go and ask the English teacher

UNIT 5 OFFERS, REQUESTS AND ORDERS

When we request others to do something for us, or offer to do something ourselves, the use of the right words and the right tone are very important. If we are too abrupt or too aggressive, there is every possibility that the request will be turned down or the offer refused. The more formal the situation and the greater the favour requested, the more indirect the subject of the request. Though it might be all right to say, 'Excuse me, sir. Could you tell me the time, please?' to someone at the bus-stop, if you wanted to take a ride with your neighbour in his car you would have to be more indirect: 'I was wondering if you would be going via Connaught Place to your office tomorrow morning, Mr Singh? If it's not inconvenient, could you drop me off at Madras Hotel? I'll be ever so grateful.' It is also useful to know how to turn down offers and requests without giving offence.

There is very little difference between the way orders and requests are framed in English. Most orders are disguised as requests even when it is the older or the superior who gives the order. When the director of the company tells the typist, 'Miss Gomes, could you please have this report ready by lunch?' everyone concerned knows that it is an order even though the question form, typical of requests, has been used. In informal speech, normally the person asked to do something is not mentioned. The speaker begins with the action word straightaway.

1 Offers

Informal	Anytime/Anywhere	Formal
Here, have (some/another)	Can I ....?	May I help you?
Here, take (some/another/a bit of)	Shall I ....?	Perhaps I could help?
Do you want	Let me help you.	Would you care for .... ?
Like a	Would you like a ....?	May I be of assistance?
Please have/take/sit down	Is there anything I can do for you?	Could I be of any help/do something for you.
Need (some) help?	What will you have?	Do have ....
I'll do it/carry it/for you.	Is there anything you want/you'd like?	
Want a hand?		
How about		

2 Responding to offers: accepting and refusing

Informal	Anytime/Anywhere	Formal
Yes, thanks.	Yes, please.	I'd be delighted.
I'd love it/that.	Thank you (very much).	If you don't mind.
Lovely/Great/Terrific.	No, don't bother/worry (really).	I'd like that very much.
Just what I needed.	No, thank you (very much).	That's very/extremely kind of you.
No, its OK, thanks.	Thank you very much but	Please don't trouble yourself.
Thanks, but its OK.		
Thanks a lot, but		

3 Requests

Informal	Anytime/Anywhere	Formal
Got a ....?	Would/Could/Can you ...., please?	Do you think it would be possible to ....?
You haven't got .... have you?	Could I ask you to ....?	Would it be possible to ..?
Have a .... on you?	Do you/Would you mind ....?	If you could .... I'd be grateful.
	May I ...., please?	I shall be grateful if ....
	May I please have ....?	

4 Responding to requests: accepting and refusing

Informal	*Anytime/Anywhere*	*Formal*
Yes, sure.	Yes, of course.	Certainly.
Yes, all right.	Of course not.	Definitely.
Why not?	By all means.	I'd be delighted to.
Here (you are).	I'm sorry I don't/ can't	I'm afraid you can't/it's not possible/it's not allowed.
Sorry.		

5 Getting things done

Informal	*Anytime/Anywhere*	*Formal*
Give/Open/Sit/Get/ Do ...., please.	Could you please ....?	Would you be so kind as to ....?
	Would you/Will you ...., please?	I'd like you to ...., please.
	Would you mind .... ?	

6 Responding to orders

Generally, informal orders don't require a verbal response. But if necessary use the following:

Informal	*Anytime/Anywhere*	*Formal*
Yeah/Sure.	Yes, of course.	Yes, sir.
Right away.	Of course not.	Certainly, sir/ma'am.
In a minute.	I'm afraid that's not possible.	No, sir. That may not be possible.
Sorry		

Samples

1 **A** : Here, have a biscuit.
B : Thanks.

2 **A** : Excuse me, waiter. Can I have another glass of water, please?
B : Certainly, sir. I'll bring it in a moment.

3 **A** : Like another cup of tea?
B : No, thanks. I've had enough.

4 **A** : Want a hand with that heavy bag, miss?
B : Oh, thank you. That's very kind of you.

5 **A** : How about a cold drink? I'm thirsty.
B : Great! That would be lovely.

6 **A** : I'm driving down to Connaught Place. Is there anything I can do for you Mr Natrajan?

B : If you don't mind Mr Wasani, could you, please, pick up my coat from the dry-cleaners? Here's the receipt and the money.

7 A : Would you like me to type this letter for you, sir?
B : Yes, please. Could you do it immediately?

8 A : You seem very busy. Need some help?
B : Thanks a lot, but it's something I must do myself.

9 A : Got a match?
B : Here.

10 A : Have some change on you?
B : Sorry, man. Not a paisa on me.

11 A : Do you think it would be possible for the Chairman to see me tomorrow?
B : I'm afraid not. He's very busy this week.

12 A : Would you mind getting me another copy of this book, please?
B : I'm sorry, we don't have any more in stock.

13 A : I'd like to call a meeting of all the teachers of the English department on Wednesday at two o'clock. Please send out the letters immediately.
B : Certainly, sir.

14 A : Could you issue me these two books, please?
B : Sorry, the issuing counter closes at five o'clock.

15 A : Do answer the phone, Pooja. Its been ringing for the last minute or so.
B : Yes, Ma.

16 A : Give me another pair of scissors, will you? These seem to be rather blunt.
B : In a minute.

Tasks

1 You are at your friend's house. You are feeling thirsty. How will you ask for a glass of water from:

(*a*) your friend?
(*b*) his mother?
(*c*) his younger sister?

2 You and your friend are at the cinema. You have got two seats on either side of an old gentleman. He offers to change his seat so that you and your friend can sit together. Which of the following would you say to him:

(*a*) Just what we needed.
(*b*) Great!
(*c*) That's very kind of you, sir.

3 You've been on a round of visits and at each place you have had tea and snacks. You are now in Mrs Khan's house. She insists that you have a cup of tea. You have really had enough tea for the day. What will you say to Mrs Khan?

4 Your elderly neighbour is trying to push his car, the battery of which has run down. What do you say to him:

(*a*) Want a hand, Mr Sharma?
(*b*) May I be of assistance to you, Mr Sharma?
(*c*) Let me help you, Mr Sharma.

Had you met your father's boss in a similar situation, what would you have said?

5 You have been working at the house of a colleague who is rather new in the office. It is late and you are hungry. His wife offers you dinner. How will you accept?

6 As you get out of a taxi, you offer the driver a fifty rupee note. The driver does not have change. Neither do you. You ask a nearby panwallah, a cold drink kiosk owner and a chemist for change. The first two refuse. The chemist changes your money. Complete the conversation below:

Taxi Driver	:	I'm sorry, I don't have any change. Why don't you get it from one of the shopkeepers.
You to Panwallah	:	....
Panwallah	:	Sorry, I don't have any.
You to Cold Drink Kiosk Owner	:	....
Kiosk Owner	:	I'm sorry.
You to Chemist	:	....
Chemist	:	Yes, sure.
You	:	....
Chemist	:	You're welcome.

7 Mr Satpati, the Chief Accountant, wants to leave. He hasn't brought his car and wants the office clerk, Mr Mehta, to call a taxi for him. What would he say:

(*a*) Mehta, taxi.
(*b*) Mr Mehta, I order you to get me a taxi.
(*c*) Could you please get a taxi for me, Mr Mehta?
(*d*) Mr Mehta, I request you to kindly call a taxi for me.

8 Your younger brother is playing his transistor radio rather loudly while you are trying to study. Suddenly your father walks in. What would he say to your younger brother?

9 Read Tasks 4 and 6 again. Do you think the speakers in these are friends or strangers? Is their speech formal or informal?

10 In the following table, List A gives your thoughts, List B an appropriate offer/request/order you could use in that situation and List C completes the offer/request/order. Match the three lists:

	List A	*List B*	*List C*
(*a*)	After class, you want your teacher to solve certain problems you have. You know she is very busy.	I was wondering if you could kindly	some food for me from the Chinese restaurant, please?
(*b*)	You are going to be working late in office. You want your secretary to order some food for you.	Ma'am, I know you're rather busy but would it be possible	carry some of your books, ma'am?

	List A	List B	List C
(c)	You want your neighbour to look after your plants while you visit your aunt in Chandigarh.	May I	You can use my scooter tomorrow if you do.
(d)	You want your younger brother to book some tickets for you at the local cinema.	Mr Mehta, can you order	for you to find time this week to help me with my work?
(e)	You see your teacher walking past carrying a big pile of books. You would like to help.	Raju, can you book some seats for me for tomorrow's show at Regal?	water my plants while I'm out of town?

UNIT 6 GETTING AND GIVING PERMISSION, AGREEING AND DISAGREEING, WARNING AND PERSUADING

Getting permission is quite similar to making a request and only a thin line divides making a suggestion from persuading people. Agreeing with others is easy (though too emphatic an agreement is sometimes a sarcastic way of disagreeing). While disagreeing, however, we have to be careful not to give offence to others as well as to leave a way open for them to change their stand without loss of face, or to drop the subject if no agreement is possible. Too pronounced a disagreement would not allow this, so we agree initially but add a 'but' after it, 'Yes, but . . . being the typical form of disagreement.

1 Asking permission

Informal	*Anytime/Anywhere*	*Formal*
Is it all right to/if ....?	Can/Could I ...., please?	Do I have your permission to ....?
All right if .... ?	Do you mind if ....?	Do/Will you have any objection to/if ....?
Let me ....?	Might/May I ....?	With/By your leave ....
Mind if I ....?		With your permission ....

2 Giving and refusing permission

Informal	*Anytime/Anywhere*	*Formal*
Sure.	Of course.	Feel free to ....
OK/Fine/All right.	Yes, certainly.	There seems to be no reason why you can't/shouldn't ....

Informal	*Anytime/Anywhere*	*Formal*
Yes,/(That's) all right.	You're welcome.	Sorry. That's out of the question.
Yes, that's fine.	Not at all.	Sorry. That's not possible.
Sorry.	Sorry, you can't.	
	No. I'm afraid not.	
	No way (I'm afraid).	

3 Asking for agreement

Informal	*Anytime/Anywhere*	*Formal*
Yes/OK/Right?	Don't you feel/think ....?	Do/Would you agree with/that ....?
Isn't that so?	Don't you agree?	I wonder if you would agree?
All right?	Don't you think so?	You wouldn't/don't disagree with that ...., would/do you?
.... is it/isn't it/ isn't s/he/aren't they?	Wouldn't you say so?	

4 Agreeing

Informal	*Anytime/Anywhere*	*Formal*
Yes/Sure!	Yes, I agree!	Oh, I agree totally/ entirely/absolutely!
Exactly/Certainly/ Precisely!	That's right/true.	I couldn't agree more.
That's it!	Oh, absolutely!	I'm exactly of the same opinion.
You're right!	How true.	
	That's just what I was thinking.	

5 Disagreeing

Informal	*Anytime/Anywhere*	*Formal*
Yes, but	(Oh) I don't agree.	I may be wrong, but ....
Oh, surely not.	Not really.	I'm sorry I just can't agree with that/you.
You can't mean that.	I disagree.	I beg to differ.
You must be joking.	I can't/wouldn't agree with that.	

Informal	Anytime/Anywhere	Formal
You can't be serious.	That's quite true, but	
Rubbish/Nonsense.	That's wrong/not right, surely.	
	Do you really think so?	

6 Warning

Informal	Anytime/Anywhere	Formal
Watch out!	Look out!	I would be extremely careful of/to/not to ....
Hey!	Be careful!	On no account should you/we/one ....
Mind	Make sure you	
Sh-hh!	Take care (not) to	

7 Persuading

Informal	Anytime/Anywhere	Formal
Come on (now)	Won't you ...., please?	Are you quite sure you won't reconsider ....?
Go on!	Why don't you ......, please?	(Surely) the most sensible thing would be to ....
Please!/Just this once.	Do	
(For my sake.)		

Samples

1 **A** : Mind if I make a phone call?
B : Not at all. Go ahead.

2 **A** : Can I borrow your book for the weekend, please?
B : Yes, of course.

3 **A** : Is it all right if I leave my children with you for the afternoon?
B : I'm afraid you can't. I'm going out myself.

4 **A** : Do you mind if I pluck some flowers from this garden?
B : I'm afraid that's not allowed.

5 **A** : Would you mind moving your car? It's blocking the road.
B : Of course not. I'm sorry for the trouble.

6 **A** : I'll be out for the day, Asha. There's some food in the fridge. Do feel free to help yourself to it.
B : Thanks a lot. Have a good day!

7 **A** : May I take my bag into the examination hall, please?
B : That's out of the question. Bags are not allowed inside the hall.

8 **A** : Hey! Look out, there's a car coming.
B : Gosh! That was close. Thanks.

9 **A** : Mind your head. The beam is rather low. You might hurt yourself.
B : Yes I know. I'll be careful.

10 **A** : Take care to reach the place of interview on time. And good luck to you.
B : Thanks! I'll take a three-wheeler and be there on time.

11 **A** : On no account should your answer exceed 300 words or you will be penalized.
B : Yes, sir. I'll keep that in mind.

12 **A** : Come on, now. You can't be serious. I'm sure you'll change your mind once you've had time to think.
B : Nonsense! I've already thought about it and I'm absolutely serious.

13 **A** : Why don't you take your driving test again? I'm sure you'll pass this time.
B : Nice of you to say that. I need the encouragement!

14 **A** : Are you quite sure you won't reconsider your decision?
B : I'm quite sure, sir. I've enjoyed working here, but I think it's time to move on.

15 **A** : We're having a little too much of cricket these days, don't you think?
B : Yes, I agree. It's become quite a bore now.

Tasks

1 What is the relationship between the speakers in the above dialogues? For instance in Sample 1, A and B are friends while in 7, B is a person in authority. Try and imagine the roles of A and B in greater detail. Can you also provide the contexts in which the conversations occur?

2 After you have defined the roles of A and B can you tell which of the samples illustrate asking for permission, which ask for agreement and which ones warn or persuade?

3 You are visiting your aunt. You would like to use her telephone. What will you say to her?

4 You want to invite a friend home for lunch. Which of the following will you say to your mother:

(*a*) Excuse me, mother. Do you think I could invite Kapil for lunch today?
(*b*) With your permission, I should like to invite Kapil for lunch today, mother.
(*c*) I was wondering if I could invite Kapil for lunch today, mother.

5 The office clerk wants to leave early one afternoon. He says to his boss:

OK if I leave early this afternoon?

Will he get the permission? What should he have said?

6 You want a book lying on a table which you cannot reach easily. How will you ask the following to hand it to you:

(*a*) your mother?
(*b*) your younger brother/sister?
(*c*) a guest in the house?

7 There is a discount sale on and your friend Sunita wants to go shopping while you want to go and see a film. Keeping this context in mind supply the missing lines in the following dialogue:

You : It's a very good film you know. It won three national awards.
Sunita : ....

You : But you already have so many dresses. Why do you want more?
Sunita : ....

You : Look, its the last show today. If we don't make it now, we will never see it.
Sunita : ....

8 You and your friend, who is on a diet, pass by an ice-cream parlour. You want to have an ice-cream, your friend wants to pass it by as quickly as she can. What will you say to persuade her to join you?

9 In a restaurant, a waiter carrying a tray full of food is not looking in the direction in which he is going. You are afraid he will bump into your friend. How will you warn your friend?

10 You catch your little nephew playing with a box of matches. How will you warn him against it and persuade him to give the matchbox to you.

11 Supply the missing lines in the following conversation:

A : What did you think of last Sunday's film?
B : ....
A : That's quite true, but ....
B : ....

12 You are talking to a senior colleague at work about technology. He says, 'The point is we can't become totally dependent on imported technology.' Which of the following will you say to him:

(*a*) I couldn't agree more.
(*b*) That's it!
(*c*) Oh, surely not.
(*d*) You must be joking.

13 You, your sister (who is a nursery school teacher) and your mother are discussing how best to bring up children. Your sister believes in a strict upbringing, you prefer leniency, while your mother prefers to mix both methods, depending upon the situation. Can you imagine a conversation between the three? Some expressions you might use are given below:

Sister	*You*	*Mother*
strict discipline spare the rod and spoil the child tight control	child's rights no violence plenty of love and affection	learn self-control balance is needed firm but gentle

UNIT 7 INVITING, SUGGESTING, ACCEPTING AND REFUSING

In informal speech, there is little difference between invitations and suggestions. Most informal invitations are usually suggestions that can be easily refused if they do not appeal to the person to whom the invitation is made. Formal invitations and suggestions usually have a longer introduction. Very often a refusal too begins like an acceptance only it ends differently.

1 Inviting

Informal	*Anytime/Anywhere*	*Formal*
Let's	Shall we ....?	We would be (very) pleased if you could ....
Like to ....?	Would you like to ....?	I'd (very much) like you to ....
Why don't you ....?	Would you care to/for ....?	We should be delighted if you could ....
What about ....?	Do	I was/We were wondering if you'd like to ....
You must	Won't you ....?	It would be nice if ....
Come and	I'd like to invite you to	

2 Suggesting

Informal	*Anytime/Anywhere*	*Formal*
Let's	Shall we ....?	Can/Could/May/Might I suggest ....
Fancy ....?	You could	I'd like to suggest ....
What about ....?	I suggest that	You may/might like to ....
How about ....?	We might as well	Have you considered ....?
Why don't we ....?	Would you care to ....?	
We'll .... shall we? shall we?		
Surely s/he/they/ could		

Informal	*Anytime/Anywhere*	*Formal*
I'd say that		
Try		
I think you'd better		

3 Accepting an invitation or suggestion

Informal	*Anytime/Anywhere*	*Formal*
(Thanks) I'd love to.	That would be wonderful/ very nice.	I'd/We'd be delighted to ....
Sounds great!/Fine.	(Thank you) I'd like to/that.	That's really (very)/ nice/most kind of you.
OK!/All right.	That sounds like a very nice idea.	It would give me/us great pleasure to ....
Yes, fine. Thanks.	Yes I will, with pleasure.	
I won't say no.		

4 Refusing an invitation or suggestion

Informal	*Anytime/Anywhere*	*Formal*
That would be great, but	Thank you (very much), but	That's very/extremely kind of you, but ....
I'd love to, but	I'd like to, but	I'm awfully sorry, but ....
Sorry, I can't. (But thanks anyway).	I wish I could, but	Unfortunately, ...
Oh, I'm sorry.	Thank you very much for	
I won't be	asking (me), but	

Samples

1 **A**: Like to come for a drink? We have a few minutes before the bell goes.
B: Love to.

2 **A**: How about meeting on Monday to finalize the details?
B: Fine, what time?
A: Would eleven o'clock be all right?
B: Yes, great!

3 **A**: Hello, Savitri! How are you?
B: Fine, thanks, Rati. And you?
A: Oh, all right. Listen Savitri, we've got two spare tickets for the Bharatnatyam recital this evening and I was wondering if you and Atul would like to come.
B: That would've been great, but we're going out for dinner tonight. Thanks all the same.

4 **A**: Mrs Bhasin, my daughter is getting married next Monday. We would be delighted if you and Mr Bhasin could join us in the celebrations and stay for dinner that evening.

B: It would give us great pleasure, Mrs Jones. Thank you very much.

5 **A**: Why don't you drop in tomorrow evening and we'll have a game of chess.

B: Sounds great! Five o'clock then.

6 **A**: Let's first decide how much we want to spend and then look for the gift.

B: Good idea.

7 **A**: I suggest that you speak in English as often as you can if you really want to improve.

B: I'd like to, but so few of my friends really know any English.

A: Try talking to your teachers if your friends won't respond.

8 **A**: We might as well go home now. We've been round this park four times and still haven't found the house.

B: I'm sure you're right, but perhaps we could try once more just to be absolutely certain.

9 **A**: If I might make a suggestion, I think there should be more classes for English than have been allotted at present.

B: Yes, but where do we fit them in? The timetable's already packed.

10 **A**: Mr Mahajan, I'd like to invite you for the release of my book by the President on Wednesday next at 4.30 p.m. at Rashtrapati Bhavan. I hope you will be able to make it.

B: Yes, indeed! I will. With pleasure.

Tasks

1 Invite your friend to come and watch a cricket match with you next Sunday at the Feroze Shah Kotla ground.

2 Your sister is getting married. You are asked to invite:

(*a*) your friend
(*b*) your teacher
(*c*) a very old family friend

What do you say to each one of them?

3 Your friend Rashid invites you to spend an evening at Appu Ghar. Your exams are near so you don't want to go. How will you decline?

4 Here are some one-sided dialogues. Supply the missing lines:

(*i*) **A**: ....
B: Oh, that would be great!
A: Around eight o'clock.
B: ....
A: ....

(*ii*) **A**: ....
B: Oh, I'm sorry, but ....
A: ....
B: ....

5 Jasjit is a student at one of the local colleges. Robert is a foreign student who has joined the college only recently. Jasjit and Robert have just been introduced. Now Jasjit wants to invite Robert to his birthday party. With the help of the clues given below devise a dialogue and act it out with the help of your partner:

Jasjit	*Robert*
(*a*) Greets Robert.	(*i*) Returns greeting.
(*b*) Invites Robert to his birthday party.	(*ii*) Accepts invitation, asks about time.
(*c*) Gives time.	(*iii*) Asks about place.
(*d*) Apoligizes for not mentioning place. Gives address.	(*iv*) Accepts apology. Offers to bring something.
(*e*) Rejects offer	(*v*) Thanks Jasjit for the invitation.

6 **Jasleen** : Hi, Sumit! Like to come to a picnic next Sunday? It'll be great fun. All our friends are coming and there'll be lots of good food.

Sumit : Unfortunately, Miss Jasleen Singh, on that particular day I shall be engaged in the task of cleaning up my room. However, it is very kind of you to invite me.

Which of the following ways is Jasleen likely to react in:

(*a*) Why is he being so formal? After all, we're friends.
(*b*) What a rude answer!
(*c*) What's wrong with him? Staying in the hostel has done something to him.

7 As you leave for college you find that your elder brother who goes to work by scooter can't start it. You suggest he check the fuel and the spark plug. What do you actually say to him?

8 A business meeting has gone on longer than you thought it would. You would like to meet again the next day, rather than continue now. Which of the following would you say:

(*a*) Let's go home now and meet again tomorrow at ten.
(*b*) I'd like to suggest that we disperse now and meet again at ten tomorrow to thrash out the matter.
(*c*) Hey, stop it! We've had enough for the day.

9 It's a lovely day and you don't feel like studying. How will you suggest to your friend that the day be spent exploring the Qutb?

10 'Fancy a cold drink?'

Would you say this to:

(*a*) your father's colleague who has come over to help you with your studies?
(*b*) your cousin who has been showing you around Bombay, which you are visiting for the first time?
(*c*) an old lady who has just fallen off the bus she was trying to board and who looks very shaken?

How would you make the offer to the other two?

UNIT 8 LIKES AND DISLIKES

Expressing likes and dislikes comes naturally to most of us. In informal speech, most of us tend to use rather strong language to convey the intensity of our feelings even when talking of ordinary things. In formal speech, however, people are more restrained and try not to give offence while expressing their preferences.

1 Expressing likes

Informal	*Anytime/Anywhere*	*Formal*
I'm crazy/mad about	I (really) like/ love/enjoy	I have a special/particular fondness for ....
You can't beat	I'm very keen on	.... is one of my favourites.
.... is really great/terrific.	.... is wonderful/really good.	What I particularly enjoy/specially like/ am fond of is ....
Wow/Lovely!	I have always liked/ loved/enjoyed	I'm (really) very fond of ....
	There's nothing I like/ enjoy more than	

2 Expressing dislikes

Informal	*Anytime/Anywhere*	*Formal*
I can't stand/bear/ tolerate	I (really) hate/dislike/ don't like	I have to admit I (rather) dislike ....
Oh no!	I'm afraid I dislike/don't like	I specially dislike ....
Oh God!	I'm sorry but I (really) don't like it at all.	I don't think .... is particularly good/ pleasant/enjoyable.
It's absolutely terrible/awful/ dreadful.	I'm not very keen on	
I never could put up with	I find it difficult to get on with	

3 Asking about likes

Informal	*Anytime/Anywhere*	*Formal*
Don't you like/love/ enjoy ....?	What do you think of ....?	Don't you find .... (very/extremely) enjoyable?
Isn't/Aren't .... great/terrific?	Do you like/love/ enjoy ....?	May I ask you if you like/ are fond of ....?

Informal	*Anytime/Anywhere*	*Formal*
Don't you think .... is nice/pleasant?	How do you like ....?	
	Are you keen on ....?	

Samples

1 **A** : I'm crazy about films. I never miss a new picture.
B : Yes, but you can't beat theatre for real entertainment.

2 **A** : Are you keen on football? We're going for a game on Sunday morning and you could join us if you like.
B : There's nothing I would enjoy more. Football is one of my favourite games.

3 **A** : Raghu, your aunt from America is arriving tomorrow on a two-week visit.
B : Oh God!

4 **A** : How do you like working with Sheila?
B : I can't stand her, she's so artificial. But one can't choose one's colleagues, can one?

5 **A** : Are you keen on skating?
B : Skating is really terrific. I love it.

6 **A** : Now that we know about your professional qualifications, Mr Narain, do tell us something about your other interests.
B : Reading is one of my favourite pastimes. I'm really fond of books.

7 **A** : What do you think of our new sales executive, Mr Hussain?
B : He's rather good. What I particularly like about him is that he's so full of enthusiasm.

8 **A** : How do you like the new budget, Salim?
B : I'm afraid I don't like the new taxes levied on entertainment.

Tasks

1 Can you guess the relationships between the speakers in the above dialogues?
2 You and your friend are at a restaurant. You are placing the order. How will you ask your friend what he would like to eat?
3 Your friend has had her hair styled in the latest fashion. You don't think it suits her. What will you say in answer to her question: 'Isn't my new hairstyle great?'
4 Your friend has bought a new music cassette. You think it's terrific. What do you say to him?
5 Complete the following conversation:

A : He's a really great batsman, isn't he?
B : ....
A : You must be joking. I think he's fantastic.
B : ....

6 Supply the missing lines:

A : ....
B : Well, the first part is terrific. I really like that and the bit that follows is quite good too. I'm afraid I don't like that section in the middle all that much, but

then I can't stand all those big words that mean very little anyway. I'm not keen on the ending either, but that I'm sure can be improved.

A : ....

7 One day a close friend says to you: 'You know, Ravi, what I particularly enjoy about the summer are the mangoes. I have a special fondness for the *Dussehri* though the *Alphonso* is one of my favourites too. I'm sp ecially keen on the ripe yellow variety. I have to admit I rather dislike the other summer fruits—specially the water melon. May I ask you if you too are fond of mangoes and whether you dislike water melons as well?'

What do you think:

(*a*) Has he gone crazy?
(*b*) Why is he being so formal?
(*c*) His English is rather good.

8 You are shopping for T-shirts in an expensive, fashionable store. The salesman has already shown you 10–15 pieces. You don't like any. You also think they are over-priced. What do you say to him?

9 Devise a conversation between Mrs Ahmed and her friend Mrs Wagle according to the clues given below:

Mrs Ahmed	*Mrs Wagle*
(*a*) Asks how she looks.	(*b*) Says the sari is lovely but she doesn't like the jewellery.
(*c*) Says it is very expensive jewellery.	(*d*) Says it doesn't go with the sari.
(*e*) Asks what she should do.	(*f*) Suggests she wear something else or do without the jewellery.

10 To whom would you say this:

'You can't beat one-day cricket matches for excitement.'

(*a*) to a friend who asks you what you enjoy most?
(*b*) at a formal interview when you are asked what your favourite sport is?
(*c*) to your neighbour in the bus, who is listening to the cricket commentary on his transistor radio?

UNIT 9 REGULATING SPEECH

To carry on a conversation, even if we are only listening, requires that we make responses to show that we are paying attention. To do this, we must know how to show understanding, surprise and attention. Sometimes we may miss or not understand what other people are saying so we must know how to ask them to repeat themselves. At other times we may have to explain or clarify something that we have said and which the other person may not have understood. Sometimes we may have to attract the attention of people who may be otherwise busy or inattentive and we must know how to do this, too, without giving offence. This unit teaches us how to regulate speech, our own as well as that of others.

1 Drawing attention and interrupting

Informal	*Anytime/Anywhere*	*Formal*
Sorry to butt in, but	Sorry to interrupt, but	May I have your attention please?
Look/Listen!	Excuse me!	Pardon me ....
Sorry, but	(Please) Ma'm/Sir!	Could I just mention/make a point ....?
		Pardon the interruption, but ....

2 Paying attention and showing surprise

Informal	*Anytime/Anywhere*	*Formal*
Oh?/Oh/Yes! Well, well.	Really!/Really/What?	Indeed!
Do you/Has it/ Does it?	I see.	Is that so?
Oh my gosh/God!	Exactly/Right.	
Goodness me!	How interesting!	
Don't tell me!	I know what you mean.	
No!	Not really.	

3 Getting someone to repeat or slow down

Informal	*Anytime/Anywhere*	*Formal*
Sorry?	Pardon (me)?	I beg your pardon?
What/When/ Where/Who?	Sorry, but could you please repeat that/the last bit/ that name/the sentence?	I'm sorry, but would you mind repeating what you just said, please?
Eh?	Sorry, what did you say?	
What was that (you said)?		

4 Repeating yourself in other words

Informal	*Anytime/Anywhere*	*Formal*
All/What I'm trying to say is	All/What I meant was	Perhaps it would be better/ more accurate to say ....
What I'm getting at is	What I mean is	If I can rephrase that ....
	In other words	To put it differently ....
	Let me put it another way.	

5 Giving examples

Informal	*Anytime/Anywhere*	*Formal*
Look at	.... for example.	Let me give an example ....
Like .... (for example).	For instance/For example, take	To illustrate this point ....
Take	.... such as	What I mean is ....
	To give an example	

Samples

1 **A** : Hey, Naresh! You've left your book behind.
B : Oh, thanks, Alok.

2 **A** : Excuse me. Aren't you Mr Wagle's neighbour? I think I've seen you before.

3 **A** : Pardon me, sir. Could I interrupt you here for a moment? I didn't get that last point you made. Would you mind repeating it, please?

4 **A** : Look, that's your bus, isn't it?
B : So it is. I must be off. Bye.

5 **A** : Sorry to interrupt, but there's someone on the phone for you.
B : Oh, thanks, Gautam. Excuse me, Adil. I'll be back in a moment.

6 **A** : May I have your attention please? Flight SQ 208 is now ready for boarding. Passengers are requested to proceed to the aircraft.

7 **A** : Pardon me, Mr Chairman, but I think that we have forgotten a rather important point. Unless we bring down the price of our product, sales will not pick up.
B : Yes, but that would leave a very narrow margin of profit for us.

8 **A** : Hey, have you heard the latest? Gita and Anil are getting married next month.
B : Really?
A : Yes, and then Gita's going to give up her job.
B : Don't tell me!

9 **A** : Excuse me. Could you shift a little, please? Hey, Pravinder, there's just enough space for you to squeeze in.

10 **A** : I think that the age for voting should be lowered.
B : Do you?
A : Yes, I think that young people mature faster these days.

11 **A** : Hello, Anjana! When did you come back from Kashmir?
B : Yesterday. We stayed a fortnight in Srinagar and the weather was absolutely great! And guess whom we bumped into there? The Chawlas!
A : No!

12 **A** : Excuse me, sir. Could you repeat the last bit again, please?
B : What I said was that when we interrupt others, we always say 'Excuse me' or 'Sorry' first.

13 **A** : Could you say that again, more slowly and a little louder, please?
B : Yes, ma'am. The meeting is scheduled for next Thursday at 2.00 p.m. in the conference room.

14 **A** : Where did you say the shop was?
B : It's in a little lane in Shanker Market right opposite the Super Bazar.

15 **A** : All I mean to say is that I am not interested, but if you are so keen you can go ahead.

16 **A** : Now what exactly did you mean by that?
B : Well, let me put it this way. You must insure your car, not because you're not a good driver but because a lot of other people on the road may not be very good drivers.
A : In other words, I must pay for the foolishness of others.

17 **A** : Vacations don't have to be spent in bed all day. One could do many interesting yet relaxing things. Take for instance photography, or cookery, or activities such as judo, playing tennis or even learning a new language.
B : But aren't all these rather expensive hobbies?
A : Not necessarily. And there are others that require even less money. To give an example, clay modelling. You don't have to spend a paisa on it.

18. **A** : There are many things that one could do to improve the efficiency of this office. Let me give an example. If tea could be served in office itself, we would save between half an hour to forty-five minutes of each employee's time everyday.

Tasks

1 Read Sample 8 again. What would you say is B's attitude to the news that Gita is going to give up her job? Is she:

(*a*) surprised?
(*b*) disappointed?
(*c*) unconcerned?

2 Read Sample 11 again. The attitude of A to the Chawlas is:

(*a*) she likes them very much.
(*b*) she doesn't like them at all.
(*c*) they really don't matter to her.

3 Supply the missing lines in the following dialogue:

Mujahid : Hello, Anil. How are you?
Anil : ....
Mujahid : I had a miraculous escape yesterday.
Anil : ....
Mujahid : I fell off a bus and would have got killed if someone had not pushed me away from the path of a speeding truck in the nick of time.

4 You go to the staff-room to ask your teacher about an assignment you handed in last week. He is talking to Mrs Varma of the English Department. You have already waited five minutes trying to catch your teacher's attention. How will you interrupt him?

5 When would you say this:

'Could I just mention that tea is served.'

(*a*) to the chief guest at an official function?
(*b*) to your best friend at a party?
(*c*) to guests who have come to stay at your home for the first time?

6 You are travelling through Bharatpur to attend a business meeting at Jaipur with your boss, Mr Ghosh, in his car. On the way you see a Siberian crane. You want to draw the attention of your boss to the bird. Which of the following would you say:

(*a*) Hey! Look!
(*b*) Sorry to interrupt you, Mr Ghosh, but isn't that a Siberian crane?
(*c*) May I have your attention please, Mr Ghosh? There is a Siberian crane flying ahead.

7 Given below is a conversation on telephone. The line is very bad and the other person cannot hear properly. Supply the missing responses:

A : .... and she was taken to the hospital last night.
B : ....
A : I said, 'she was taken to the hospital last night'.
B : ....
A : (Speaking very loudly into the receiver) I SAID ILA WAS TAKEN TO THE HOSPITAL LAST NIGHT. CAN YOU HEAR ME NOW?
B : Yes I can. What did you say?

8 Here is a dialogue between two friends who will be travelling from Bombay to Delhi on the Rajdhani Express. Supply the missing lines following the directions given in brackets:

A : Now, when exactly does our train leave?
B : At five past four in the everning.
A : (Ask him to say that again.)
B : At five past four in the everning. At least that's what's given in the timetable. But you know what our trains are like. Never on time.
A : (Shows he is listening.)
B : And we may not reach Delhi before noon.
A : (Agrees.)

9 Two foreigners on their first visit to India, are talking to each other. Supply the lines following the directions given in brackets:

A : I must say, the Indian style of hospitality is unique.
B : What do you mean?
A : (Say it another way: 'No other people are so insistent in their hospitality.')
B : I still don't get you.
A : (Gives examples: They are always trying to make you eat and drink even if you don't want to. They won't let you do anything for yourself.)
B : (Shows surprise.) I don't think I agree. I've had rather pleasant experiences myself. (Illustrates: He found people open and friendly and was very well looked after.)

UNIT 10 ENDING A CONVERSATION: SAYING GOODBYE

Ending a conversation normally involves two steps: signalling that the conversation is coming to an end, and the actual leave taking. Signals of ending usually consist of thanking a person or making an excuse or apology. It is important to be able to recognize these signals, for in formal situations it is considered rude to ignore them. It is normally the superior in age or status who signals the end of a conversation. On the telephone, it is the caller who does so.

Parting salutations, like greetings, are set phrases and do not necessarily mean what they say. People who meet regularly generally take leave informally. Formal leave takings are more eleborate. People who will not meet each other for long periods usually shake hands too. On leaving a party or a gathering, one must seek out the host and hostess, thank them and bid them goodbye.

1 Pre-closings

Informal	*Anytime/Anywhere*	*Formal*
Thanks for a (really) lovely	Well, I'd better be going.	Thank you very much for your attention/interest/ support.
Well, it was (really) nice talking to you.	I'm sorry but I've (really) got to go.	Well, I think that's all. Thank you for seeing me.
Well, I must leave/be off. Great seeing you.	Thank you so much for	I hope you'll excuse me, but ....
We must get together again soon.	I'm sorry I can't stay any longer. I have	
(Sorry, I've) Got to go now. Come over/Drop in some time.	It's been very nice/ interesting talking to you, but	
OK then	It's been a pleasure.	

2 Responses

Informal	*Anytime/Anywhere*	*Formal*
Yes, I('ve) enjoyed it (too).	Good/Nice to see you.	It's been a pleasure.
Right then.	You're welcome.	The pleasure has been mine.
Same here.	Not at all.	Thank you for coming.
Sure/Yes, I will.		

3 Closings

Informal	*Anytime/Anywhere*	*Formal*
Bye!	Bye-bye!	Goodbye!
See you soon/later/ tomorrow/next week.	Good night!	Hope to see you soon again some time. Bye-bye!
Look after yourself. Until next time then.		I look forward to seeing you soon/again. Goodbye!
So long.		
Take care.		

Note: In responding to closings we generally repeat the same expression that has been used by the 'leave taker', except for 'Take care' and 'Look after yourself' where the response is 'And you/You too'.

Samples

1 **A:** Well, Naaz. I'd better be going or I'll miss the special.
B: Bye, Kiran! See you tomorrow.
A: Bye!

2 **A:** Dr Pandit, when can I come and discuss my problem with you?
B: Would three o'clock this afternoon be all right?
A: Yes, that would be fine. Thank you very much. I'll see you at three.
B: Well, goodbye till then.
A: Goodbye, sir!

3 **A:** O my gosh! It's five o'clock. I'd better rush. Mum will be wondering what happened to me.
B: We must get together again soon.
A: Yes, we must. Bye now!
B: Bye!

4 **A:** Excuse me, Mr Sinha. Here is the report that you wanted.
B: Ah yes. Thank you, Mrs D'Souza.
A: Er, I was wondering, sir, if I could leave an hour earlier today. My son is rather ill and needs to be taken to the doctor.
B: Oh, what is the matter with him?
A: He's been running temperature for the past few days, and the doctor had asked for certain tests to be done. I must pick up the reports before the hospital closes at five o'clock today.
B: Well, all right. But do be on time tomorrow morning. I have some important papers that I want typed urgently.
A: Thank you, sir. I will. Goodbye, Mr Sinha!
B: Goodbye, Mrs D'Souza!

5 **A:** Thanks for a really lovely evening, Meera. It was nice meeting old friends again and the food was absolutely delicious.
B: I'm glad you enjoyed yourself. Do drop in again, whenever you have time.
A: Yes, I will. Good night, Meera, and thanks once again.
B: Good night and take care.

6 **A:** Does that solve your problem?
B: Yes, sir. You've been most kind.
A: I'm glad to have been of help. Feel free to drop in again if there's anything you need.
B: Thank you very much, Dr Singh.
A: Well, goodbye, Rakesh! I hope you are working hard for your exams.
B: Yes, I am, sir. Goodbye, sir! And thank you once again, sir.
A: Goodbye!

7 **A:** Hi, Rakesh! Fancy bumping into you here!
B: Oh! Hello, Sudha! Nice to see you again after such a long time. Shopping?
A: Yes, buying some vegetables. And you?
B: I've come to see Dr Bali who has a clinic here. I'm sorry I can't stay. I'm already late for my appointment.
A: Drop in at my place after your consultation.
B: Yes, I will. Bye!
A: Bye!

8 **A**: And that brings me to the end of my report. Thank you very much gentlemen, for your attention. I am now ready to answer any questions that you may have.

9 **A**: Anything else you'd like to discuss?
B: Well, I think that's all. Thank you for seeing me.
A: Goodbye!
B: Goodbye, sir!

10 **A**: That's the whistle for your train. Goodbye and take care of yourself.
B: Yes, I will. Don't forget to write and look after yourself too.
A: Yes, I will. Goodbye!
B: Goodbye!

11 **A**: Talking to you has been a great pleasure. Thank you very much for sparing me so much of your time.
B: Not at all. The pleasure's been mine. Thank you for coming.

Tasks

1 **A**: Ghosh, it's late. I'd better be going.
B: Yes, you should. You've already taken up too much of my time.
Who is saying something inappropriate? What should he have said?

2 An important client who has come from another city is leaving after negotiations. As he leaves he says:

Thank you for looking after me so well. I look forward to seeing you again soon. Goodbye!

You reply:

(*a*) What for?
(*b*) I hope not.
(*c*) It's been a pleasure having you with us.
(*d*) Sure. Bye!

Choose the correct reply and say why the other replies are inappropriate.

3 You are talking to your English teacher about your performance in the last test, but you now want to end the conversation because you are getting late for the next class. What will you say to her/him?

4 You're talking to an elderly gentleman at the bus-stop as you wait for your bus. He talks incessantly about the lack of seriousness in today's youngsters. Your're bored and want to end the conversation. Fortunately your bus arrives just then. What will you say to the gentleman?

5 You're going home after college. How will you take leave of:

(*a*) your best friend?
(*b*) the college principal?
(*c*) a teacher who is friendly with you?

6 To which of these people would you say 'Good night':

(*a*) To a person whom you won't see till the next morning. The time now is 3 p.m.
(*b*) To a person who has just now invited you for a late night movie. The time now is 7 p.m. and the movie begins at 9.30 p.m.
(*c*) To a person of whom you are taking leave at 8 p.m. and won't see till next morning.

7 You are saying goodbye to your host and his family after having stayed a week with them. The host's part of the conversation is given below. Fill in your part of the dialogue:

Host : Not at all. We enjoyed your stay with us very much. The pleasure was ours. Do come again.

You : ....

Host : Yes, we will.

You : ....

Host : Bye-bye! Have a nice journey.

8 Here is a piece of incomplete conversation. Supply the missing parts:

A : .... And that's the way the film ended.

B : Oh, I nearly forgot. I've got to see .... in a few minutes.

A : ....

B : ....

9 Read the conversation given below:

A : It's half past four already!

B : Goodness me! The last special leaves at quarter to five. I must leave. I don't think I'll be able to show you the photographs.

A : I hope not. Now off you go and don't worry about me.

Is this conversation appropriate, or is there something wrong with it? Can you improve it?

10 Your office had some serious problems. You invited a specialist to solve them. He is now going back after solving the problems. You and your boss are seeing him off:

You : Well, we hope you have a pleasant journey back, Mr Dangwal.

Your boss : And thank you for everything you have done. Goodbye!

The specialist : Hardly done anything boys. Have a nice time. And hope to see you again.

Your boss is surprised at what the specialist says. Why? What should the specialist have said?

Reading Comprehension

UNIT 1 NON-VERBAL COMMUNICATION

(Cartoon by Ajit from *Target*, New Delhi, July 1987)

Exercises

Study the cartoon above and answer the following questions:

1 Can you guess who the man on the left is?
2 Can you guess who the man on the right is?
3 Where are they?
4 Why is the man with the briefcase pointing at the man on the left?
   (*a*) Because he is talking about this man.
   (*b*) Because that is the way he wants to go.
   (*c*) He is not pointing.
5 What do the dots on the coat of the man to the left represent?
6 What do the dots on the right represent?
7 Does the expression on the face of the man on the left show:
   (*a*) surprise
   (*b*) anger
   (*c*) fear
8 Guess from the expression on the face of the man on the right if he is:
   (*a*) drunk
   (*b*) tired
   (*c*) sleepy
9 What mistake, do you think, has the man on the right made? Is such a mistake possible in real life?
10 If you could give one line of dialogue to any of these characters, to whom would you give it and what would it be?

(From the *Times of India*, New Delhi, 16 Aug 1987)

Put the pictures given above in the right order. If you have difficulty in doing it by yourself discuss it with your friends.* Then answer the following questions:

1 Does the word 'Hey' in picture 3 express:
   (*a*) anger
   (*b*) surprise
   (*c*) fear

2 Can you guess the relationship between Beetle and the fat man? Is it that of:
   (*a*) master and servant
   (*b*) friends
   (*c*) superior and subordinate

3 Do you think Beetle and the fat man are:
   (*a*) policemen
   (*b*) soldiers
   (c) custom officers

4 'You saw me buy a candy bar at the PX, didn't you?' The 'didn't you' at the end

* If the teacher feels that this is too difficult for the class s/he can provide the correct sequence and then let the class proceed with the rest of the exercises.

(called question tag) changes a statement into a question. Rewrite all sentences in the cartoon with question tags as proper questions. Begin your questions, 'Did you. . . .'

5. Notice how a positive sentence takes a negative question tag and a negative sentence a positive question tag. Now rewrite the following sentences with question tags:
   (*a*) He is late.
   (*b*) You are clever.
   (*c*) He didn't take it.
   (*d*) They are such bores.
   (*e*) You put the books somewhere.
6. Everytime the fat man gives Beetle a kick the drawing shows a star. What do the stars stand for?
7. Do you think that this sequence is funny? If so, what is the joke?

UNIT 2 COMMUNICATING THROUGH ADVERTISEMENTS 1

TO LET

COMMERCIAL space with telephone facility available on rent in Connaught Place contact Telephone 3314032.

ONE independent large room set available in Nizamuddin nurses public sector or government employees preferred rent approximately 1500 contact 698541 8 a.m. – 10 a.m.

ONE room attached bath independent entrance first floor K-14 South Extension to contact phone 6449454 preferable bachelor.

ANNEXE Vasant Vihar a 1/3 two rooms with kitchen attached bathroom lady doctor or couple with small family preferred telephone 671018 rent rupees 2000 negotiable.

VIKASPURI ground/second floor, two beddings, drawing, dining space, balcony, bath, latrine only on company lease 676305.

KE 34/9 Kavinagar Ghaziabad spacious bungalow two beds drawing dining dressing store kitches toilets etc. on company lease contact 849418.

JANAKPURI B1/131 two room independant set ground floor single storey house rear entry preference Souths Indians, Maharastrians, Christians. Contact site or phone 590699.

TO LET

JANAKPURI first floor three bedroom DDA self financing flat public sector company lease contact 693876 or DII/181 Kaka Nagar.

INDEPENDENT one room set available only foriegner or bachelor preferred, contact 645 Vasant Kunj (SFS) time 9 a.m. to 11 a.m. near J.N. University.

NEWLY constructed/three room groundfloor independent set Rajapark Jaipur decent locality transferrable small family preferred Box IE-1725, Indian Express, New Delhi-2.

AVAILABLE two bed one drawing room set on lease in NOIDA please contact Vijh telephone 6833115 after office hours.

INDEPENDENT two room set B-173 Ashok Vihar Phase I contact at site after 5 p.m.

DECENTLY planned entirely independent first floor set three rooms dining kitchen store bath verandah open yard parking 171 sector 15 Faridabad, Phone 8123639.

LAJPAT NAGAR-III first floor spacious/airy/two-bed attached baths front balcony glazed verandah. Young couple/small family company lease preferred. Telephone 6836937.

TO LET

D-26 Anand Niketan, two floors three bed rooms each with attached bathrooms drawing dining servant quarter third story one bedroom foreigners preferred phone 392488.

ONE room set (Janata) for South Indian, (Service Class) Rent 700/-. Ask Deepak Type College, 26, Shopping Complex, Sheikh Sarai-II, before 5 p.m.

WELL located ground floor drawing dining two beds non Punjabis preferbaly. South Indian Contact: E-77, South Extension-I on holidays or evenings after seven.

THREE room set with kitchen bathroom first floor. Contact: Teja Singh C-22, Vishnu Garden, near Punjabi Market, New Delhi-110018.

PASCHIM Vihar B 5/165, three bed rooms, D/D Verandah terrace independent, first floor. Contact: Site Phone 5431248.

EAST of Kailash drawing/dining three bedrooms, attached baths servant quarter, parking for guest house/office. Limited Company. G-1, Lajpat Nagar-III. Phone 6835170.

47 Community Centre East of Kailash, New Delhi 1500 sq. ft. basement. Contact telephone 698289/698258.

Exercises

Read carefully the 'To let' advertisements, taken from a newspaper, given on the previous page and then do the following exercises:

1 (*a*) What does the word 'lease' mean? Find out its meaning with the help of a dictionary.
  (*b*) Why do advertisers prefer to give out houses on company lease? Discuss your answer with others.

2 Why do landlords prefer foreigners, bachelors and non-Punjabis? Do you think they have good reasons to do so or are they prejudiced?

3 (*a*) How would you advertise the house in which you live, if you wanted to rent it out?
  (*b*) Imagine that you are married and have three children. Devise an interesting dialogue between yourself and the landlord with reference to the fourth advertisement in the first column and act it out before the class.

4 Amar Sinha has just got his first job. His office is in Connaught Place. He is drawing a salary of Rs 2000/-. He can afford to pay Rs 600/- to Rs 800/- as rent. He is now looking for a place to stay. Look at the 'To let' advertisements and suggest the ones that will be most suitable for him. Compare your choice with that of the others and justify it.

5 Pick out the misspelt and wrongly used words from the advertisements and provide the correct equivalents. Can you also provide suitable punctuation?

KULU–MANALI

Finding your feet in Kulu–Manali

Winter sports activities close to Manali

General information

Altitude

Kulu: 4,000 feet
Katrain: 4,800 feet
Naggar: 5,800 feet
Manali: 6,200 feet
Solang: 8,200 feet
Rohtang Pass: 13,348 feet

Visiting Months

Summer: April–June and September–November; Winter: February–March (Rohtang Pass and beyond is accessible only during summer, June–October).

Clothing

Summer: Cotton and tropicals at altitudes up to Manali and light woollens at higher altitudes.

Distances

(All measured from Kulu)

Bhuntar Airport	10 km
Raison	16 km
Katrain	20 km
Naggar	26 km
Manali	40 km
Solang	52 km
Rohtang Pass	91 km
Keylong (in Lahaul Valley)	157 km

How to reach

Air

Daily Vayudoot flights from Delhi/Chandigarh to Bhuntar in Kulu Valley.

Rail

Convenient rail heads are Shimla, Chandigarh and Pathankot, from where one must travel by road.

Road

Delhi–Manali: 570 km
(via Chandigarh, Ropar, Mandi & Kulu)
Shimla–Manali: 270 km
(via Bilaspur, Mandi & Kulu)
Chandigarh–Manali: 312 km (via Ropar, Bilaspur & Mandi)

Bus service: Delhi to Manali

State Transport's daily bus service (from Inter State Bus Terminus, Delhi)
Deluxe: 6.50 a.m., Rs 160; Semi-Deluxe: 8.30 p.m., Rs 120: Ordinary: 5.30 and 6.30 p.m., Rs 90.
Himachal Pradesh Tourism Development Corporation's Luxury (video) buses operate from April to mid-November (from Chandralok Building, 36 Janpath). AC: 6.00 a.m., (Sun & Tue), Rs 250; Non-AC: 6.00 a.m., (Fri) Rs 170.

Package tours

The types of package tours and their rates vary from season to season. They mostly operate during the off-season (mid-November to mid-April). The prevailing package tours are:

Vayudoot's in collaboration with HPTDC (4 days & 3 nights), Rs 1499 per adult and Rs 799 per child.

Span Resorts Holiday Special (4 days & 3 nights) during 15 November–15 April and 15 July–15 September 1987, Rs 1655 per adult and Rs 575 per child below 12, plus a car at the disposal for 2 days or a maximum of 200 km.

Sightseeing tours

Tour no. 1 (Daily during season)
Manali–Nehru Kund–Rahla Falls–Marhi–Rohtang Pass–Manali. Time: 9 a.m. to 4 p.m. Fare: Rs 60 per seat by Luxury coach and Rs 500 by car for 5 persons.

Tour no. 2 (Daily during season)
Manali–Naggar–Manali. Time: 9 a.m. to 4 p.m. Fare: Rs 35 per seat by Luxury coach and Rs 225 by car for 5 persons.

Tour no. 3 (Daily during season)
Manali–Manikaran via Kulu–Manali. Time: 9 a.m. to 4 p.m. Fare: Rs 70 per seat by Luxury coach and Rs 600 by car for 5 persons.

Taxi service

There are a large number of taxis in the valley which can be availed. Though there are no fixed rates, the rates in general between Bhuntar Airport and Kulu are Rs 15 per person, and Rs 75 per person from Bhuntar Airport to Manali.

The enchanting countryside between Kulu and Manali

Where to stay

KULU

Hotels

ITDC Ashok Travellers Lodge, Tel: 79. Rs 230–285
HPTDC Hotel Sarvari, Tel: 33. Rs 100–150
Rohtang Transit, Tel: 303. Rs 100–150.

Budget accommodation

HPTDC Hotel Sarvari (Dormitory). Rs 12 per bed
Circuit House, Tel: 35. Rs 40
Central Hotel, Tel: 46. Rs 45–90
Naveen Guest House, Tel: 228. Rs 25–50
Empire Hotel, Tel: 97. Rs. 50–100

RAISON

HPTDC Camping Site, Rs 50 (14 double bedded cottages on river bank)

KATRAIN

Span Resorts Rs 950–1,100, Suite Rs 2,300, extra bed Rs 350. (For bookings in Delhi, Tel: 3311434
HPTDC Apple Blossom, Full cottage (of 3 bedrooms) Rs 275, Suite no. 1 Rs 140, Suites no. 2 & no. 3 Rs 80.
PWD Rest House Rs 30

NAGGAR

HPTDC Castle Hotel, Rs 150–200
Forest House, Rs 15

MANALI

Hotels

HPTDC Log Huts (double bedrooms & kitchenette), Rs 900–1,100
HPTDC Hotel Manaslu, Rs 200 (New wing), Rs 100 (Old wing)
HPTDC Hotel Beas, Rs 75–150
HPTDC Tourist Cottages (with kitchenette) Rs 300
ITDC Ashok Travellers Lodge, Rs 235–530
Pinewood Hotel, Rs 150–300
Hotel Piccadilly, Rs 300–500
Hotel Holiday Home International, Rs 200–275

KULU–MANALI

Hotel Cedar, Rs 150–250
HPTDC Hamta & Birch Cottages, Rs 300

Guest houses/Resorts

John Banons Guest House, Rs 200–400
May Flower Guest House, Rs 225–500
New Hope Guest House, Rs 150–300
Woodlines Hotel, Rs 175–520
Sunshine Guest House, Rs 200
Hotel High Land, Rs. 225
Brightways Guest House, Rs 100

Budget accommodation

HPTDC Tourist Lodge (Dormitory), Rs 20 per bed
HPTDC Youth Hostel (Dormitory), Rs 5 per bed
Blue Heaven Hotel, Rs 30–50
Hotel Shantiniketan, Rs 40–65
Capital Hotel, Rs 30–50
Hotel Neel Kamal, Rs 25–100
Thakur Hotel, Rs 50–75
Rising Star, Rs 30–50
New Himland Hotel, Rs 50
Renuka Guest House, Rs 40–75

Club house

An ideal place to hold seminars, conferences and meetings in the entire valley. It has an auditorium with a capacity for 250 persons and a good PA system. In addition it has a restaurant attached which can serve Indian or Mughlai, Continental and Chinese cuisine.

The Club House also serves as the community centre both for the residents and the tourists, on permanent and temporary membership basis. The facilities provided by the Club House, in addition to the ones mentioned above, are billiards, tennis, indoor games and a good TV lounge. Located in sylvan surroundings it is a lovely picnic spot.

Outdoor activities

Angling

Summer months are ideal for trout fishing in River Beas. There are a number of fishing spots between Manali and Katrain. Fishing permits are issued by the Fisheries Officer at Katrain.

Trekking

Kulu is a favourite start point for various treks. Details on treks and routes, as well as the agencies who organize the treks, can be obtained from HPTDC offices.

Excursions

Kulu is popularly known as the 'Valley of the Gods'. With over 6,000 temples, there are fascinating spots to visit. The other excursion sites, a walking distance from Manali township, are Hadimba Devi temple, Vashisht hot sulphur springs and old Manali Village. Rohtang Pass, Nehru Kund, Solang ski valley, Jagatsukh, Naggar Castle and Roerich Art Gallery at Naggar are other places of interest.

Tourist information centres

Calcutta
25 Camac Court Street
Tel: 446847

Chandigarh
SCO, 1047–48, Sector 22-B
Tel: 26494

Madras
14 Ganga Nagar, Kodambakkam
Tel: 812955

Bombay
36 World Trade Centre
Cuffe Parade
Tel: 219191/284

New Delhi
Chandralok Building, 36 Janpath
Tel: 345320

Kulu
Dholpur Maidan
Tel: 7

Manali
Mall Road
Tel: 25

Note:
The above mentioned offices also undertake bookings of HPTDC managed hotels/cottages/log huts and the Club House at Manali.

(From *Destination India*, April 1987)

Exercises

Read the travel brochure reproduced above on Kulu–Manali and answer the following questions:

1 You are a college student in Chandigarh who would like to visit Kulu and Manali. You can go only during your summer vacation. You have a budget of Rs 1000/-. Plan a trip for yourself with the help of the information provided. You must decide:

(*a*) how you will travel.
(*b*) where you will stay.
(*c*) what places you will visit.
(*d*) how many days you plan to spend there and the dates on which you will travel.

2 A Bombay based company wants to take its employees on a trip to the mountains. On this trip the company wants to combine seminars and conferences on sales promotion with treks, fishing expeditions and visits to nearby tourist spots. Imagine you are the programme officer who has been asked to plan the trip:

(*a*) What arrangements will you need to make?

(*b*) What are the things you are going to do to make the trip a success?

(*c*) Which people will you contact (through correspondence or personal contact) to make the necessary advance bookings? Don't forget to arrange transport for sight-seeing.

(*d*) In groups of three or four discuss and write a letter to the Manager, Club House, Manali, reserving the Club House for a three-day seminar which you wish to hold on its premises.

UNIT 3: COMMUNICATING THROUGH ADVERTISEMENTS 2

Oil is one of the most important items in our life. We need it to travel in cars, buses, trains, aeroplanes and ships. We need it to produce electricity for our lights and to run our factories. We need it to cook food. But inspite of the importance of oil, people waste it carelessly. And unfortunately there is only a limited amount of oil in the world.

P.C.R.A. (Petroleum Conservation Research Association) is working to save your friend, Oil. We need your help too.

Here are three things you can do to help save oil:

1. The gas burner in the kitchen should be turned off when it is not being used.
2. Walk to school, if it is nearby.
3. Turn off the lights and fans when they are not in use.

These simple ways and many more like it will help your friend Oil, to stay with us longer.

Petroleum Conservation Research Association,
306 Sethi Bhawan, 7 Rajendra Place,
New Delhi-110 008.

Oil isn't going to last much longer. Use it with wisdom.

Exercises

1 An advertisement is an announcement or notice in a newspaper or TV. It is meant (*a*) to sell certain products like soaps, clothes, TV sets, etc. (sometimes by making false claims), (*b*) to make a public announcement like the last date for the payment of income tax, etc., (*c*) to warn us against certain dangers (drugs, cancer), and (*d*) teach us about the value of certain things (like keeping our city clean). Advertisements can also be used by the government for propaganda. Discuss with your friends and make a list of other purposes for which advertising is used.

2 Read the advertisement given on the previous page carefully and decide if it is meant:

(*a*) to persuade us to buy something.
(*b*) to make a public announcement.
(*c*) to warn and teach us.

Who has paid for the publication of this advertisement?

3 In this advertisement oil is represented by a drop. What are some of the other ways in which oil can be represented? Discuss with your group and make a list.

4 List A gives some difficult words and phrases used in this advertisement. List B has their meanings but not in the correct order. Can you match the words with their meanings?

List A	*List B*
item	despite, even so
in spite of	without thought or consideration
carelessly	unit in a list, thing
conservation	group of people working together
association	preservation, to save

5 How can one save oil by turning off lights and fans?

6 The advertisement says, 'These simple ways and more like it, will help our friend Oil to stay with us longer'. Why is oil called 'our friend'? Discuss ways of saving oil with your friends and prepare a list of these.

7 Given below is a list of ideas contained in this advertisement. Pick out the three most important ones and justify your choice:

(*a*) Oil is very important in our everyday life.
(*b*) It makes our machines and factories work.
(*c*) Without it cars, buses, planes, etc., would not run.
(*d*) It is required to produce electricity.
(*e*) People waste oil due to carelessness.
(*f*) We must not waste gas in the kitchen.
(*g*) We must turn off lights and fans when not needed.
(*h*) We must walk when we can, in order to save petrol.
(*i*) The world has limited resources of oil which are drying up fast.
(*j*) Oil is our friend.

8 Is this advertisement meant for people who live in villages or people who live in towns and cities? Do people in cities waste more oil than people in villages? Discuss in small groups and justify your opinion.

9 Look at the word 'carelessly'. It has been formed by adding two suffixes to the word 'care': care + less + ly. Similarly 'unfortunately' is made by adding a prefix and a suffix to the word 'fortunate': un + fortunate + ly.

(*a*) Pick out the prefixes and the suffixes in the following words:

needlessly	walkable	traveller	simplify
importantly	reproduce	disuse	reporter
unlimited	helpless	wasteful	mismanagement

(*b*) Make as many new words as you can by adding prefixes/suffixes to the following:

limit	help	important
work	friend	break

10 Look at the word 'Let's'. It is a combination of two words, 'Let' and 'us'. In spoken English we often join together words and pronounce two words as one. When we write them down we put an apostrophe (') to mark the place where letters have been dropped. Contracted forms (two words spoken as one) should not be confused with possessive nouns, which denote possession or something that belongs to the person mentioned, e.g. Sita's bag, Sunil's book. Given below is a list of contracted forms. Expand them to their full form and practice saying them aloud:

I'm, you're, it's, can't, shan't, we're, I'll, you'll, don't, he's, here's,
I've, you've, isn't, won't, they're, that's, wasn't, shouldn't.

UNIT 4 UNDERSTANDING TECHNICAL TERMS

A Dilosyn

Anti-allergic Expectorant

Warning: It is dangerous to take this preparation except under medical supervision.

Dosage:

ADULTS: 1 to 2 teaspoonfuls 3 or 4 times daily.
CHILDREN: ½ to 1 teaspoonful 3 or 4 times daily.

Caution: Although Dilosyn Expectorant is known to be safe, drowsiness may occur. Patients are warned that if drowsiness does occur, they should not drive a vehicle or be in charge of moving machinery.

Keep in a cool place away from direct sunlight.

Retail price not to exceed Rs 10.54
Local taxes extra

Lot N 271

MFD. Mar 91
EXP. Feb 93

B Raricap HT

Hematinic Tablets

Dosage: 1 tablet daily or as directed by the physician.

Store in a cool dry place.

Maximum retail price Rs 25.01 for 40 tablets + L.T.

Batch No. 117
MFD. 1/91 EXP. 6/92

C Betnosol-N

Eye/Ear Drops

For external use only. Not for injection.

Keep in a cool place protected from sunlight.

To be used only under medical supervision.

Use the solution within one month of opening of the container.

5 ml

Retail price not to exceed Rs 6.18
Local taxes extra

Lot 2194

MFD. FEB 91
EXP. JUL 92

D Spasmo-Proxyvon

Anti-spasmodic analgesic Capsules

Schedule H drug

Warning: To be sold by retail on the prescription of a registered medical practitioner only.

Dosage: 1 capsule 2 to 3 times a day.

Precautions: Spasmo-Proxyvon may impair mental/physical ability required for performance of potentially hazardous tasks such as driving a car or operating heavy machinery in which case extra precaution is required. Patients should not consume alcohol when on Spasmo-Proxyvon therapy. Spasmo-Proxyvon has to be used with care in patients having or suspected to have glaucoma.

RP not exceed Rs 9.55 for 6 capsules L.T. extra

Batch No. 8326

MFD. Nov 90
EXP. Oct 93

E Savlon
Antiseptic Cream
For external use only.

Directions: For minor burns and scalds, small wounds, scratches, cuts and abrasions: Squeeze cream on to cotton wool or a piece of lint and gently wipe over the damaged area to remove any dirt or extraneous material. A second application of the cream should then be made for greater protection against bacterial infection.

Avoid contact with brain, meninges or middle ear.

Nett 35 g

Retail price not to exceed Rs 5.51

L.T. extra
Batch No 0067
MFG. Date Jan 90
EXP. Date 36 months from date of manufacture

F Sloan's Balm

Dr Sloan created this balm with unique 'Heat-Action' to relieve body pains such as: muscular pains, sprains, pains in joints, backache, pains of arthritis, lumbago, bruises, etc. Also relieves local congestion due to bronchitis and colds.

Directions: Apply Sloan's Balm freely on the affected area. Rub gently. Apply 1 to 3 times daily as needed. Avoid contact with open wounds, eyes, etc.

Net weight 10 g
Maximum price Rs 5.86
Local taxes extra
Batch 711
MFG. Date 10/90

Exercises

Reproduced above are some labels of common medicines. Read them carefully and answer the following questions:

1 A solution is a water/liquid based preparation; an ointment is a cream-based preparation; a tablet is a solidified preparation or drug compressed into a convenient shape; a capsule is a tiny soluble container for a dose of medicine. How many different types of preparations are mentioned in the list of medicines?

2 MFD./MFG. means the manufacturing date; EXP. means date of expiry, i.e. when the medicine becomes useless.
   (*a*) How many medicines do not have the date of expiry mentioned on them? Why?
   (*b*) If we opened Betnosol-N on 1 June 1991, could it still be used on 1 April 1993?
   (*c*) If we started using Savlon in March 1990, would it still be fit for use in August 1993?

3 If you were a bus driver and were suffering from a bad cough which medicine would you avoid taking while on duty?

4 What is meant by the phrase 'For external use only'? Does it mean that the medicine is:
   (*a*) not to be eaten or drunk?
   (*b*) not for use in eye or ear?
   (*c*) to be used outside the house?

5 Where will you keep medicines marked 'Keep in a cool dry place':
   (*a*) in the fridge
   (*b*) in a cupboard
   (*c*) on a window sill

6 Which of the medicines in the list can be bought only after consulting a doctor and getting a prescription from him? How can you tell?

7 (*a*) In deciding how much medicine to take and at what intervals to take it, should we follow the doctor's instructions or the instructions given by the manufacturers? Why?

(*b*) Can we give two teaspoonfuls of Dilosyn six times a day to a one-year-old child? Give reasons for your answer.

8 Are medicines available at the prices printed on them? What words on the packaging allow the chemist to charge more than the printed price?

UNIT 5 REFERENCE SKILLS

How to use a dictionary

A dictionary is an invaluable aid to learning, and to get the best out of it, we must know how to use it. A good dictionary gives us not only the definitions of words of a language but much more. It tells us about spelling and pronunciation, usage and style, grammar and idiom. It contains words, compound words, derivatives and idiomatic expressions and explains their meanings through examples and even illustrations.

Words in a dictionary are arranged in alphabetical order, i.e. words beginning with **a** are listed before words beginning with **b** and words beginning with **ab** are listed before words beginning with **ac**. If the first two or three letters of two words are the same, we must look at the next letter in each word to find out where it is listed. Thus, **park** comes before **part** and both come before **party**. If two words have the same spelling but are different parts of speech, they are listed one after the other, and numbered thus: **man**[1] and **man**[2] (where **man**[1] is a noun and **man**[2] is a verb). The first and last words listed on each page are printed on the top left-hand or right-hand corners of that page as running heads or headers, so that by turning the pages quickly we can guess the words that might be included on a particular page.

The main entry (or headword as it is called) is printed in bold type, i.e. with heavy lettering and in dark ink (e.g. **man**), so that the eye can pick out the main entries easily and quickly. Immediately after the headword, the correct pronunciation of the word written in phonetic symbols is given (e.g. /mæn/). Since in English, the same letter can be pronounced in many ways (as **a** in at, art, able and alone, or **g** in gate and ginger, or **c** in cat and cinema), the correct pronunciation of a word can become a tricky business. Therefore, the International Phonetic Association has devised a system of writing in which each sound is represented by a different symbol. With the help of this system one can show the exact pronunciation of a word in writing. This system may be said to give phonetic spellings. So **cat** in phonetic spelling becomes /kæt/ while **table** is written /'teɪbl/ and **cart** /'kɑ:t/ and so on. Two words that are spelt differently but pronounced in the same way will have the same phonetic spellings. Thus **write** and **right** will both be written /'raɪt/ in phonetic spelling.

Some words in the dictionary show two phonetic spellings of the same word. These words can be pronounced in two different ways, e.g. **direct** as /di'rekt/ or /dai'rekt/. Sometimes certain words are pronounced differently by the English and the Americans, e.g. **missile** in British usage is /'mɪsaɪl/ but in American usage it is

/ˈmɪsl/. American pronounciation is usually shown by the words *US* written just before the word.

The grammatical category of the word is given in italics immediately after the phonetic spelling—thus, *n* stands for noun, *vt* for verb transitive, *adj* for adjective and so on. Each dictionary uses its own abbreviations and one must know the short forms used in one's dictionary. So our entry for 'man' now reads **man**[1] /mæn/ *n*. The plural of a noun is generally formed by adding an '-s' or '-es' to it. If a noun forms its plural in any other way the dictionary will show in brackets what the plural is together with its pronunciation, if necessary. Thus, **man** (*pl* men/men/) will be given at the beginning of the entry. Similarly, if the past tense of a word is not formed by adding '-d' or '-ed' after it, that too will be indicated within brackets as in **sing** (*pt* sang).

If a word has more than one meaning, the meanings are numbered **1, 2, 3, 4** within the entry. Number **1** will give the commonest meaning while number **4** will give the rarest. For example, the noun **man** has eleven meanings. Of these, the first four are: **1** male adult human being. **2** person. **3** (*sing* only, no *article*) the human race; all mankind. **4** husband. When we are looking for the meaning of a word we must keep in mind the context in which it has been used and then decide which meaning fits the word. In the sentence 'Man is a social animal', **man** is used in the third sense, whereas in the sentence 'This is a man's job' the same word is used in the first sense. The correct meaning of a word can only be decided upon when it is placed in context.

Idiomatic expressions are given after the meanings have been listed. An idiom is a phrase or sentence of two or more words that has a meaning different from the meanings of the words that make it up. We have already seen some of the meanings of the word **man**. When, however, it is used in a fixed expression it can have a very different meaning. For instance, **a man of letters** is a writer or scholar; **to be one's own man** means to do as one pleases, to act freely; and **every man for himself** means that each person must take care of his own safety. Very often the meaning of phrases and idioms may have no connection with what the words say. For example, **to hit the nail on the head** means to give a correct explanation and **to be all ears** means to listen eagerly. The meanings of phrases and idioms should be looked for under the most important word in the phrase or idiom, e.g. to **hit the nail on the head** should be looked for under **nail** and **to be all ears** under **ears**.

Compound words, i.e. words formed by adding another word to the original are listed after idiomatic expressions and are written in bold type within the entry. The compound word can sometimes be written as one word (**manhole; manpower**) sometimes as two (**child care; income tax**) and sometimes it can be hyphenated (**man-eater; man-made**).

Derivatives, i.e. words formed by adding suffixes like '-less', '-able', '-ance', '-ly', '-ment', '-ness', etc., to a headword are listed at the end of the entry. The grammatical category of the derivative is also indicated, e.g. **harmful** *adj*; **harmfully** *adv*. If, however, the spelling or meaning of the derivative is markedly different from that of the headword, then the derivative is listed as a separate entry, e.g. **manly** *adj*; **picturesque** *adj*.

Before we end, a word about the swung dash or tilde sign (~). In some dictionaries, to save space, whenever the headword is repeated in the entry, the swung dash is used. For example, under **book** there will be **~stall** for bookstall, **~seller** for bookseller, **~worm** for bookworm, etc. Any other information that is needed to understand the functioning of the dictionary will be found in the introduction to the dictionary you are consulting.

Most dictionaries also contain many useful appendices (something added at the end of a book), which give a lot of useful information. One should be aware of what is contained in the appendix so that one can use it when required.

A dictionary is a very useful book and a storehouse of information. It is a friend and a guide. Learn to use it frequently and see how much it can tell you. ❑

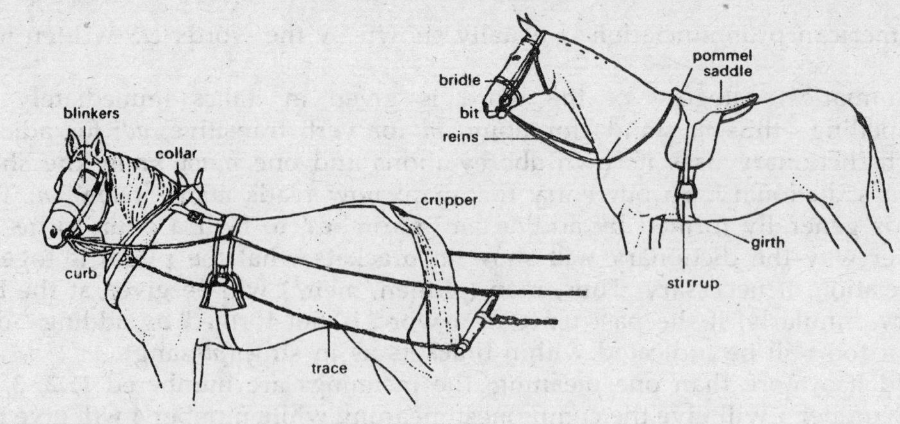

a harness

~-*boiled woman,* (fig) one lacking in the gentler feelings; one without sentiment or sympathy. ˈ~-ˈ**baked,** baked until ~. ˈ~-ˈ**boiled,** (e g of eggs) boiled ~; (fig) callous. ˈ~-ˈ**bitten** *adj* (of a person) stubborn in fighting; tough because of a difficult life, etc: *a ~-bitten colonel.* **5** closely; immediately: *follow ~ after/upon/behind someone.* **~ by,** close by: not far away.

harden /ˈhɑdn/ *vt, vi* [VP6A,2A] make or become hard, strong, hardy, etc: *~ steel; ~ the heart; a ~ed criminal,* one who is callous, who shows no signs of shame or repentance; *~ the body,* e g by taking exercise. ***be ~ed to,*** made insensitive to. [VP15B,2C] **~ off,** (of young plants, esp seedlings) make or become hardy and ready for planting out in the open.

hardi·hood /ˈhɑdɪhʊd/ *n* [U] boldness; audacity.

hard·ly /ˈhɑdlɪ/ *adv* **1** only just; not quite; scarely: *I ~ know her,* have only a very slight acquaintance with her. *We had ~ got/H~ had we got into the country when it began to rain.* Cf No sooner... than. *I'm so tired I can ~ walk.* **2** (used to suggest that sth is improbable, unlikely or unreasonable): *He can ~ have arrived yet. You can ~ expect me to lend you money again.* **3** (neg in meaning) almost no; almost not: *He ~ ever* (= very seldom) *goes to bed before midnight.* Cf His wife *almost always* goes to bed before midnight. *I need ~ say* (= It is almost unnecessary for me to say) *that I am innocent. There's ~ any coal left. H~ anybody* (= Very few people) *came to the meeting.* **4** (from hard[2](3)) severely: *~ treated.* **5** (from hard[1](6)) with effort or difficulty. For this sense the *adv* 'hard' is usu preferred. Cf *hard-earned money* and *salary that was ~* (i e only just, barely) *earned.*

hard·ship /ˈhɑdʃɪp/ *n* **1** [C] circumstance that causes discomfort or suffering: *the ~s borne by soldiers during a war.* **2** [U] severe suffering: *bear ~ without complaining.*

hardy /ˈhɑdɪ/ *adj* (-ier, -iest) **1** strong; able to endure suffering or hardship: *A few ~ men broke the ice on the lake and had a swim.* (of plants) able to endure frost without being injured: *~ annuals.* **2** bold; ready to face danger. **hardi·ness** *n*

hare /heə(r)/ *n* fast-running field animal with long ears and a divided upper lip, like but larger than a rabbit. ***~ and hounds,*** paper-chase, a game in which two persons called the ~s run across country dropping torn-up bits of paper and are followed by others, called 'hounds', who try to catch them. ***run with the ~ and hunt with the hounds,*** try to keep the favour of both sides in a dispute; play a double game. ***mad as a (March) ~,*** very wild. ***start a ~,*** raise a topic, augment, etc unrelated to the main issue. ˈ**~·bell** *n* round-leaved plant with blue bell-like flowers (in Scotland called *bluebell*). ˈ**~-ˈbrained** *adj* rash; wild. ˈ**~-ˈlip** *n* person's upper lip divided (from birth) like that of a ~. □ *vi* [VP2C] run fast or away: *They ~d off.*

harem /ˈheərəm/ *n* women's part of a Muslim household: women living in it.

hari·cot /ˈhærɪkəʊ/ *n* (also ˈ**~ bean**) kidney bean; French bean.

hark /hɑk/ *vi* **1** (chiefly imper) **~ to/at,** (colloq) listen to: *Just ~ at him!* **2** ***~ back (to),*** refer back to sth done or said earlier.

har·le·quin /ˈhɑləkwɪn/ *n* character in Italian comedy; mute character in English pantomime, full of tricks and very lively; (hence) person fond of practical jokes; buffoon. **~·ade** /ˈhɑləkwɪnˈeɪd/ *n* part of a pantomime in which a ~ plays the chief part.

Har·ley Street /ˈhɑlɪ strit/ *n* London street where many fashionable doctors and surgeons live.

har·lot /ˈhɑlət/ *n* (archaic, or as a term of abuse) prostitute.

harm /hɑm/ *n* [U] ***do sb ~,*** cause damage; injury: *It will do you no ~. He probably meant no ~,* did not intend to hurt anyone or anyone's feelings. *There's no ~ in your staying up late occasionally,* no reason why you should not do so. ***out of ~'s way,*** in a place of safety. □ *vt* [VP6A] cause ~ to: *It hasn't ~ed you, has it?* **~·ful** /-fl/ *adj* causing ~ *(to).* **~·fully** /-flɪ/ *adv* **~·less** *adj* **1** not doing ~ *(to): ~less snakes.* **2** innocent; inoffensive: *Several ~less spectators were wounded during the rioting.* **~·less·ly** *adv*

har·monic /hɑˈmɒnɪk/ *n* (music) higher note produced (by vibration of strings) with a note that is played, and having a fixed relation to it.

har·mon·ica /hɑˈmɒnɪkə/ *n* name of several musical instruments, esp (in GB) the mouth-organ.

har·moni·ous /hɑˈməʊnɪəs/ *adj* **1** pleasingly or satisfactorily arranged: *a ~ group of buildings.* **2** in agreement; free from ill feeling: *~ families/neighbours.* **3** sweet-sounding; tuneful; **~·ly** *adv*

har·mo·nium /hɑˈməʊnɪəm/ *n* musical instrument

with a keyboard like a small organ, supplied with wind by means of bellows worked by pedals, but with metal reeds instead of pipes.

har·mon·ize /ˈhɑmənɑɪz/ *vt,vi* **1** [VP6A,14] bring (one thing) into harmony (with another); (music) add notes (to a melody) to make chords. **2** [VP2A,C] be in harmony or agreement: *colours that* ~ *well* (*with the decorations/with each other.*) **har·mon·iz·ation** /ˌhɑmənɑɪˈzeɪʃn/ *n*

har·mony /ˈhɑmənɪ/ *n* (*pl* **-nies**) **1** [U] agreement (of feeling, interests, opinions, etc): *There was not much* ~ *in international affairs during those years.* ***be in*** ~ ***(with),*** match; agree (with): *His tastes are in* ~ *with mine.* **2** [C,U] (instance or example of) pleasing combination of related things: *the* ~ *of colour in nature,* e g the greens, browns, etc of trees in autumn. **3** [C,U] (music) pleasing combination of notes sounded together to make chords.

har·ness /ˈhɑnɪs/ *n* [U] (collective *sing*) all the leather-work and metal-work by which a horse is controlled and fastened to the cart, waggon, plough, etc, that it pulls. ***in*** ~, (fig) doing one's regular work. ***die in*** ~, die while engaged in one's regular work, not after retiring. ***work/run in double*** ~, work with a partner, or with a husband or wife. □ *vt* [VP6A] **1** put ~ on (a horse). **2** use (a river, waterfall, etc) to produce (esp electric) power.

harp /hɑp/ *n* freestanding musical instrument with vertical strings played with the fingers. ⇨ the illus at **string**. □ *vi* **1** play the ~. **2** ~ ***on sth,*** (fig) talk repeatedly or tiresomely about: *She is always* ~*ing on her misfortunes.* ~**er,** ~**-ist** /-ɪst/ *nn* player on the ~.

har·poon /hɑˈpun/ *n* spear on a rope, thrown by hand or fired from a gun, for catching whales and other large sea animals. □ *vt* strike with a ~.

harp·si·chord /ˈhɑpsɪkɔd/ *n* piano-like instrument used from the 16th to the 18th cc (and today for music of these centuries). ⇨ the illus at **keyboard**.

harpy /ˈhɑpɪ/ *n* (*pl* **-pies**) **1** (old Gk stories) cruel creature with a woman's face and a bird's wings and claws. **2** cruel, greedy, hard-hearted woman.

har·ri·dan /ˈhærɪdən/ *n* worn-out, bad-tempered old woman.

har·rier /ˈhærɪə(r)/ *n* hound used for hunting hares; (*pl*) pack of these with huntsmen. **2** cross-country runner.

har·row /ˈhærəʊ/ *n* heavy frame with metal teeth or discs for breaking up ground after ploughing. □ *vt* [VP6A] pull a ~ over (a field, etc); (fig) distress (the feelings): *a* ~*ing tale of misfortunes.*

harry /ˈhærɪ/ *vt* (*pt,pp* **-ried**) [VP6A] **1** lay waste and plunder; attack frequently: *The Vikings used to* ~ *the English coast.* **2** annoy or worry: *money-lenders* ~*ing their debtors.*

harsh /hɑʃ/ *adj* (**-er, -est**) **1** rough and disagreeable, esp to the senses: *a* ~ *texture/voice/contrast;* ~ *to the ear.* **2** stern, cruel, severe: *a* ~ *judge/judgement/punishment.* ~**-ly** *adv* ~**-ness** *n*

hart /hɑt/ *n* adult male of (esp red) deer; stag.

har·tal /ˈhɑtɑl/ *n* (in India) closing of shops as a mark of sorrow or for a political reason.

harum-scarum /ˈheərəm ˈskeərəm/ *n* reckless, impulsive person.

har·vest /ˈhɑvɪst/ *n* **1** (season for) cutting and gathering in of grain and other food crops; quantity obtained: *this year's wheat* ~*; a succession of good* ~*s.* ˈ~ ˈ**festival** *n* service of thanksgiving in Christian churches after the ~ has been gathered. ˈ~ **home** *n* festival given by farmers to their workers when the ~ is gathered in. ˈ~ ˈ**moon** *n* full moon nearest to the autumn equinox. **2** (fig) consequences of action or behaviour: *reap the* ~ *of one's hard work,* be rewarded for it. □ *vt* [VP6A] cut, gather, dig up, a crop: ~ *rice/potatoes.* ~**er** *n* **1** person who ~s; reaper. **2** machine for cutting and gathering grain, esp the kind that also binds it into sheaves or (ˈ**combine-**ˈ~**er**) threshes it. ⇨ the illus at **combine**.

has ⇨ **have**[1].

has-been /ˈhæz bin/ *n* (colloq) person who, or thing which, has lost a quality, skill, etc formerly possessed; sb or sth now out of date.

hash /hæʃ/ *vt* [VP6A,15B] ~ ***(up),*** chop or cut up (meat) into small pieces. □ *n* **1** [U] (dish of) cooked meat, ~ed and re-cooked. **2** ***make a*** ~ ***of sth,*** (fig) do it very badly, make a mess of it. ***settle sb's*** ~, deal with him in such a way that he gives no more trouble. **3** (colloq) hashish.

hash·ish, hash·eesh /ˈhæʃiʃ/ *n* [U] dried hemp leaves made into a drug for smoking or chewing; cannabis.

hasn't /ˈhæznt/ = has not. ⇨ **have**[1].

hasp /hæsp/ *n* metal fastening for a door, window, etc used with a staple. ⇨ the illus at **padlock**.

has·sock /ˈhæsək/ *n* cushion for kneeling on, e g in church.

hast /hæst/ (archaic): *thou* ~, you have.

haste /heɪst/ *n* [U] quickness of movement; hurry: *Why all this* ~*?* Why are you in such a hurry? *He went off in great* ~. ***Make*** ~***!*** Hurry! ***More*** ~, ***less speed,*** (prov) The more you hurry, the less real progress you will make.

hasten /ˈheɪsn/ *vi,vt* **1** [VP2A,C,4A] move or act with speed: ~ *away/home/to the office;* ~ *to tell sb the good news.* **2** [VP6A] cause (sb) to hurry; cause (sth) to be done or to happen quickly or earlier: *Artificial heating* ~*s the growth of plants.*

hasty /ˈheɪstɪ/ *adj* (**- er, -iest**) **1** said, made or done (too) quickly: ~ *preparations for flight; a* ~ *departure;* ~ *words that are regretted afterwards.* **2** (older use) quick-tempered: *a* ~ *old colonel.* **hast·ily** /-əlɪ/ *adv* **hasti·ness** *n*

hat /hæt/ *n* covering for the head, usu (for men) with a brim, worn out of doors. Cf *cap* and *bonnet* without a brim. ***go/come hat/cap in hand,*** obsequiously, apologetically. ***send/pass round the hat,*** ask for, collect, contributions of money (usu for sb who has suffered a loss). ***take one's hat off to,*** (fig) express admiration for. ***talk through one's hat,*** (sl) talk foolishly. ***a bad hat,*** (sl) bad person. ˈ**hat-band** *n* band round the crown of a hat, above the brim. ˈ**hat-pin** *n* long pin used (formerly) by women to fasten a hat to the hair. ˈ**hat trick** *n* (cricket) taking of three wickets with successive balls; similar success in other sports or activities. **hat·ful** /-fʊl/ *n* as much as a hat holds. **hat·less** *adj* not wearing a hat. **hat·ter** *n* man who makes or sells hats. ***as mad as a hatter,*** very mad.

hatch[1] /hætʃ/ *n* **1** (movable covering over an) opening in a door or floor, esp (ˈ~**-way**) one in a ship's deck through which cargo is lowered and raised; opening in a wall between two rooms, esp a kitchen and a dining room, through which dishes, etc, are passed. ***under*** ~***es,*** below deck. **2** lower half of a divided door.

hatch[2] /hætʃ/ *vt,vi* **1** [VP6A,2A] (cause to) break

(From *Oxford Advanced Dictionary of Current English* by A S Hornby, OUP, Oxford, ELBS edn of 3rd edn, 1974)

Exercises

Carefully read the sample pages from a dictionary given earlier and do exercises 2 to 13:

1 List the following words in alphabetical order: across, account, ascent, akin, acknowledge, accustom, arch, air, about, arrest.
2 What are the plurals of 'harmony' and 'harpy'?
3 How many times is the word 'hatch' listed? Why?
4 What parts of speech are the following words: haste, hasten, hasty, hastiness?
5 How many idiomatic expressions are listed under 'hat' and 'hare'?
6 How many derivatives can you make from 'harm'?
7 How many compound words can be made with 'harvest'?
8 What do the following phrases mean?

(*a*) to make a hash of something
(*b*) to harp on something
(*c*) to die in harness

9 In what sense is the word 'hardly' used in the following sentence?
That's hardly the right thing to say at a time like this!
10 Only one entry starts with a capital letter. Which one and why?
11 How should the following words be pronounced?
hark, hare, harp, harry

(*a*) Is the 'r' in all these words pronounced?
(*b*) In how many different ways is the 'a' in these words pronounced?

Practise saying the words out loud.

12 How do the British pronounce the Indian word 'hartal' (closing of shops as a mark of sorrow or for political reasons)?
13 Can you guess what was the entry before 'harden'?
14 A dictionary is a very useful thing and we would be lost without it, yet we don't go running to a dictionary everytime we sit down to read something. If we come across a new or unfamiliar word, we usually try to guess its meaning from the context. The following paragraphs have some words in italics with jumbled up letters. Can you guess what these words are:

A pyramid is a *cusrettur* with a square base and with triangular sides which meet in a point at the top. They are the *botms* of ancient Egyptian kings who believed that their bodies needed to be *fretpecly* preserved for their future lives. The dead were therefore *belamedm* and the mummies were hidden below the veell of the ground in these pyramids.

The *rypmaid* of King Cheops was built around 2575 BC and according to Herodotus, the King *pomelyde* 100,000 men for 20 years to *dubil* it. It was made of limestone and *gratine*, each block of stone weighing about two tons. The pyramid *semaures* 755 feet at the base and is 482 feet high.

(From *Target*, New Delhi, Sept 1986)

UNIT 6 UNDERSTANDING JOURNALESE

From Our Special Representative

NEW DELHI, AUGUST 14.

ENTIRE DELHI KEPT AWAKE TO WITNESS THE HISTORIC EVENT OF USHERING IN THE FREEDOM OF INDIA AT THE HOUR OF MIDNIGHT.

Unprecedented scenes of enthusiasm were witnessed both inside and outside the Constituent Assembly Chamber, where seething, swaying humanity wildly cheered the momentous event, heralded with the blowing of conches.

Raising to the height of the occasion, Pandit Nehru made a speech in the Assembly which was at once notable and a masterpiece of literature.

"Years ago we made a tryst with destiny", he said, "and now the time comes when we shall redeem our pledge, not wholly or in full measure, but very substantially. At the stroke of the midnight hour, when the world sleeps, India will awake to life and freedom".

(From the *Times of India*, New Delhi, 15 Aug 1947)

Exercises

Read the passage above and answer the following questions:

1 Which of the following titles is most suitable for this text?

- (*a*) The stroke of the midnight hour
- (*b*) Pandit Nehru's speech in the Assembly
- (*c*) The freedom of India
- (*d*) 'A tryst with destiny'
- (*e*) Nation wakes to new life
- (*f*) A historic event

2 (*a*) How many of the suggested titles are actually used in the text?
- (*b*) How many of the titles are expressed differently in the text? What are the different sentences or phrases?
- (*c*) Why is title in 1(*d*) within inverted commas?

3 Notice how the titles do not form complete sentences yet we have no problem understanding them if we know the context. How many of these titles can be expanded to form full sentences? What do you gain or lose by doing so?

4 Was this passage originally:

- (*a*) a newspaper report
- (*b*) an essay
- (*c*) a letter

How can you tell?

5 (*a*) Given below are certain words from the text and their meanings. Match the words in *List 1* with their meanings in *List 2*:

List 1	*List 2*
momentous	agreement or appointment
usher	a large spiral shell
conch	publicly announced
seething	important
tryst	crowded
heralded	lead, show in

(*b*) Explain the meanings of the following phrases from the text. Use a dictionary if necessary:

rising to the height of the occasion
a tryst with destiny
redeem our pledge
in full measure
historic event

Photo: Pradeep Mandhani

6 The title of one of the articles of a newspaper is 'A Step in Time'. Can you guess what the article is about? Make a list of the themes suggested by the members of your group.

7 If the picture above was given with the title, would it help you to guess better? Make another list of the themes now suggested by the title 'A Step in Time' and the picture taken together.

8 The following extract is also given along with the title and the picture:

Walking is the key to fitness for people of all ages. Started at an early age and continued till later years, it is a sort of life insurance, that can have significant preventive effects on some major health problems.

Now say if the subject of the article is:

(*a*) Safety
(*b*) Health
(*c*) The importance of time

9 (*a*) From the list given below choose three major health problems that can be prevented by walking:

Obesity
Backache
Sluggish liver
Flu
Heart disease
Arthritis
Bad stomach
Common cold

Consult the dictionary if you aren't sure of the meaning of some of these words.

you're the detective

CAN YOU SOLVE IT

By E.K.

The thief ran down the corridor pursued by the Inspector, two uniformed policemen, and two guards. The hotel manager brought up the rear. But by the time they reached the corridor, the thief had disappeared.

'You check these rooms,' the Inspector orders the guards. He and the policemen, accompanied by you and the manager, proceed to the kitchen at the end of the corridor.

Inspector Smith questions the guard stationed outside the kitchen's rear entrance. 'No,' he answers, 'no one came out this way.'

You look around the kitchen. The chef has resumed giving orders to one of his assistants while three others return to their duties. One is washing lettuce for the salad; another is watching a lump of doughnut batter fry at the bottom of a pot of boiling oil; the third is stacking clean dishes in preparation for the dinner crowds.

The two guards enter the kitchen empty-handed. 'There are only storerooms along the corridor,' says one. 'They don't have any outside windows or doors and there's no one in them.'

'I didn't expect you to find anyone', says Inspector Smith. The manager wrings his hands. 'When I invited the coin exhibition here, I thought it would bring us publicity. But now what kind of publicity will we get when a rare gold coin is stolen?'

'Did anyone get a good look at the man?' asks the Inspector. 'Only that he was wearing white, like the kitchen people here,' one of the guards says. Everyone else agrees.

'There's no other way out,' says the Inspector. 'It must be one of the kitchen staff.'

'I didn't see anyone run in here,' protests the chef.

'He didn't'' you state. 'He walked in so he wouldn't attract attention. But I know who it is.'

(From the *Times of India*, New Delhi, 26 July 1987)

Exercises

Read the passage given above and answer the following questions:

1 How many people are there in the story? List them.
2 What crime has been committed?
3 Inspector Smith questions the guard stationed outside the kitchen's rear entrance. What question did he ask the guard?
4 Who is the 'you' in the title, paragraph 4, line 1, and the last paragraph line 1.
5 Why does the Inspector think that the thief could only be one of the kitchen staff?
6 Why does the thief in the story return to the kitchen? If you were the thief what would you have done?
7 Name at least four things that the kitchen staff in the hotel were doing.
8 Who do you think is the culprit? If you cannot guess look for the answer at the end of this unit.
9 (*a*) 'The manager wrings his hands.' In this sentence 'wring' means:

(i) to dip in water repeatedly
(ii) to hit with a piece of iron to produce a sound
(iii) to squeeze and rub one's hands

(b) 'The chef has resumed giving orders.' In this sentence 'resumed' means:
(i) to stop after beginning
(ii) to begin after stopping
(iii) to make brief

(c) 'I thought it would bring us publicity.' In this sentence 'it' refers to:
(i) his hands
(ii) the exhibition
(iii) the theft

10. Retell the story as if you were the thief.

Answer: The doughnut in the pot of boiling oil should have floated. It didn't because the thief who made it hid the coin in it which made the doughnut heavy and thus sink.

UNIT 8 UNDERSTANDING EXTENDED PROSE

Men are lazy

Even though more and more women have started taking up full-time jobs outside the house, they still end up doing nearly all the housework. In spite of a demanding career, a woman is expected to be an efficient housewife but most men still do not make good house-husbands. When it comes to helping with the housework many men feel totally helpless. When they decide to do a few jobs around the house they only pick the ones they enjoy. Sometimes if they are in the mood they don't mind doing a bit of gardening or mending a few things but they refuse to do any boring jobs like cleaning the house, washing and ironing the clothes, looking after the children or cooking dinner. Most of these jobs have to be done immediately and regularly while household repairs, the job that men enjoy doing most, can always wait till a more convenient time or till one feels like doing them.

According to a survey done recently, the lady of the house does three-quarters of the boring household chores even if she has a full-time job. But, surprisingly, housewives don't seem to mind, for most women still see their family role as the one that matters most. Only 20 per cent of the women interviewed said they would like their husbands to help more with the housework; 75 per cent were satisfied with things as they were and the remaining 5 per cent preferred to have their husbands keep away from housework. Most women tended to use electrical appliances to make up for male laziness. Makers of household appliances and electrical gadgets are delighted, of course.

Exercises

Read the passage given above and answer the following questions:

1. Which household jobs do men find boring? Which household jobs do you find boring and why?

2. Name some household appliances and electrical gadgets that can make household work easier.

3. (*a*) 'When it comes to helping with the housework many men feel totally helpless.' Does this mean that:

   (*i*) men have very little energy?
   (*ii*) men don't know how to do housework?
   (*iii*) men don't like to help?

   (*b*) 'When they decide to do a few jobs around the house they only pick the ones they enjoy.' Does this mean that:

   (*i*) men are always ready to do work around the house which is enjoyable?
   (*ii*) men sometimes do housework but only those tasks which they find enjoyable?
   (*iii*) men never enjoy housework and they rarely do it?

4 Why, in your opinion, do men feel totally helpless when it comes to doing housework? Is it because:

   (*a*) men are lazy?
   (*b*) men have been taught since childhood that household jobs are women's work and therefore not meant for them?
   (*c*) household jobs are specialized jobs and men need training before they can handle them?

5 (*a*) What are some of the words used in this text for *man, woman* and *work*?
   (*b*) What does 'ones' in the sentence 'When they decide to do a few jobs around the house they only pick the ones they enjoy' stand for?

6 Why, in your opinion, do most women not mind when their husbands avoid housework? Discuss in small groups and present a reasoned answer.

7 If a woman did not have a full-time job would it be all right to expect her to do all the household jobs? Do you think that it would be a good idea to pay women for housework? Discuss with others in your group and justify your answer.

8 (*a*) Look up the dictionary and see how 'ones' and 'once' are pronounced. Find out the pronunciation of the following words too and practice saying them correctly:

   women, enjoy, refuse, housewives, chores, ironing, repairs.
   satisfied, processors, appliances, preferred

   (*b*) Look up the meaning of the word 'housewife' in the dictionary. Can you find the word 'house-husbands' in it too? If not, can you guess what it means and why it is not to be found in the dictionary?

9 Do you think that 'Men are lazy' is a suitable title for this piece? Are men really lazy or are they lazy with regard to only certain types of work? Can you think of a better title for this piece?

10 Conduct a survey in your class to find out what percentage of your classmates:

   (*a*) have working mothers/wives.
   (*b*) have full-time domestic help or servants.
   (*c*) use household appliances and electrical gadgets and which ones are the most commonly used.

UNIT 9 UNDERSTANDING POETRY

AN INVITATION

Sukumar Ray

Oh don't be scared—please don't be scared! I don't intend to beat you.
Believe me, if we fought a bout, I never could defeat you.
My heart is of a kindly sort, I'm gentle in my habit—
I really couldn't crunch your neck or even try to grab it.
Perhaps it's these unfortunate horns that complicate the issue?
My forehead's in a tender state, I cannot biff or squish you.
So come and see my humble home, and take a little rest:
We wouldn't spare the slightest care to please an honoured guest.
Ah, now I know! This cudgel, then, is really why you linger?
Why bless my soul, it's light as pith, it wouldn't crack a finger!
What, still unsure? Why really, sir, you'll start to hurt my feelings:
I'll twist your neck or crush your leg to add to my appealings.
There's me, my missus, nine stout sons, the whole lot at your service—
We'll bite you all together, now, if you don't stop being nervous.

(From *The Select Nonsense of Sukumar Ray*,
trans Sukanta Chaudhury, OUP, Delhi, 1987)

Exercises

Read the poem carefully and answer the following questions:

1 (*a*) Who is the 'I' of the poem:

(*i*) the poet
(*ii*) a beast with horns, claws and a tail
(*iii*) an aggressive and violent man

(*b*) Who is the 'you' of the poem:

(*i*) the reader
(*ii*) a cautious man
(*iii*) a frightened mouse
(*iv*) an honoured guest

2 What is the 'invitation' for:

(*a*) a party
(*b*) a visit to the house of the speaker
(*c*) the invitation is only a trick

3 Which of the following Statements accurately describe the speaker:

(*a*) He has a bump on the forehead.
(*b*) He has horns and a cudgel.
(*c*) He is married and has nine sons.
(*d*) He runs a guest-house.
(*e*) He is a kindly man with gentle habits.
(*f*) He will not attack anyone.
(*g*) He is an aggressive violent man.

4 What, according to the speaker, are the two things that have frightened the guest?

5 Can you think of another word that could be used instead of 'scared' in line 1?

6 You will notice that the last words of all the odd numbered lines (1, 3, 5, 7, etc.) rhyme with the last words of the even numbered lines (2, 4, 6, etc.). Thus, we have: you/you, habit/grab it, issue/you, linger/finger, feelings/appealings, service/nervous. Can you find, besides 'issue', another word to rhyme with 'you'? You will also notice that service/nervous though spelt differently rhyme very well. Can you find other examples, in the poem, of words that look different but rhyme perfectly?

7 Given below are three summaries of the poem. Which one would you say is most accurate?

(*a*) A clever man invites a simple man to his house but the simple man refuses because he is nervous.
(*b*) An aggressive monster tries to trick a cautious man into his house, first by trying to persuade him and later by threatening him.
(*c*) A brave man tries to reassure a nervous guest that there is nothing to be afraid of, that he will be honoured and well looked after; but if he persists in being nervous, his hospitality will turn into enmity.

8. The columns below list some of the things the speaker of the poem will do or will not do. Put a tick in the appropriate column.

Actions	*Will do*	*Will not do*
beat		
defeat		
crunch his neck		
biff		
squish		
crack a finger		
twist his neck		
crush his leg		
bite		

9 What does 'it' in lines 4 and 10 stand for?

10 In what sense is the word 'now' used in line 14? Does it mean:

(a) immediately?
(b) soon?
(c) without doubt?

11 (*a*) Is this poem an invitation or a threat? Point out the words which make you think that it is:

(*i*) an invitation
(*ii*) a threat

(*b*) Is there any change of tone in the poem? Where does it occur and which words indicate this change?

UNIT 10 UNDERSTANDING NARRATIVE

Under Consideration

RAMESH KAPOOR

Marriages are made in heaven they say. Or are they? Feasting on the rich food and expensive sweets usually served at marriage parties, I would often wonder. . . .

One day, on a sudden inspiration, my father decided that I must be married off. Accordingly he placed a matrimonial advertisement in a popular English daily. Prompt came a reply from Lala Dhaniram claiming that his son would make an ideal match. It was decided that the two parties should meet at the Qutb Minar as the precincts of the Birla Mandir and the hotels of Connaught Place were already overflowing with prospective matchmakers.

We reached the Qutb Minar well in time. Lala Dhaniram and his dear son were quick to arrive too. There was little to differentiate between father and son, except, perhaps, for a minor variation in the sizes of their girth.

The negotiations started immediately. My father, who had quickly launched into the merits of his well-qualified and well-endowed daughter, was cut off in mid-stream by the Lala: 'That is hardly a matter to be discussed.' Cautiously my father asked if he had any demands. 'Indeed, no! You are a respectable man and you will yourself ensure that your dignity is not compromised,' said Lala Dhaniram. In the meantime his son, who had been eyeing the Qutb, exclaimed, 'Bapu, the Qutb Minar.' Immediately the Lala declared, 'Since the boy is insisting upon it, do let him have the Minar.' The son's gaze had, by now, wandered off to the Iron Pillar and soon enough he whined, 'Bapu, the Iron Pillar.' Lalaji promptly asked my father to let him have the Pillar as well.

We moved forward to examine the Qutb Minar and the Iron Pillar. My father was in a fix. He did not know how to go about acquiring protected monuments. But he did know that he had to marry off his daughter. After some deliberation, he ventured to ask the Lala how he would transport the Minar and the Pillar to his house and where he would instal them once they were gifted to him. 'Don't you worry,' came the reply. 'The government is very kind. I have always managed to get what I wanted.'

(*contd.*)

My father wrote out an application to the government asking for the Minar and the Pillar. The government, ever obliging, wrote back to say that it had no objection but rightfully my father should obtain the permission of Qutb-ud-din Aibak and Emperor Ashok for the monuments.

Magic and table rapping were used to summon the spirits of Qutb-ud-din Aibak and Ashok the Great. Qutb-ud-din bluntly told my father that minars were not meant for such purposes. 'Horses, elephants and slaves are gifted in marriages, not minars,' he added. Emperor Ashok pleaded that after all these centuries he should not again be dragged into the earthly cycle of possession and dispossession. 'After the battle of Kalinga, I renounced everything,' he said. With one voice they cautioned, 'We have long been dead. Think not of us but of your daughter.'

My father did not give up hope just as the Lala did not give up his demands. He wrote again to the government explaining everything in detail. The government, ever helpful, set up a commission to look into the case. The matter is under consideration and so is my marriage. . . .

(Translated from the original in Hindi by Promodini Varma)

Exercises

Read the above story and answer the following questions:

1 Who is the 'I' of the story? Why is this person not described in the story?

2 (*a*) To whom does 'they' in the first line of the story refer? What does 'they' in 'or are they?' refer to?
  (*b*) Who are the 'two parties' mentioned in paragraph 2?

3 In response to the question if he had any demands, Lala Dhaniram replies, 'Indeed, no!' Does he mean what he says? Does the rest of his answer support his denial?

4 'My father wrote out an application to the government asking for the Minar and the Pillar.' Whom does 'government' here refer to:
  (*a*) the Prime Minister?
  (*b*) the Home Minister?
  (*c*) the Director General of the Archaeological Survey of India?
  (*d*) anyone in authority?

5 The writer describes the attitude of the government once as 'ever obliging' and again as 'ever helpful'. Is the writer being serious or ironic? What is your experience of a government office?

6 Do you think that the Qutb Minar and the Iron Pillar would make good gifts for a newly married couple? Why, in your opinion, did the Lala want them?

7 The word 'consideration' comes from **consider** (to think about). Other derivatives are 'considerate' and 'considerable'. Look up the dictionary and see what they mean.

8 Why is the story titled 'Under consideration'? Can you give the story any other title?

9 It is clear that the story criticizes Lala Dhaniram and his son. What is the attitude of the writer towards the 'I' of the story and her father? Does it:
  (*a*) sympathize with them?
  (*b*) show them to be clever and resourceful?
  (*c*) show them to be as guilty as Lala Dhaniram and his son?

10 The first and last paragraphs of the story end not with a full stop but with four dots or ellipsis. What do the dots represent?

BOOK II

Writing Skills

Mita Bose
Naresh Jain
Sheela Srivastava

Narrating

UNIT 1 NARRATING PAST EVENTS

All of us have constantly to report or narrate past events. Things happen to us and we like to tell others about them. And when they happen to others, we like to hear accounts of them. This is how stories are made. We like to narrate and hear stories. Most stories are generally in the past tense and tell of things that have happened in a sequence over a period of time. So the ability to narrate past events is an important language skill.

Activity 1

Given below are a set of pictures showing the different things a girl (whom we shall call Anita) did to seek admission to her college.

Things to do

1 The pictures are not in the correct order. Discuss with your partner/group and rearrange the pictures in the correct sequence.
2 Write one sentence about each of the pictures.
3 Add the following sentences. Discuss with your partner/group the best places to add them:

   (*a*) The clerk told Anita to come again after four days.
   (*b*) Anita gave the happy news to her mother.
   (*c*) Anita went back home.

4 We can improve the story of Anita's admission. We can use pronouns instead of nouns. We can also join the sentences together by using certain words and expressions that serve to indicate sequence (i.e. what comes first and what next or after).

   (*a*) *List of pronouns*:

he/his/him	they/theirs	I/my/mine
she/her/hers	your/yours	it/its

   (*b*) *List of words and expressions to indicate sequence*:

   first, after that, after which, then, thereafter, and then, finally, in the end

   Note: Remember, this list is not exhaustive. Use any other appropriate sequencer that comes to your mind.

   Now rewrite the story of Anita's admission so that it reads like a connected account.

Exercise 1 That was Anita's story. Now write the story of your own admission to college.

Hint: First, write down the different steps that you took to seek admission and then write a connected account.

Exchange your story with your partner/group and find out if s/he thinks the account is complete. You can also offer similar comments on her/his story.

Exercise 2 Rewrite the story from the point of view of a student who faced some difficulty in getting admission. Discuss with your partner/group, put down the different steps such a student took and then write a connected account.

Hint: Here you will need to make use of the *past tense in the negative*.

Example: found/did not find/didn't find

Jagjit did not find his name in the first list.

Activity 2

The students of your college recently took out a procession against the practice of *sati*. Discuss with your partner/group the various steps that the students took for taking out the procession, make a list of them, and then write the account. Please also mention the route of the procession.

You could make use of the past forms of the following verbs in writing your account:

assemble, address, end, carry (placards), decide,
join, march, shout (slogans)

Hint: Here are some questions that will help you to write the account:

1 What was the immediate occasion for the procession? Was it a recent case of *sati*? Or was the college observing a Social Awareness Week? There could be other occasions too.
2 Who decided to take out the procession? The Students' Union? Or the Social Awareness Society? Or some other group of students? Identify the group that took the lead.
3 How many students took part in the procession?
4 Where did the students assemble?
5 What was the route they took?
6 Did they carry any placards?
7 What slogans did they shout?
8 Where did the procession end?
9 Who addressed the students?

Exercise 1 Write an account of an anti-dowry procession taken out by students/residents of your locality. First discuss the details of the procession with your partner/group, make a list of them, and then write.

Activity 3

Study the following sentences on the life of Jawaharlal Nehru:

Nehru met Mahatma Gandhi in February 1920.
In the same year, i.e. 1920, he joined the freedom movement.
He married Kamla Kaul in 1915.
A daughter, Indira, was born to them in November 1917.
Jawahar Lal Nehru was born in Allahabad on 14 November 1889.
He returned to India in August 1912 and joined the Indian National Congress.
In 1907 he went to Trinity College, Cambridge.
In 1905 he was sent to London to study at a school called Harrow.
Nehru became President of the Congress in 1936.
He died on 27 May 1964.
Nehru became the first Prime Minister of independent India on 15 August 1947.
He took his degree in law in 1912.

1 Rearrange these sentences in the correct chronological order. Then write a connected account of the life of Nehru. While doing so, make use of sequencers, connectives and pronouns where necessary.
2 Add the following sentences to the account. Discuss with your classmates the best places to add them:

Nehru spent several years in jail.
Nehru was not only a great political leader, he was also an important writer.
His books include *The Discovery of India, Glimpses of World History,* and his autobiography.

3 Do you think this is a complete outline of Nehru's life? If not, make additions on your own. Then rewrite the account.

Exercise 1 Choose six or seven important dates in the life of Mother Teresa or Indira Gandhi or P T Usha, and write them down along with the event which happened at the time. On the basis of this information write an account of her life.

Further practice

1 Go back to Exercise 2 of Activity 1 and write the story from the point of view of the parent of the student who faced difficulty in getting admission to a college.

2 A friend of yours is interested in knowing how your younger brother got selected for a commission in the army. Write an account of the various things that your brother had to do for his selection. Make use of the following outline:

— applied to the Union Public Service Commission for admission to the National Defence Academy, Kharakvasla.
— appeared in an Entrance Test.
— qualified in the test.
— was called for an interview by the Services Selection Board at Meerut/Bangalore.
— did well there.
— was selected by the Board.
— was medically examined and found fit.
— received a call from the Academy to come and join the course.

Describing

UNIT 1 DESCRIBING SIMPLE TASKS AND GIVING INSTRUCTIONS

All of us have to learn to do simple tasks like making tea/coffee, polishing shoes, making a telephone call or looking for a book in the library. Sometimes we need to describe how we do them, at other times we need to write instructions on how others could perform these tasks.

Activity 1 Describing a task

How to prepare tea

1 Think for a moment and note down the different things that you do to make tea.
2 Show the list to your partner and make sure that you haven't left out any important step.
3 Then write a paragraph describing how *you* prepare tea. *Remember, you have to describe, not to write instructions.*
4 When you have written your description, check whether you have answered the following questions:
   (*a*) Do you heat milk separately?
   (*b*) Or do you add it to the boiling water along with tea leaves?
   (*c*) When do you add sugar?

   Revise your description, if necessary.
5 Exchange what you have written with your partner and find out where it is different from her/his account.

Exercise 1 Now list the different things we do to prepare either *lassi* or *nimbu pani.* Check your list with your partner. Then describe how *you* prepare either *lassi* or *nimbu pani.* Finally, compare your account with that of your partner.

Exercise 2 A foreign friend wants to know how we prepare *chappatis.* Describe the process for her/him. Some useful words are: flour, dough, knead, rolling pin.

Activity 2 Giving instructions

Let's now turn to another common task: polishing leather shoes.

Discuss with your partner/group and note down the different things that you do to polish leather shoes.

Hint: The following questions will help you prepare your list:

1 How do you remove dirt? With a hard brush or with an ordinary brush?
2 How do you apply polish? With fingers? With brush?
3 Why do you allow the shoes to dry after applying polish?
4 What happens when we brush the shoes vigorously?
5 What do you do to give a further shine to the shoes?

Now write your *instructions*. Exchange your instructions with your partner and find out whether the instructions are complete. Then prepare a final draft.

Exercise 1 Write for the benefit of a cousin from a small town how he could make use of a public telephone in Delhi. Before starting follow the usual procedure, i.e. list the different steps. Then discuss the list with your partner to ensure that it is complete. Thereafter go on to write the instructions. Add a warning to avoid the most common mistakes we make while using the public telephone.

Further practice

1 Write instructions for the following:

(*a*) on how to locate a book in the library.
(*b*) on how to prepare tea with the help of tea bags.
(*c*) on how to revive a person lying unconscious on the road.

Hint: Use the procedure called ABC. A stands for Air passage, B stands for Breathing and C for *Circulation*. Consult a doctor in the neighbourhood and find out the entire procedure. (*Don't forget to add the things one must avoid doing.*)

2 Explain to an interested friend how to get a bus pass made.

UNIT 2 DESCRIBING OBJECTS

There are many occasions when we need to describe objects. We may want to sell something and put in an advertisement about it in a newspaper. Or we may have to seek the help of others to trace an object that has been lost. In both cases we will need to write a fairly detailed and accurate description of it. Or we may want to write to our friends or relatives living at a distance about the gifts that we have received or that we propose to give. Let's therefore try and learn how to describe objects.

Activity 1

Look at your watch carefully, jot down important points about it and then write at least four sentences describing the watch. Your sentences should give information about those features of the watch that are most important. When you have written your description, check whether you have included information on the following points:

(*a*) manufacturer/brand name
(*b*) kind of watch—handwound, quartz or digital
(*c*) shape
(*d*) colour of the dial
(*e*) does it have a seconds' hand
(*f*) does it show day and date
(*g*) does it run on battery
(*h*) is it waterproof or shockproof
(*i*) cost

Revise or add to your description, if necessary.

1 Exchange your description with your partner who will match your description with your watch. Similarly, you will match his description with his watch. Revise again, if necessary, in the light of his comments.
2 Add at least four more sentences about the watch. Apart from other information, do say how it keeps time. (Is it slow? Is it fast? Does it give accurate time?) Also mention how you acquired it. (Is it a gift from someone or did you buy it yourself?)
3 Rewrite the entire description so that it reads like a connected account.

Hint: Use *is/has* in framing sentences. But you are free to frame sentences in other ways also.

Activity 2

Look at the picture of a wall clock given here and describe it in at least five sentences. You could write about its size, shape, material, dial, hands and cost.

Here is a list of some words commonly used to describe objects.

List of helpful words:

Size : tiny, small, big, large, huge

Shape : circular, round, rectangular, spherical, oval, heart-shaped, cylindrical

Material : glass, wooden, steel, plastic, (is) made of

Weight : light, heavy, weighs, in weight

Age : old, new

Volume : contains/holds

Use : is used for/to

This list is not exhaustive. As you read descriptions of objects, keep adding to this list. You could maintain a small notebook for this purpose.

Activity 3

Now fill in the blanks in the following descriptive sentences.

Size : This geometry box is 17.7 cm .... 7.3 cm .... and has a .... of 1.9 cm.

Shape : An egg is ...., and a football is ....

This talcum powder container is .... in shape.

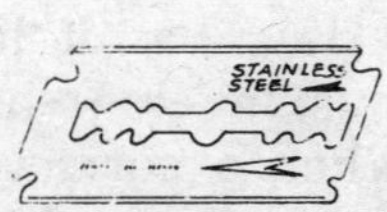

Material : The blade is .... stainless steel.

The jug is ....

Colour	:	Most common roses are red .... but some are ...., some .... and some ....
Weight	:	This piece of cheese .... 160 grams. That one is 500 grams or half a kilogram.
Use	:	A knife .... cutting things.

Check your answers with that of your partner or other members of your group.

Activity 4

Given below is a list of everyday objects with which we are all familiar. Describe them in sentences as indicated against each object:

(*a*) *Bicycle* : height
material of (frame)
manufacturer/brand name
additional features like carrier, chain cover

(*b*) *Refrigerator* : length
width
height
material
use

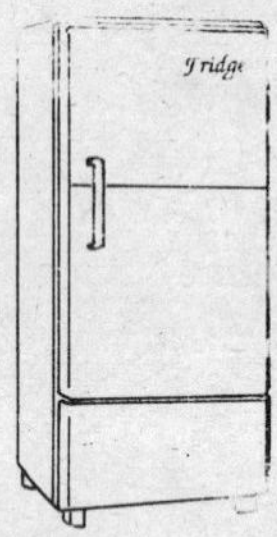

(*c*) *Television* : size of the screen
black and white/colour
material
cost (expensive/cheap)
manual control/remote control
quality of service

(*d*) *Study Table* : size
material
facilities (like drawers, shelves at the back for books and papers)

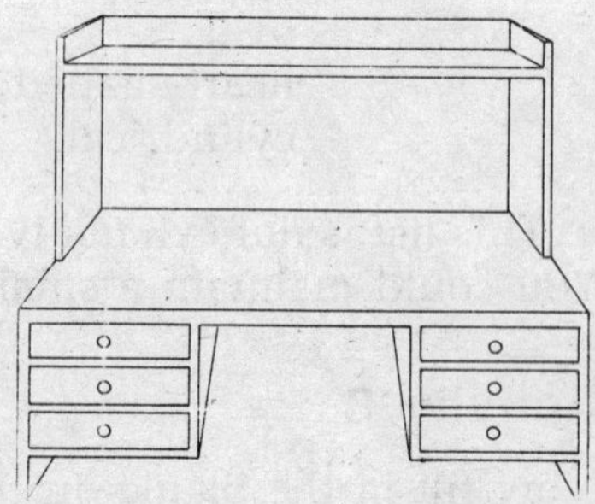

Exercise 1 You have lost a pen which your sister had presented you on your birthday. Describe the pen so that a notice can be put up about it on the college notice-board. You could write about the make, material of the cap and the body, colour and any other special features of the pen.

Activity 5

Let us now play a guessing game. The class is divided into two groups. One group decides upon an everyday object (like a shoulder bag, ball-point pen, sun-glasses, sofa or a chair) and describes it in four to six sentences without naming the object. The second group must guess what the object is, but can ask for more information if it cannot do so. When a correct guess has been made, the groups switch roles. For the game to succeed it is important that the group describing the object provides all the important information to the other group.

Here are some groups of objects with pictures:

sun-glasses

spectacles

fountain pen

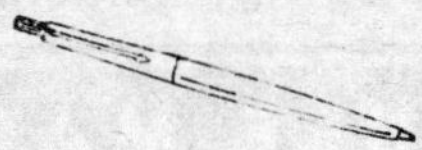

ball-point pen

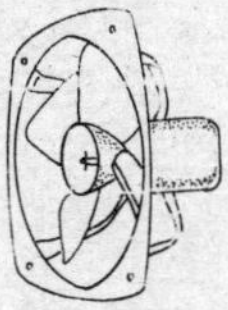

exhaust fan

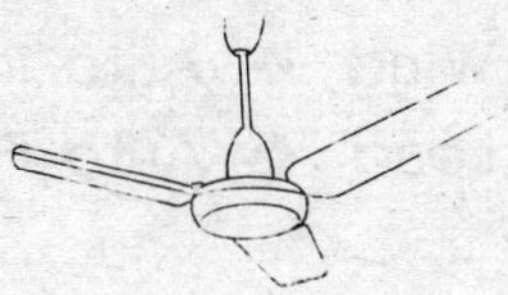

ceiling fan

pedestal fan

chair

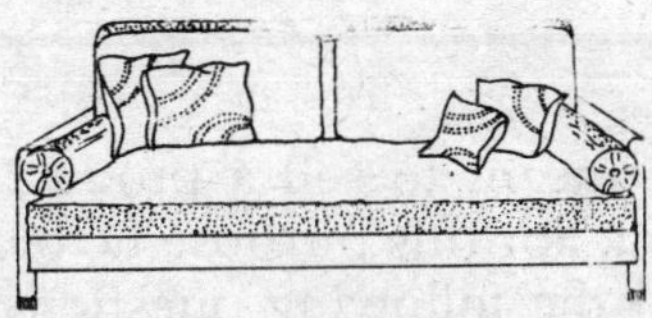

sofa

stool

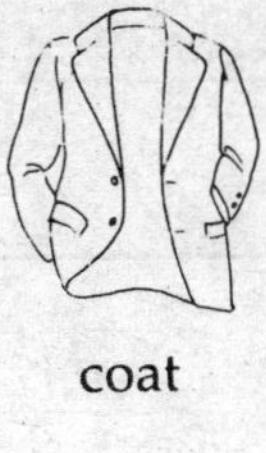

coat

dressing-gown

overcoat

After the game is over, each group could revise its description, if necessary.

Activity 6 Separating facts from opinions

Let's now try another kind of exercise. We all live in an age of advertisements. Those who have things to sell tell us that their things are the best and we must buy them. Some of the things they say may be facts but often these facts are mixed with opinions. This makes it necessary for us, the buyers, to learn to separate facts from opinions.

Look at the following descriptive sentences:

Keycee TV is the best TV in India.
It has an 18 inch screen.

Do you see any difference between the two sentences? The first sentence expresses an *opinion* about the TV. It praises it. But the second gives you an important *fact* about the TV, i.e. the size of its screen. The first sentence depends upon the point of view of the writer/speaker. The second one does not.

We come across both *facts* and *opinions* in advertisements.

Look at the following advertisement of a camera:

PURE MAGIC
Pixon AF 35M II

Autofocus ❖ Auto Exposure
Auto Wind ❖ Auto Rewind
Auto Load ❖ Auto Flash

Now you can get great pictures. Anytime.
Everytime. The Pixon AF 35M II makes it so easy.
Everything is automatic. All you have to do is to push a button.

A commercial advertisement is meant to sell a product. In the above advertisement the advertiser wants to sell a camera. For this purpose he praises the camera. Try and analyse the advertisement. Ask yourself the following questions:

1 What facts does the advertisement give you about the camera?
2 Where does the advertiser praise the camera and persuade you to buy it?

In other words fix your attention on words and sentences that give you *facts* and on words and sentences that give you the advertiser's *opinion* about the camera. Write them down separately. Now check your answer with the following suggested answers:

Words and sentences that give facts about the camera	*Words and sentences that express an opinion about the camera*
Pixon AF 35 II Autofocus. Auto Exposure. Auto Wind. Auto Rewind. Auto Load. Auto Flash.	Pure magic Now you can get great pictures. Anytime. Everytime. The Pixon AF 35 II makes it so easy. Everything is automatic. All you have to do is to push a button.

Exercise 1 Here is another advertisement. Try and separate facts from opinions and put them in a table as you did in the last activity.

MINISAHA–MIRAJ LMB

The toughest, raciest, safest motor cycle of them all.
Japanese technology effectively adapted for Indian roads.

The LMB is brought to you by Miraj, India's premier two- and three-wheeler company, and Minisaha, the Japanese high technology giant. Minisaha has nailed history to its door by making the fastest motor cycle in the world.

Ride the Minisaha–Miraj LMB and you'll appreciate why you just can't beat a Miraj.

Exercise 2 Now write out the facts in complete sentences.

Exercise 3 In Activity 4 you described a TV. Discuss with your partner/group and write an advertisement (also called *copy*) of the same TV in about 100 words. Compare this with your earlier description. Is there any difference?

UNIT 3 DESCRIBING PEOPLE

We often need to describe people on a number of occasions. We sometimes write to others about people we have met or the ones we admire, or the ones we/they are going to meet. On occasions descriptions may become necessary for physical identification. Such descriptions may also be found in newspapers and magazines, and novels and short stories and also in stage directions in plays. Therefore, it is useful and important to know how to describe people.

Activity 1

Look at the following data about Manjit Singh, a doctor:

Name	:	Manjit Singh
Job	:	Doctor
Age	:	35 years
Home	:	S 72 Green Park Extension, New Delhi
Marital status	:	Married with two children
Place of work	:	Safdarjung Hospital
Income	;	Rs 5,200/- per month
Interests	:	Reading detective fiction, watching cricket

What to do

1 Discuss with your partner and write a paragraph about Dr Manjit Singh.
2 Separate eight key verbs and enter them in the table on the next page.

Note: The table that follows provides four columns—for a doctor (Manjit Singh), a politician, a housewife and a rickshaw puller. Information about each of these is to be filled in the table. See Exercises 1, 2 and 3.

Key verbs	*Manjit Singh*	?	?	?
is	a doctor	a politician	a house-wife	a rickshaw puller
is	35	?	?	?
lives	at S 72 Green Park Extension, New Delhi	?	?	?
is	marrried	?	?	married
has	two children	?	?	one child
works	at Safdarjung Hospital	?	?	at Tilak Nagar bus stop
earns	Rs 5,200/- per month	?	?	?
likes/is interested in (any other)	reading detective fiction and watching cricket	?	?	films, watching TV

Can you add some other details about Dr Singh? Rewrite the description as a connected paragraph.

Exercise 1 Now complete the table for any political figure who has been in the news. After you have completed the table, see if you can add some more details. Then write a brief paragraph about the person. Exchange paragraphs with your partner and check whether the description is accurate.

Exercise 2 The next task is to fill the table for a housewife. The housewife should preferably be someone you know. It could be your mother, an aunt, a married sister, or a neighbour. Find out the details that you don't have with you and put the information in the appropriate columns in the table.

There are some columns that you cannot fill in for her. Which columns are these?

One of the suggested answers says: 'she works at home'. Do you think this is enough? Wouldn't you like to expand it? Wouldn't you like to say briefly what she does? Ask yourself the following questions:

Who manages the household?
Does she do the cooking?
Does she wash the clothes?
Does she clean the house?
Does she have a maidservant to help her?

Add some other details also and write a paragraph about her.

Exercise 3 We shall now attempt to describe the life of a rickshaw puller. It would be interesting if you could contact a rickshaw puller of your area and find out all the required details from him. Some of the columns may not be easy to fill in. For instance, where does he live? He may be living in a *jhuggi*, but often a rickshaw puller has no fixed place to live. Then:

Where does he *work*?

Here we will have to use some other verb to define his *work*. We shall have to say:

.... plies his rickshaw in the Tilak Nagar bus stop area.

Again:

How much does he earn?

Apparently he has no fixed income. He lives from day to day. Here, too, the answer will have to be suitably modified.

Discuss the problems in writing a description of the life of a rickshaw puller with your partner, make suitable changes in the verbs to be used in the description, make notes and then write down the description.

Exercise 4 Fill in the blanks in the following sentences:

Mohammad Habib .... a rickshaw puller. He is 25 but l........................... at least 35. He hails .... Rajasthan. He has no house to .... He is .... and .... a child but he .... afford to bring .... to .... He s........................ outside the shop of the o.............................. of his rickshaw.

He .... his rickshaw .... the Tilak Nagar a....................... . His earnings are un............................. . They .... from day to day. On an a............................... he is .... to earn Rs 20/- per .... Out of this, he .... Rs 10/- to the .... of the rickshaw as h.................................... charges. He m............................ also send .... money to .... in Rajasthan. His ambition is to be a.................. to earn .... money so .... he can .... a rickshaw and t.......................... it to ....

A distant uncle from a village is coming to visit the family, but you have never seen him before. You are to go to the railway station to meet him. Write to him, carefully describing yourself and the clothes you will be wearing so that he will be able to recognize you.

Activity 2

The task is to describe the persons in the pictures given below:

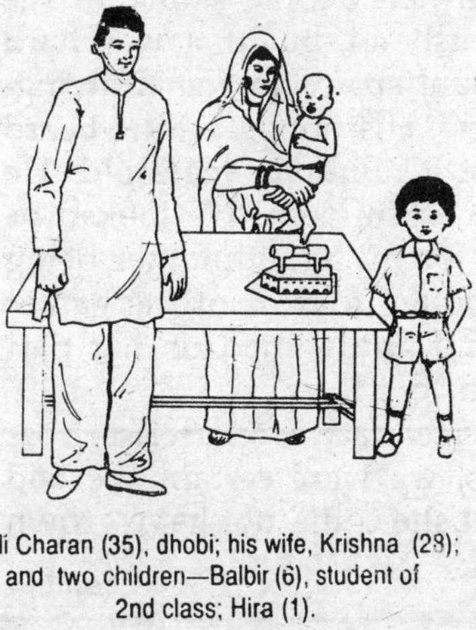

Kali Charan (35), dhobi; his wife, Krishna (28); and two children—Balbir (6), student of 2nd class; Hira (1).

Ram Prakash (42), policeman; his wife, Parvati (37), housewife; and two children—Harish (14), student of 10th class; Rekha (9), student of 4th class.

Mr B John (52), railway ticket collector.

In the first instance, look at pictures one, two and three. Picture one gives some information about the person shown in it. Make a list of all such items for which we get information from the picture and its caption. Here are some questions that will help you to describe the persons.

Who is the person in the first picture?
How old is he?
What work does he do?
Is he tall or short?
Is he fat or well-built or thin?
What sort of hair has he?
Has he got a beard or a moustache?
Is he married or single?
What dress is he wearing?
Is he wearing spectacles/glasses?

Discuss with your partner and write separate sentences about each of the items about which we have information. Check if anything has been left out. Thereafter, join the sentences and produce a connected paragraph.

Follow a similar procedure for the persons in pictures two and three.

Patterns to use

As in the previous exercises in this Unit, you will of course make use of *is/has* construction. But you will find that this construction is not enough. You will make use of the following patterns also:

.... is working/studying.
.... is a railway clerk.
.... is employed as ....

Exercise 1 Write descriptions of all the characters on the basis of the pictures given earlier.

Activity 3

Here is a passage taken from Khushwant Singh's 'The Portrait of a Lady'.

My grandmother, like everybody's grandmother, was an old woman. She had been old and wrinkled for the twenty years that I had known her. People said that she had once been young and pretty and had even had a husband, but that was hard to believe. My grandfather's portrait hung above the mantlepiece in the drawing-room. He wore a big turban and loose-fitting clothes. His long, white beard covered the best part of his chest and he looked at least a hundred years old. He did not look the sort of person who would have a wife or children. He looked as if he could only have lots and lots of grandchildlren. As for my grandmother being young and pretty, the thought was almost revolting. She often told us of the games she used to play as a child. That seemed quite absurd and undignified on her part and we treated it like the fables of the Prophets she used to tell us.

She had always been short and fat and slightly bent. Her face was a criss-cross of wrinkles running from everywhere to everywhere. No, we were certain she had always been as we had known her. Old, so terribly old that she could not have grown

(contd.)

older, and had stayed at the same age for twenty years. She could never have been pretty; but she was always beautiful. She hobbled about the house in spotless white with one hand resting on her waist to balance her stoop and the other telling the beads of her rosary. Her silver locks were scattered untidily over her pale, puckered face, and her lips constantly moved in inaudible prayer. Yes, she was beautiful. She was like the winter landscape in the mountains, an expanse of pure white serenity breathing peace and contentment.

(From *The Collected Short Stories* by Khushwant Singh, Ravi Dayal Publisher, Delhi, 1990, p. 29)

Now take out information about Khushwant Singh's grandmother described in the text and put it in the following table:

Name	....
Age	....
Family background	....
Height	....
Build	....
Complexion	....
Face	....
Hair	....
Dress	....
Nature/character	....
(Any other not covered above)	....

If the above categories are not sufficient, add some of your own. Also notice how the information is organized in the passage. Read the passage again and do the following exercises:

Exercise 1 Tick off whichever of the following you think is correct. The passage describes:

(*a*) the grandmother's dress
(*b*) her beauty
(*c*) her religious and peaceful nature
(*d*) her family background
(*e*) her physical appearance
(*f*) her life as a young woman

Exercise 2 Rearrange the correct items above in the same order in which the information is presented in the passage.

Exercise 3 Now write four sentences about your own grandmother/grandfather.

Activity 4

Let's now try fuller descriptions:

1 Imagine that Daisy, a girl, and you study in the same college. You have been to her home several times and you like her very much. Write about her to a close friend in another town. Here you will write not only about *who* she is and *what* she looks

like but also about *her character* and her *manners*. You could make use of the vocabulary given later in this unit.

Hints: Divide the description into three paragraphs as follows:

Para 1 : Say who she is, and when and where you met her.
Para 2 : Describe what she looks like and what sort of clothes she wears.
Para 3 : Give a description of her character and write about the qualities that you like in her.

2 A friend of yours is going to Bombay to study, and he will be staying with your cousin for a month before he gets a room in the hostel. Your cousin is to receive him at the station.

(*a*) Write a description of your friend so that your cousin can recognize him at the station.

(*b*) Since your friend will be staying for a month, you want the two to get to know each other. Write a fuller description of the friend for the benefit of your cousin.

Before you write, discuss with your partner the qualities that make people likeable; make notes and then write.

Useful vocabulary

The following table lists useful words and phrases in ten areas of physical appearance and dress:

Aspect	*Words/Phrases*
Age	teenaged/teenager/in his or her teens, young, middle-aged, elderly early / mid- / late } forties/fifties/sixties, etc.
Complexion	(colour) fair, wheatish, dark (texture) smooth, oily, dry
Hair	black, brown, blond (feminine: blonde), grey, silver/silver-haired wavy, curly, straight, thick, thin, long, short
Build	slim, thin, well-built, fat, plump, stocky
Height	is (e.g. 162 cms/5' 6") tall about (give approximate height) tall, short, medium height
Face	round, square, long, thin, wrinkled
Nose	big, small, straight, flat, snub-nosed, hooked nose/hook-nosed
Mouth/Lips	small, wide, thin, thick, full
Looks	good-looking, attractive, beautiful, charming, cute, pretty, handsome, smart, distinguished, homely, ordinary, ugly
Dress	wears/is wearing is dressed in (has a/an ....) on

Additional exercise

You can repeat the game using:

(*a*) public figures—national and international
(*b*) sports personalities
(*c*) persons present in your classroom

Here is another list of words and phrases used to describe people's character and manners. Rearrange them in two columns. Column 1 should list what you think are *good qualities* and Column 2 the *bad qualities*. Make a third column, if necessary, of the qualities about which you are not sure.

hard working	neat	nervous	reserved
dull	shabby	tense	careless
stupid	loud	irritable	talkative
honest	punctual	tense	polite
generous	soft-spoken	quick-tempered	selfish
miserly	mild-mannered	ambitious	frank
well-dressed	mean	tolerant	considerate
friendly	kind	easygoing	rude
well-mannered	aggressive	shy	cheerful
(has) a sense of humour			

Further practice

1 Describe a teacher who taught you at school.
2 Describe someone in your family who you like particularly or who you dislike intensely.
3 A five-year old child of your locality has been missing for the past few days. Write a description of the boy so that it can be given to the police and can also be announced on the radio and television.

The description should mention the age, height, complexion, dress, any identification marks, the town or locality he belongs to and the date from which he is missing. (For help listen to such announcements over the radio and television. You could also look for such announcements in the newspapers.)

UNIT 4 DESCRIBING PLACES

Often we have to describe places to other people for a variety of reasons. We may have to describe a house or a building they haven't seen, a town or a city or a village or a historical monument they haven't visited, a street or a scene they aren't familiar with. Descriptions may form part of letters written to friends living abroad or part of directions on how to reach a place or a destination.

Activity 1 Describing a route

We shall begin by describing how to reach a particular place.

On page 90 is given a route map of an area of New Delhi. You are at Bahadur Shah Zafar Marg and you want to reach Sri Ram Centre to purchase tickets to see a play. Write at least three sentences describing the route from Bahadur Shah Zafar Marg to Sri Ram Centre on College Road near the Mandi House roundabout. Sri Ram Centre is a well-known place in New Delhi where plays are staged.

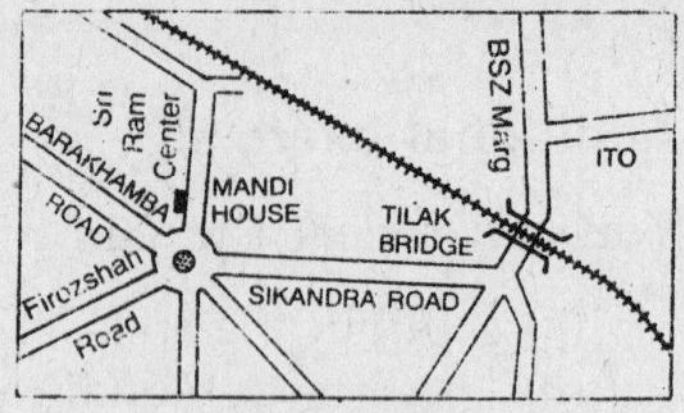

Discuss your description with your partner/group.

Exercise 1 Describe the route that you will take from Sri Ram Centre to Bahadur Shah Zafar Marg after the play is over.

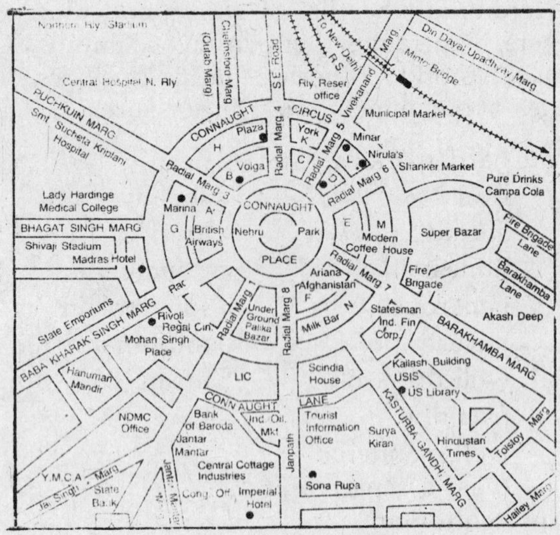

Exercise 2 Here is a map of Connaught Place indicating roads and important places in it. You are with a friend who is new to the area. You have left him at the Super Bazaar to do some shopping. An hour later you will meet him at the Shivaji Stadium where both of you are to see a hockey match. Give him directions on how to reach Shivaji Stadium from the Super Bazar.

Discuss the route with your partner/group and later check what you have written with them.

Exercise 3 Your 18-year old cousin who is new to the city intends to come to visit you. Write to him how he should reach your place from the railway station/bus stand. Also indicate *how* he should travel (by bus or scooter or rickshaw or on foot). If he has to travel by bus, provide him with the exact bus numbers and tell him where he has to get down. Be precise and do not neglect details in your instructions.

Describing the location of a building/place

List of useful words/expressions:

Here are some useful words and expressions that will come in handy in describing locations:

in front of	adjacent to	on the left of
opposite	behind	there is/there are
by the side of	on the right of	on the hill/by the river
across		

Activity 2

When we describe the location of a place, we do so in relation to the things near it. For example, we describe the location of a building with reference to the other buildings around it or to a nearby road or roads, or some other landmark. Here are some sentences describing the location of Regal cinema in Connaught Circus.

It is situated between Baba Kharak Singh Marg and Sansad Marg.
It lies on the outer circle.
There are three circles in Connaught Place—the outer circle, the middle circle and the inner circle.
Regal cinema is in Connaught Circus.
It is at a walking distance from another cinema, Rivoli, on Baba Kharak Singh Marg.

Read the description and see if the sentences are in the right sequence. If they are not, arrange them in the proper order. Then discuss your sequence with your partner/group. If you find the description incomplete, add a sentence or two of your own.

Exercise 1 Now describe the location of Jantar Mantar in four to six sentences.

Hints: Where is it? Name two important buildings nearby.
Name the road on which it is situated.
How far is it from the Parliament House?

Describing a house/flat

List of useful words/expressions:

Here is a list of terms/words that can be used to describe a house/flat:

ground floor/first floor/second floor
drawing room
dining room
bedroom
living room
balcony
terrace
a rented house/flat
my own/our own
kitchen
lobby
water closet (WC)/toilet or bathroom
floor area
garden
compound wall
staircase

Here are some adjectives that describe the house/flat and how you feel about it:

small
big
spacious
airy
stuffy
congested
dark
well ventilated
old/old fashioned
dilapidated
well planned
well built
badly constructed

Activity 3

On page 92 is the plan of a flat. Study the plan carefully. Each student should take his turn to describe one feature of it.

But before you start describing, decide on the following:

How are you going to describe it?

Will you describe each room or feature of the flat as it comes or will you first give a general description and then come to the details? For example, you could begin like this:

The flat is on the ground floor. The entrance leads to the drawing-cum-dining room.

Alternatively, it is possible to say:

It is a flat with two bedrooms. It is airy and spacious.

Moreover, while describing don't forget to mention the special features of the flat. For instance, the flat in question may have an unusually big drawing-cum-dining room. In some other flats the kitchen may be large and airy. Or there may be two balconies instead of one. In other words, while describing this or any other flat or house ask yourself:

Does it have any special facility/facilities that other flats/houses don't have?

After the entire flat has been described, put the sentences together and see that they form a connected paragraph.

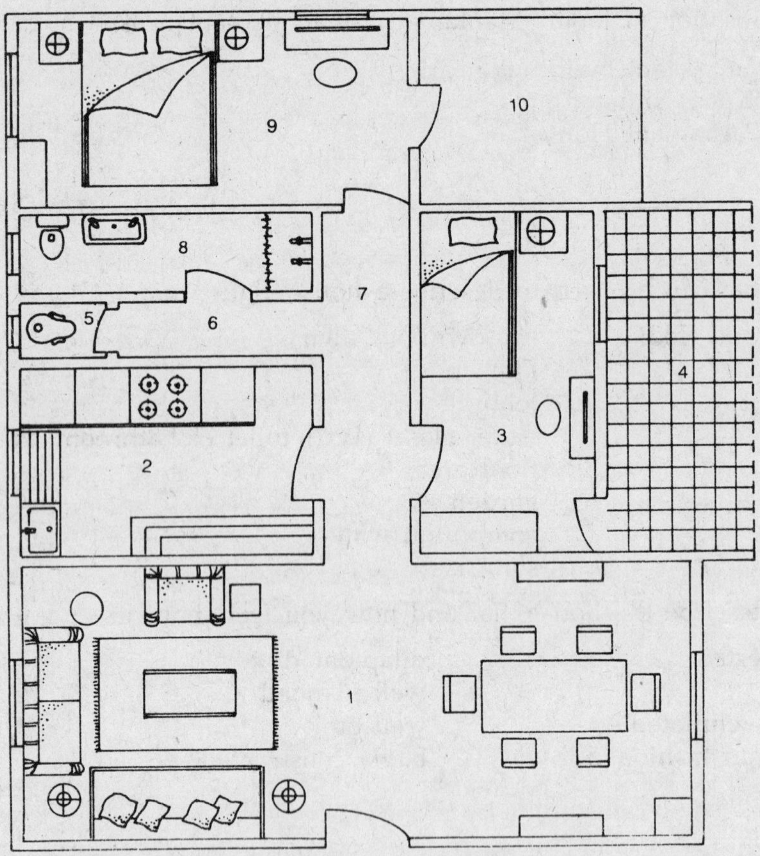

1 Drawing-cum-Dining room
2 Kitchen
3 1st Bedroom
4 Covered Balcony
5 Lavatory (Indian style)
6 Passage
7 Passage
8 Bathroom with western w.c.
9 2nd Bedroom
10 Open Terrace

Here are some questions that will help you:

1 Where is the kitchen?
2 Where is the first bedroom?
3 Where is the second bedroom?
4 Are they large or small?
5 Where is the balcony?
6 Where is the terrace?

Plan of flat

Exercise 1 Now treating the above flat as a model, describe your own flat/house.

This is how you should proceed. Each student should answer some questions relating to the flat. For example, the first question could be:

Where does the entrance open?

Here are some more questions:

How big is the drawing-cum-dining room?
Are the drawing and dining rooms combined or are they separate?
How many bedrooms are there in the flat?
What are their sizes?
Where is the kitchen?
How big is it? Is it airy?
What is the size of the bathroom?
Where do you study?

The list is not complete. One could ask similar questions about the other aspects of the flat. Also add a sentence or two about its location and surroundings. And don't forget to point out any special features that make it different from the others.

There is another thing that you should do. Mention how you feel about the flat. Do you like it? Do you think it is adequate for the needs of the family?

Activity 4 Attempting bigger descriptions

Let's turn to bigger descriptions. What do you do, for instance, when you describe a college? Discuss with other members of your group, make notes and then check whether you have included all the points raised in the following paragraph. You are of course free to make additions/deletions.

When we describe a college, we describe its location, its surroundings, its looks and its general plan. We also take a closer look at the college and give certain physical details. Then we could describe one special feature or aspect to it. Finally, we could write about how we feel about it.

Here is how the class could do the task. The entire description could be split up into the following parts:

1 Location of the college and its surroundings; its area (exact figures if possible), its general plan and shape (whether, for instance, the building is L-shaped or H-shaped, etc.).
2 A closer look at the college; number of rooms, laboratories, library, playgrounds and similar facilities.
3 Its special feature(s).
4 Conclusion—how you feel about the college.

Each of these parts could be taken up by a different group which could concentrate on the part alloted to it. Later, each group could read out the description of its part or area alloted to it. The other groups will of course comment on whether the description is adequate and accurate. There can be a difference of opinion about the special feature of the college. If there is such a difference, the students who hold a different view could be asked to identify what they consider to be the special feature of the college and then to produce an appropriate description. Thus, each group will contribute at least one paragraph to the description. After the entire college has been described the class as a whole can go over the whole description and see that it is a connected piece of composition.

Exercise 1 Now describe your old school or house or any other place of which you have fond memories. Exchange your description with your partner and draw a plan of each other's school/house from the written description.

Activity 5 'Identifying the place' game

Each student/group chooses or 'adopts' two or three or more well known places of historical, religious, or other interest, and writes out four sentences or more describing each of them without naming them. The sentences are then read out and other students/groups have to identify the place. Here is an example:

1 It is a tall tower.
2 It was built by a king and later by his son-in-law.
3 It is situated in Mehrauli near Delhi.
4 The tower has five storeys.

Now make a guess.

Some of the other places that could be thus adopted for description are—the Sun Temple at Konarak, Gol Gumbaz at Bijapur, Charminar at Hyderabad, Meenakshi Temple at Madurai, the Taj Mahal, Vijay Stambh (Victory Tower) at Chittorgarh, Vrindavan Gardens at Mysore, India Gate, Parliament House, Kovalam Beach at Trivandrum, Jallianwala Bagh, the Golden Temple at Amritsar and the Dal Lake in Srinagar, Kashmir. There are any number of such places that could be taken up for description.

This simple exercise can lead to longer descriptions of places which the student *has really* visited and been interested in. For instance, the student who has visited Qutb Minar may like to go beyond the four sentences given earlier. He may note down other details that he has observed or that he has gathered from other books. He may like to mention the details of its height, its material, the inscriptions on it, etc. He would certainly like to dig a little deeper into its history. And he would like to describe its location and its surroundings more precisely.

Use of past tense

Sometimes when we describe past events, we use the past tense. Look at sentence 2 given above describing the Qutb Minar. Whereas the other sentences are in the present tense this one is in the past tense. Keep this in mind while describing places.

Further practice

1 You have received a letter from a person who is interested in taking on rent a flat in your neighbourhood. He may even buy it. Describe the flat bringing out its special feature(s).
2 Describe a place you knew well when you were young. Explain how and why it was important to you. Write 10 to 15 sentences.
3 Describe in 10 to 15 sentences places of religious interest along Chandni Chowk in Delhi. (Only for those who have visited the area.)

UNIT 5 DESCRIBING PROCESSES

Describing processes is a common feature of scientific writing. We may be asked to describe how things work or how things are done.

Activity 1

Do you know how the Delhi Milk Scheme or Mother Dairy milk that you drink in the morning comes to you in a big city like Delhi? It doesn't come straight from the buffalo. The entire process is in fact quite long and complicated.

1 Discuss the process with your partner/group and write down the different steps as they occur to you. Consult someone who knows, if necessary.
2 Arrange the steps in the order in which they are taken.
3 Now compare what you have written with the following list of steps:

(*a*) Milk is collected from villages and towns of northern India.
(*b*) Milk is delivered to the plant.
(*c*) Milk is tested in the plant.
(*d*) Milk is pasteurized at a temperature of 72 °C.
(*e*) Milk is cooled.
(*f*) Milk is bottled/packed in polypacks.
(*g*) Milk is distributed to milk booths.
(*h*) Milk is sold to customers.

4 Again, discuss with your partner/group and make any changes or additions to the steps, if necessary.

5 Each step is important and leads to the next. The importance of sequencing will become clear if we draw a flow chart showing the different steps.

Flow chart showing the processing of milk

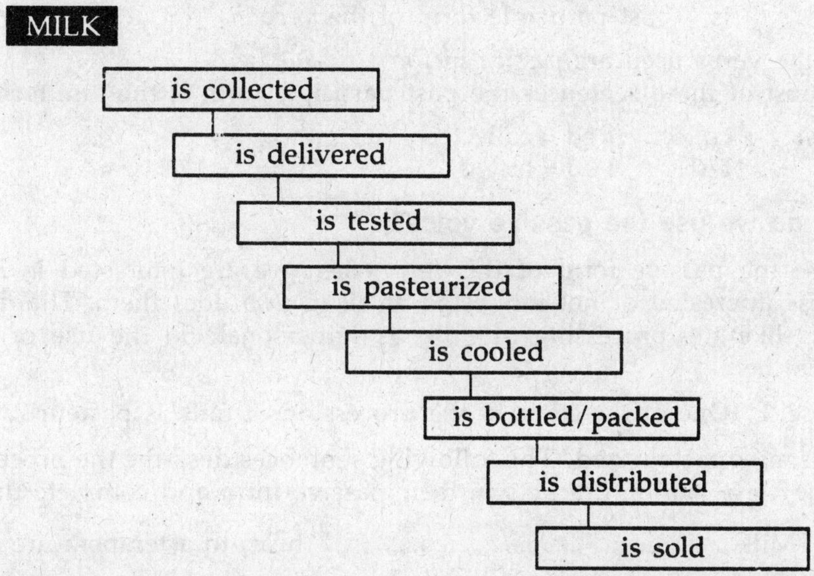

6 Now join your sentences together using pronouns instead of nouns, and sequence words or sequencers like:

First/To begin with
Then/Next/After that/Thereafter/Later
Subsequently/Finally

7 *How to join*: Let's see how the joining can be done.
Here are the first two sentences from the list given above:

Milk is collected from villages and towns of northern India.
Milk is delivered to the plant.

The word 'Milk' is repeated in both the sentences. This repetition can be avoided by using the pronoun 'it'.

Milk is collected from villages and towns of northern India.
It is delivered to the plant.

The sentences could be joined still more closely by using 'and' and leaving out 'It'.

Milk is collected from villages and towns of northern India and
is delivered to the plant.

There is another way in which the two sentences could be joined together. We can add a word to indicate the next stage in the process.

Milk is collected from villages and towns of northern India.
Then it is delivered to the plant.

We could also use 'and' to join the sentences and leave out 'It' altogether.

Milk is collected from villages and towns in northern India and is
then delivered to the plant.

Now try and join the other sentences and write a connected account.

Activity 2 Use of passives

Do you notice anything in common about the verbs used in the sentences listed in Activity 1. Identify these common features and write them down.

Each verb item consists of two elements:

is + past participle form of the verb

All the verbs used are *passive* in form.

In most of these sentences the past participle form is the *base* form of the verb + ed.

Example: collect + ed = collected
test + ed = tested

When do we use the passive voice?

We use the passive form of the verb when we are interested in *how* things are done and less interested or not interested at all in *who* does them. The description of a large process like the processing of milk, is impersonal. So the use of the passive form is essential here.

Exercise 1 One of the steps in the processing of milk is pasteurization.

How is milk pasteurized? The following sentences describe the process of pasteurization. Use the verbs within brackets in their passive form and complete the sentences:

Milk .... (heat) to a temperature of 72 °C.

The temperature .... (maintain) for about 15 seconds.

Milk .... (cool) rapidly to 4 °C.

This .... (do) to kill bacteria and make the milk safe for drinking.

After you have filled in the blanks, join the sentences together by using connectives and sequencers, where necessary. For more exercises in the use of passive voice please refer to Book III, i.e. the 'Workbook'.

Activity 3

All of us write and receive letters. How is the mail collected and sent out? Try and find out and make notes. Here is a flow chart that indicates the different stages in the process.

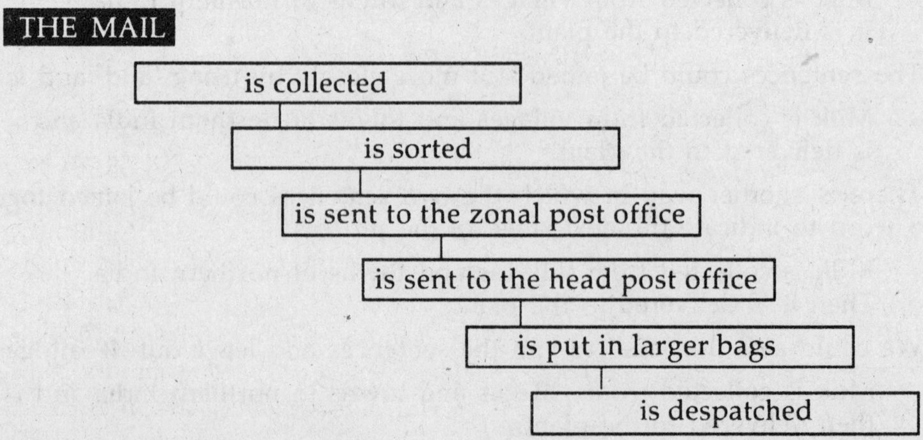

Consult someone in your local post office, if possible, and make any additions or changes, if necessary. Now write a connected account of the process on the basis of your notes. While doing so, make use of the following phrases to complete the sentences:

1 to the local post office
2 from different post-boxes in the area
3 at the local post office
4 to different destinations

Don't forget to use the connectives and sequencers to join the sentences together

Exercise 1 Now describe for a friend how the incoming mail is processed till it is delivered to individuals.

Again consult the local post office, if possible, make a flow chart of the process and consult your partner/group and then write.

Activity 4

People all over the world see films, but very few know much about film-making. Here is a list of incomplete sentences that describe the process.

1 Fill in the blanks by supplying the passive forms of the verbs in brackets. The first one has been done for you:

A producer and a director are appointed (appoint).

Scenes .... (shoot) according to convenience and not in the same order in which they appear in the film.

The story .... (convert) into a film script.

A story .... (select).

These separate scenes .... (join) together in the proper order by the film ....

Sound .... (add) to the scenes.

Sometimes sound .... (record) separately.

The film .... (release) to be shown in cinema houses.

Copies of the film .... (make).

2 Next discuss with your partner/group and rearrange the sentences in the right order.

3 Do you think this is a complete list of the stages in film-making? Discuss and make additions, if necessary.

Hint: What role does the Censor Board play in the process?

4 Now join the sentences together, using pronouns and sequence words.

Activity 5

The following sentences deal with the process of selection of candidates for some jobs Again, they are not in the right order:

Applications are read carefully (screened).
Eligible candidates are short-listed.
Applications are invited.

The selected candidates are asked to appear for a medical test.
Successful candidates are issued letters of appointment.
Those who are found medically fit are finally selected.
The short-listed candidates are interviewed.
Selection is made out of the candidates interviewed.

1 Arrange these sentences in the proper order.
2 Discuss with your partner/group and add details to the sentences wherever necessary.

Example: Applications are invited.

This could be expanded to read:

Applications are invited through an advertisement in newspapers.

The following questions will help you to expand or add details to the sentences:

(*a*) Who screens the applications?
(*b*) Who short-lists the candidates?
(*c*) Who interviews them?

The details that you add may take the form of a phrase as shown above or the form of complete sentences.

Example: Selected candidates are asked to appear for a medical test.
The medical examination lasts several hours.

3 Now join the sentences together into a connected account.

Exercise 1 These candidates also have to appear in a written examination. Add appropriate sentences to the above list wherever required and rewrite the account. Imagine that you yourself have gone through the process and been selected for the job and are explaining the process to a friend in Madras who wants to apply for a similar job this year.

Further practice

1 The following sentences concern the process of planning and building a new road. Rearrange them in the right order and join them together:

The route is cleared and levelled.
The needs of the people of the area are carefully assessed.
Samples of the soil are tested.
The best route is chosen.
The top surface is laid.
Traffic signs and guides are added.
Thick layers of concrete are deposited.

2 Describe the process of baking bread in a large bakery to a friend who is thinking of starting his own bakery.
3 Find out how bricks are made and write a simple description of the process.
4 Find out how silk is produced. Write a simple description of the process.

Note: One of the best ways of obtaining information is to consult the *Encyclopaedia Britannica* or the *Encyclopedia Americana*, both of which you will find in your college library. If you have any difficulty in locating them, ask the librarian for assistance.

Transferring Information

UNIT 1 SENDING TELEGRAMS

Activity 1

In an emergency we need to send messages, information and good or bad news urgently. A letter takes time. Hence, we send telegrams. It is, therefore, important to know how to write such messages.

Read the following:

> Your mother had planned to go to Kanpur for the marriage of her niece Maggie. But there is a last minute change in her programme. Your sister has suddenly taken ill and she can't go. Draft a suitable telegram to your uncle in Kanpur. Put down your message on a piece of paper and fold it up.

How to shorten the message

Every word in a telegram costs money. So we must use the minimum or the least number of words to convey our message. But our meaning should be absolutely clear. The important thing in *a telegram, therefore, is to be at once brief and clear.*

To achieve this take the following steps:

First step: Ask yourself: What is the essence of the message? Discuss with your partner/group and write it down in complete sentences.

The message of the telegram may be something like this:

> MARY HAS SUDDENLY BEEN TAKEN ILL. SO MOTHER CANNOT ATTEND MAGGIE'S MARRIAGE. SHE SENDS HER BLESSINGS.
>
> SHEENA

Now check whether anything essential has been left out.

Second step: Since every extra word increases the cost of the telegram, try and reduce the number of words. When you read the message again, you will find that you can leave out some words without losing any of the meaning. Discuss with your partner/group and put all such words within brackets.

> MARY (HAS) SUDDENLY (BEEN) TAKEN ILL. (SO) MOTHER CANNOT ATTEND (MAGGIE'S) MARRIAGE. (SHE) SENDS (HER) BLESSINGS.
>
> SHEENA

Third step: Now ask yourself if the meaning of the message is clear. Then read it again and see if you can shorten it still further. The shortened version may read like this:

> MARY SUDDENLY ILL. MOTHER CANNOT ATTEND MARRIAGE. SENDS BLESSINGS.
>
> SHEENA

Now look at your telegram and compare it with the above.

Specimen form

Here is a sample form used in sending telegrams.

रसीद RECEIPT

दूर संचार विभाग
DEPARTMENT OF TELECOMMUNICATIONS
तार TELEGRAM
क/A

प्रभार CHARGES		हस्ताक्षर INITIALS		भेजने ब्यौरे XMN. PARTICULARS			
रु. RS.	पै. P.		स्था.सं. LN	सर्किट CCT	समय Time	हस्ताक्षर Initials	तारीख मोहर Date Stamp

संदेश का आरंभ S O M	टर्मिनल संदेश सं. TMNLMSGE. NO.	प्राथमिकता PTY. CLASS	गन्तव्य कोड DESTINATION CODE	वि.लि. संकेत D S I
ZCZC				

श्रेणी CLASS	समय TIME	क्र.सं. SL. NO.	मूल-तार घर OFFICE OF ORIGIN	तारीख DATE	सेवा अनुदेश S.I.	शब्द WORDS

सेवा संदेश SERV. IND.	नाम/NAME .... पता/ADDRESS ....
तुरंत/Exp.	टेलीफोन TELEPHONE .... टेलैक्स नं. TELEX NUMBER .... पिन/PIN
साधारण/Ord.	
बधाई/Gtgs.	
जवाबी/R.P.	
वि. शु./L.F.	
सरकारी/State	

भेजने वाले का नाम :
SENDER'S NAME (TO BE TELEGRAPHED)

COL.

कृपया इस तार को विभागीय तार के नियमों के आधीन भेजें।
PLEASE FORWARD THE ABOVE TELEGRAM SUBJECT TO THE PROVISIONS OF THE INDIAN TELEGRAPH ACT RULES OVERLEAF

पता Address ____________ फोन Phone ____________ भेजने वाले के हस्ताक्षर Sender's Signature

Let's put our message on it:

V V JOHN
5 Ram Gali, Kanpur

MARY SUDDENLY ILL. MOTHER CANNOT ATTEND MARRIAGE. SENDS BLESSINGS. SHEENA Not to be telegraphed: Sheena John F 9/6 Model Town, Delhi

Activity 2

Your brother plans to go to Hyderabad to stay with your uncle during the summer vacation. Draft a suitable telegram to your uncle. Since your brother is travelling alone for the first time, request your uncle to meet him at the station.

Here is a draft message in complete sentences. Read the message and shorten it for the telegram:

HAMID IS TRAVELLING BY AP EXPRESS IN COACH NUMBER D 3309 AND WILL BE REACHING SECUNDERABAD ON WEDNESDAY THE THIRTEENTH MAY AT 3 P.M. THIS IS HIS FIRST MAJOR OUTING. PLEASE MEET HIM AT THE STATION.

FARIDA

Hint: Encircle the words that could be left out without losing the meaning. Discuss with others what you plan to leave out. Then write the message on the blank form.

Activity 3

Now shorten the following sentences without any loss of meaning:

1 I am leaving Delhi immediately.
2 I will be back on Tuesday.
3 There has been no letter from you. Father is worried.
4 We are sorry to say that mother is seriously ill.
5 We shall receive Hamid at the station.
6 My sister Neena is marrying Vijay in November.
7 We regret that the Government of India is unable to accept your demand.
8 There is good news for you. Father has given his consent to your marriage with Shyam.
9 I shall not marry unless father and mother refuse to take dowry.
10 The rehearsals of the play are over. The performances will start from 30 January.

Activity 4

Here are some messages in complete sentences. Shorten them to be telegraphed. (STOP) stands for the full stop at the end of the sentence:

1 ANIL HAS SUDDENLY BEEN TAKEN ILL AFTER EATING AT A RESTAURANT TODAY (STOP) KINDLY COME AT ONCE (STOP) THERE IS HOWEVER NO CAUSE FOR WORRY (STOP)

HARBANS

2 I HAVE REACHED BANGALORE SAFELY (STOP) THERE IS NO TROUBLE OR TENSION IN THE UNIVERSITY AREA (STOP) LETTER GIVING FULL DETAILS FOLLOWS (STOP)

SUNIL

3 You have been selected as a Sales Officer after an interview in Bombay. You are required to join immediately. But on reconsideration you find you have no liking for the job and wish to decline the offer. Wire your father for his permission to do so:

I HAVE BEEN FINALLY SELECTED AND AM REQUIRED TO JOIN DUTY BY MONDAY AT THE LATEST (STOP) BUT ON RECONSIDERATION I FIND I HAVE NO REAL APTITUDE FOR THE JOB AND WISH TO DECLINE THE OFFER (STOP) I HOPE YOU HAVE NO OBJECTION (STOP) WIRE REPLY (STOP)

MAHADEVAN

Also wire back your father's reply.

Further practice

Write telegrams for the following occasions:

1 Your friend from Madras is planning to come and stay with you for a fortnight. But suddenly you have to go out of town. Ask your friend to postpone his visit, and suggest a suitable date for this purpose.
2 You are staying in a hostel and you need extra money for purchasing some books and for paying the examination fee. Wire your father for some money.
3 You are a hosteler and you have information from your sister that your parents are finalizing her marriage against her wishes. Wire your parents not to act in haste and to reconsider their decision. Say that she wants to study further, or that she wants to marry a boy of her own choice.

UNIT 2 INTERPRETING CHARTS, MAPS, TABLES AND GRAPHS

We often need to interpret diagrams, charts, maps and graphs to take action. Conversely, we may be required to transfer information from a given text on to a diagram, a chart, a map, a table, or a graph. Sometimes information given in a map has to be converted into a table.

Activity 1

Do you know that the year 1987 was the year of the worst drought of the century for the country? There was little rainfall in most parts of the country. On page 103 is a map showing the rainfall in the various states from 1 June to 5 August 1987.

Now play the following game:

1 Each member of the group should adopt a state or a union territory and should state in a sentence what the rainfall was in respect of his state or union territory. For instance, the student whose state is J & K will write and later read out: 'The rainfall in Jammu and Kashmir was deficient.'

Note that the same adjective ('deficient' in the above example) must not be used more than once. Other synonyms should be found.

This activity can continue for several rounds till all the states are covered.

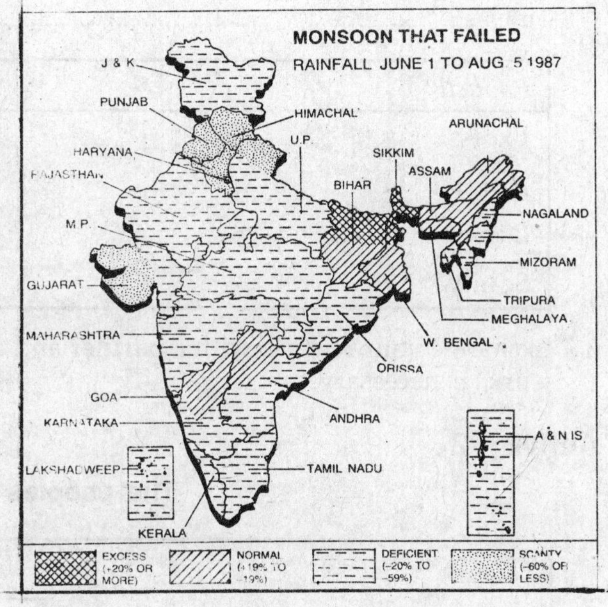

2 Now look again at the map provided and fill in the blanks in the following sentences:

(*a*) There was excess rainfall in .... and parts of ....

(*b*) Rainfall was .... in ...., ..., ... and certain areas of West Bengal, ... and ....

(*c*) .... in J & K, Rajasthan, M.P., Orissa, Tripura, Nagaland, ..., ..., ..., ..., ..., Andaman and Nicobar Islands, Lakshadweep Islands and parts of Gujarat, ..., ... and ....

(*d*) .... scanty in Himachal Pradesh, Punjab, ... and parts of .... and ....

3 Do you know the meaning of the + and – signs and the percentage figures given within brackets at the bottom of the map? These signs and figures define the sense in which the words 'excess', 'normal', 'deficient' and 'scanty' are used in this map. For instance, 'excess' here means that the rainfall in the areas shown thus was 20 per cent or more than the normal rainfall in these areas.

Now fill in the blanks in the following sentences:

(*a*) 'Normal' means that the rainfall in areas shown thus ranged between 19 per cent more to 19 per cent .... than the .... rainfall in these areas.

(*b*) 'Deficient' means that the .... in .... thus ranged between 20 per cent .... to .... per cent .... the .... rainfall in these these areas.

(*c*) 'Scanty' means .... (write the sentence yourself).

4 Finally, put the completed sentences in 2 above together as a paragraph using connectives.

5 Now rearrange this information about the rainfall in the following table. Also provide a suitable heading for it:

Title: ....

Rainfall	*Areas*
Excess	
Normal	
Deficient	
Scanty	

6 Exchange your writing with a partner and comment on each other's work. Revise your work, if necessary.

Activity 2

The peoples of Islam

Country	*Population*		
	Total (000's)	*Muslim (000's)*	*Per cent Muslim*
Indonesia	165,000	140,250	85
Pakistan	95,000	92,150	97
Bangladesh	101,500	90,335	89
India	750,000	90,000	12
Soviet Union	277,000	49,860	18
Egypt	48,000	43,680	91
Iran	43,000	42,140	98
Nigeria	89,000	40,050	45
Morocco	23,000	22,770	99
Algeria	22,200	21,798	99

1 Given above is a table showing the population of Muslims in the world. Study the table and fill in the blanks in the following sentences:

(*a*) .... has a total population of 750,000,000.

(*b*) Of the total Indian population, ... are Muslims.

(*c*) .... constitute .... per cent of the .... Indian ....

(*d*) Interestingly, Indonesia has the .... total Muslim population in the ....

(*e*) The .... place belongs to Pakistan which has a .... population of 92,150,000.

(*f*) Bangladesh comes .... with 90,335,000 Muslims.

(*g*) India with .... occupies the ....

2 Rewrite these sentences as a paragraph using connectives and making other changes wherever necessary.

3 Exchange your writing with your partner and comment on each other's work. Rewrite, if necessary.

Activity 3

Here is a diagram showing the progress made in a gas pipeline project, the Hazira–Bijaipur–Jagdishpur pipeline. The pipeline is meant to carry treated natural gas from the Bombay High offshore complex to the various users.

The shaded portion in the diagram shows the completed section of the pipeline. It also shows the power plants and the fertilizer plants that will benefit from the pipeline, when the project is completed.

Study the diagram carefully and fill in the blanks in the following sentences:

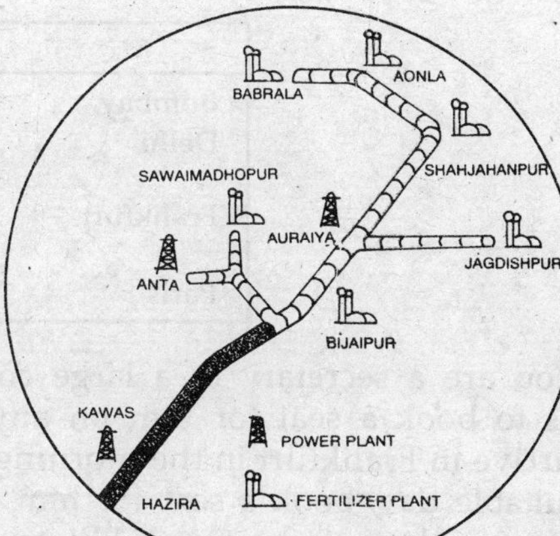

1 (*a*) The portion of the .... that has been completed extends from .... to ....

(*b*) The first beneficiaries of the pipeline are the .... at Kawas and the .... at ....

(*c*) The pipeline when finally completed will benefit .... fertilizer plants.

(*d*) The pipeline when finally completed will supply .... to three ....

(*e*) The power plants are located at ...., ... and ....

(*f*) The fertilizer plants are located ...., ..., ..., ... and ....

2 Now rewrite these sentences as a paragraph.

3 Exchange your writing with your partner and discuss each other's work. Revise your work, if necessary.

Activity 4

We shall now attempt a task which requires you to take action on the basis of a given table. Here is a table showing Air-India flights to Frankfurt (Germany) and beyond.

AI-123			*AI-129*		
Bombay	Dep	2300 (MON)	Bombay	Dep	2300 (THUR)
Delhi	Arr	0050 (TUE)	Delhi	Arr	0050 (FRI)
	Dep	0150		Dep	0150
Frankfurt	Arr	0715	Frankfurt	Arr	0715
	Dep	0830		Dep	0830
Paris	Arr	0950	Paris	Arr	0950

AI-165			*AI-131*		
Bombay	Dep	0345 (WED)	Bombay	Dep	2340 (FRI)
Delhi	Arr	0535	Delhi	Arr	0130 (SAT)
	Dep	0650		Dep	0410
Frankfurt	Arr	1215	Rome	Arr	0935
	Dep	1325		Dep	1045
Paris	Arr	1445	Frankfurt	Arr	1245

AI-155		
Bombay	Dep	0515 (SUN)
Delhi	Arr	0705
	Dep	0810
Frankfurt	Arr	1335
	Dep	1445
Paris	Arr	1605

You are a secretary in a large company in Delhi and you have been asked by your boss to book a seat for him on any working day after the coming Monday. He wants to arrive in Frankfurt in the morning so that he has the whole day at his disposal. Choose a suitable day, book a seat for him and leave a note at his table about the booking.

Here is the note you may like to leave for him. Fill in the blanks:

I have booked a seat for you from .... to .... on Air-India flight no. .... for .... The plane .... at 1.50 a.m. and will reach .... at .... on ....

Exercise 1 Look at the schedule of Air-India flights to Frankfurt and answer the following questions:

(*a*) How many times a week can one fly from India to Frankfurt by Air-India?
(*b*) Which are the days on which one cannot fly to Frankfurt from Delhi?
(*c*) How many flights touch Rome and on which day(s)?
(*d*) How many flights reach Paris in the morning?
(*e*) What weekend flights are there for Frankfurt from Bombay and Delhi? Give details.

Exercise 2 Study the train timings given below and answer the questions that follow:

TRAIN TIMINGS

Delhi		
East bound	**Dep.**	**Arr.**
Kalka–Howrah Mail	0800	1930
Kalindi Exp. to Farukhabad	1715	0945
Delhi–Howrah Exp.	2215	0445
Tinsukhia Mail to Guwahati	1845	0600
Guwahati Ganga–Jamuna Exp.	2145	0800
West bound		
Punjab Mail to Bombay V.T.	0730	2040
Frontier Mail	0800	1930
Dehradun Exp. to Bombay	2110	0710
Chetak Exp. to Udaipur	1215	1415
* Pink City Exp. to Jaipur	0550	2215
* Ahmedabad Mail	2200	0730
* Ashram Exp. Mon, Tue, Fri, Sat.	1815	1000
* Shekawati Exp. to Jaipur	2245	0500
Aravali Exp. to Ahmedabad	1600	0530
* Jodhpur Mail	2030	0615
Bikaner Mail	2100	0700
* All Metre Gauge Trains		
North bound		
Jammu Tawi Mail	2100	0440
Kalka Mail	2245	0630
Punjab Mail to Firozepur	2125	0615

New Delhi		
East bound	**Dep.**	**Arr.**
Neelanchal Exp. to Puri Tue., Thu., Sun.	0600	2115
Puri Exp. Mon., Wed., Fri., Sat.	0715	1730
Toofan Exp. to Howrah	0930	2030
A.C. Exp. to Howrah (via Patna) Thu., Sun.	1615	1045

	Dep.	Arr.
A.C. Exp. to Howrah (via Gaya) Mon., Tue., Fri.	1615	1045
Rajdhani Exp. to Howrah Mon., Tue., Wed., Fri., Sat.	1715	0950
Vaishali Exp. to Barauni	1930	1030
Magadh Exp. to Patna	1945	1145
N.E. Exp. to Guwahati	0630	2015
Tatanagar Exp.	1400	1330
Kashi, Vishwanath Exp. to Varanasi	1330	0640
Gomati Exp. to Lucknow except Tue.	1445	1315
Lucknow Mail	2130	0745
Awadh, Assam Exp. Tue., Thu. Sat., Sun.	0900	1600
Unchahar Exp. to Allahabad	2015	0600
Prayagraj Exp. to Allahabad	2200	0645
West bound		
Dadar Exp.	2050	0710
Jhelum Exp. to Pune	1115	2035
Taj Exp. to Gwalior (via Agra)	0700	2215
Malwa Exp. to Indore	1930	0905
Sarvodaya Exp. to Ahmedabad Thu., Sun.	1700	0915
Rajdhani Exp. to Bombay Central Mon., Tue., Wed., Fri., Sat.	1700	0915
Jammu Tawi to Bombay Central Super Fast, Wed., Sat.	0250	0155
A.C. Paschim Exp. to Bombay Central	1710	1025

South bound	Dep.	Arr.
A.P. Exp. to Secunderabad Mon., Wed., Thu., Sat.	1400	0740
Tamil Nadu Exp. to Madras Mon., Tue., Thu., Fri., Sat.	2245	0645
Karnataka Exp. Mon., Fri.	1200	1100
New Delhi–Bangalore Exp.	1200	1100
Tue., Thu.	1200	1100
G.T. Exp. to Madras	1915	0515
Him Sagar Exp. to Kanyakumari Sun.	1200	1530
Chhattisgarh Exp. to Bilaspur	0620	2000
North bound		
Dadar–Amritsar Exp.	0800	2000
A.C. Exp. to Amritsar	1145	1440
Tatanagar Exp.	1530	1445
Shalimar Exp. to Jammu	1600	1100
Jhelum Exp. to Jammu	2135	1015
Bhiwani Exp.	1840	0920
Nizamuddin		
South bound		
Dakshin Exp.	2030	0550
Kalinga Exp. to Puri	1250	1300
Nizamuddin–Bangalore Exp. Sat.	0915	1440
Mangalore Exp. Mon., Tue., Wed., Thur., Fri.	0915	1440
North bound		
Flying Mail	1140	2115

(*a*) Which is the most convenient train for Kanyakumari?
(*b*) On which day of the week does it leave and from which station in Delhi?
(*c*) Which train should you take for Madras if you have to leave on a Sunday?
(*d*) Which are the trains that one can take for Calcutta? Which station do they start from in Delhi and where do they terminate?

Note: The particular day or days of the week on which a train leaves is indicated by abbreviations like Mon. (Monday), Tue. (Tuesday), etc. When no such abbreviation is given, it means that the train leaves everyday of the week.

Activity 5

Study the table on page 108 showing the thematic classification of Indian films and fill in the blanks in the following paragraphs. Some of the key words have been left incomplete:

The most pop.......................... films in India are .... films. In 1981 out of a total of .... films, ... were made on .... themes. They, thus, constitute more than ....fifth of the films produced in .... Such films were .... in pre.......................... years also. In 1970, for instance, as many as .... films out of a total of .... films made were on social themes. In other words, over .... per cent of the total number of films produced were social films. A comparison with the 1981 figures shows that the popularity of .... has ....ed.

The number of films on devotional sub.......................... is .... but when one compares it with the .... of similar films made in 1970 one notices a .... increase in the figure. In 1970 there was just .... film on .... theme out of a .... of 396 .... In 1981 as many as .... films were made on the .... out of a total of 737.

On the other hand, myth.......................... themes are .... popular with Indian film-.......................... . Though the total number of films made increased from 396 in 1970 to 737 in 1981, the number of ....al pictures de.......................... from .... to .... Films on c.......................... and f.......................... have also become less popular with ....

Thematic classification of Indian films

Theme	*Year*											
	1970	*1971*	*1972*	*1973*	*1974*	*1975*	*1976*	*1977*	*1978*	*1979*	*1980*	*1981*
Social	254	283	273	305	268	313	332	420	458	594	605	602
Crime	80	83	82	102	98	89	86	55	78	37	63	56
Fantasy	13	8	9	1	5	7	9	5	13	11	6	3
Historical	2	5	2	5	4	7	10	6	6	9	—	5
Biographical	3	2	3	1	2	1	2	4	5	3	3	2
Mythological	18	16	16	19	27	19	27	20	16	23	20	11
Legendary	18	12	5	5	13	14	27	22	13	15	5	6
Devotional	1	8	6	8	14	12	6	19	14	8	15	27
Children	7	13	2	1	1	7	4	5	7	12	19	12
Stunt	—	1	6	—	—	1	2	—	7	1	3	1
Adventure	—	—	3	—	—	—	—	—	—	—	—	—
Political	—	1	2	—	—	—	—	—	—	—	—	—
Documentary	—	1	4	1	2	1	2	1	1	—	—	—
Educational	—	—	—	—	—	—	—	—	—	2	1	5
Horror	—	—	1	—	—	—	—	—	1	1	1	4
Scientific	—	—	—	1	1	4	—	—	—	—	—	—
Technical others	—	—	—	—	—	—	—	—	—	1	1	3
Total	396	433	414	448	435	475	507	557	619	714	742	737

UNIT 3 MESSAGE WRITING

Sometimes we have to attend to telephone calls that are meant for someone else who isn't there to receive them herself/himself. The caller may want to talk to your parents or your sister or brother who may be out. Or s/he may want you to convey a message to a neighbour. In an office the call may be for a colleague of yours who is not around. In such cases you can either give the message personally or leave a note for the person called. This unit is concerned with conveying a message through a written note.*

Activity 1

Read the following telephone conversation:

Caller	:	May I speak to Shalini, please?
Asha	:	I'm afraid she's not in. May I know who is speaking, please?
Caller	:	I'm John, a classmate of hers. When is she expected back?
Asha	:	Sorry, I've no idea. But can I take a message?
John	:	Please ask her to call me back. She has my number.
Asha	:	I will.
John	:	Thank you. Bye.

You are Asha and you too are going out and may not return before Shalini comes back home. So you wish to leave a note for her. What will you write? Think about it and then write your note. When you have done so compare your note with that written by your partner.

How to handle this task

Clearly, two things are important:

1 Your message must be complete.
2 And it must be clear.

You should identify the caller. And you should say what the caller wanted you to tell her. In other words, your note should answer three questions:

1 Who called?
2 What was the message?
3 When was the message received (date/time)?

Let's pick out this information from the telephone conversation given above. It would read something like this:

John, your classmate, rang up.
He wanted you to call him back.
He says you have his number.

Go over the conversation again and see that you have missed nothing important. And don't forget to put the date.

Now we can draft the note. Here is a sample:

For Shalini:

> John, your classmate, telephoned. (He) wanted you to call him back. (He) said you had his number.
> —Asha

The note need not be in complete sentences. So you can leave out the subject in the last two sentences:

For Shalini:

> John, your classmate, telephoned. Wanted you to call him back. Said you had his number.
> —Asha

Often the exact time of the call is also important. So mention the time also:

*The conversations presented in this unit could be taped and played to the students. That would make the activities more authentic.

For Shalini:

John, your classmate telephoned at 3.00 p.m. Wanted you to call him back. Said you had his number.

—Asha

Activity 2

1 Read the following telephone conversation and write notes for the persons called:

Caller : Is this five four one three one seven one?
Girish : Yes.
Caller : May I speak to Asha, please?
Girish : Sorry, she's just gone out. May I know who is calling, please?
Caller : This is Raghavan. We're in the same class. Could I leave a message for her, please?
Girish : Sure.
Raghvan : Please tell her, I have got two tickets for the play 'Ek Tha Gadha' for this evening at the Shri Ram Centre.
Girish : I'll tell her.
Raghvan : Please tell her to reach there by six fifteen sharp.
Girish : I will.
Raghvan : Thanks a lot. Bye.
Girish : Bye.

2 **Caller** : Is this Mr Srinivasan's residence?
Sridhar : Yes, it is. Whom do you wish to speak to?
Caller : May I speak to Geeta, please?
Sridhar : Sorry, she's not here at the moment. She's out visiting an aunt. May I know who's speaking, please?
Caller : This is Rita. What time is she expected back?
Sridhar : By this evening, I think. Would you like to leave a message?
Rita : Yes, could you please tell her, I am having a small get-together of friends tomorrow evening at my place. I would like her to come at four thirty. Also, could she tell Asha to come, rather could she bring her along. You see, Asha has no phone and I haven't been able to contact her. Sorry to bother you.
Sridhar : Not at all. I'll tell her everything.
Rita : Many thanks. Bye.
Sridhar : Bye.

3 **Caller** : Is this the Scholarship Banch, please?
Section Officer : Yes.
Caller : May I speak to Mr H S Hans, please?
Section Officer : I'm afraid Mr Hans is not in the office at the moment. May I know who is speaking, please?
Caller : This is Subhas Banerjee. Hans and I are neighbours. Could I leave a message for him? Its' rather urgent.
Section Officer : Sure.
Subhas : Please tell him that his father has met with an accident and has been taken to Ganga Ram Hospital.
Section Officer : I'm sorry to hear that! I hope it's nothing serious?

Subhas	:	His left arm has been fractured but its nothing serious. His wife has already gone to the hospital. Will you please ask him to reach there immediately?
Section Officer	:	I sure will. As soon as he comes.
Subhas	:	Thank you. Bye.

Activity 3

In real life, conversations on the telephone may be longer. Or at least the message may contain an address, a telephone number, a date or dates or some figures. So it is advisable to make a note as you talk over the telephone. Here is one such conversation:

Caller	:	Is this four three one two eight eight five?
Kuldeep	:	That's right.
Caller	:	May I speak to your neighbour Mrs Sushma Sharma, please? I'm her brother, Harish, speaking. Sorry to bother you.
Kuldeep	:	Not at all. But actually there are some friends with me and there is no one else at home at the moment. Would you mind telephoning again after about an hour or so? Or can I take a message?
Harish	:	Please tell her that her sister Saroj has come from Madras and is staying with her in-laws in their new house at sixty-four D Shalimar Garden.
Kuldeep	:	Just a second. Let me write it down. Where's she staying?
Harish	:	At sixty-four D Shalimar Garden.
Kuldeep	:	Sixty-four B .... ?
Harish	:	No, it's, sixty-four D, D for Delhi. And her number is seven two one three six six three.
Kuldeep	:	Seven two one three six six three. Is that right?
Harish	:	Right
Kuldeep	:	I'll send the message as soon as someone comes.
Harish	:	Thank you very much. Bye.

Here the message is not complicated, but it contains an address and a telephone number. So the message must be accurate. Read the conversation again and write the message. Compare it with what others in the class have written.

UNIT 4 FORM-FILLING

In the course of our daily life we are constantly filling in forms of all sorts—forms for admission to schools and colleges, for jobs, for depositing money in a bank and for getting money out of the bank, for a passport and for railway reservations and for a host of other purposes.

Most of the time we fill in forms for ourselves or for members of our family. But on occasions we do so for others on the basis of given information. In either case it is important to know how to fill in forms.

Activity 1 Simple forms

Do you know Kerala is the first state in India to achieve hundred per cent literacy? This is remarkable, isn't it? Wouldn't you like to do your bit and help make someone like Kamala literate?

This is Kamala today.

Turning her into

कमला

is a matter of pride.

Your pride.

By teaching Kamala the basics of reading and writing, you will be giving her more than just a name. You will be giving her a start to a new, better life.

And you could well discover a new meaning in your own life—with the immesurable sense of pride and satisfaction you will feel.

All you have to do is spend some time teaching someone in your neighbourhood.

Someone who needs just the basic learning that it takes to fill in a ration card, identity card or bank slip. Enough to make him or her confident of facing the world.

If you're ready to take up this challenge, just fill in the coupon below and mail it to us. We'll send you information on how to go about the teaching process.

Do remember the National Literacy Mission is with you all the way. All it needs is a little of your time.

Teach someone.
It's the greatest gift you can give.

Yes. I'd love to teach someone to live a more complete life by learning to read and write. Please send me more information in Hindi/English/________ (please specify language)

Name : ________________

Address : ________________

Mail to: National Literacy Mission
Post Box No. 9999, New Delhi-110 011.

Now read the above advertisement and fill in the coupon to ask for more information about the literacy programme and how you can join it.

There are two ways of filling in the blanks:

1 Name : Indu Jain
Address : A 221 Paschim Vihar
Delhi 110 063

2 But a better way is to write in block letters or capitals. Do you know what block letters or capitals are? Writing in block letters is *writing words in which each letter is formed separately and written in its capital form.* If we use block letters the form will look like this:

Name : INDU JAIN
Address : A 221 PASCHIM VIHAR
DELHI 110 063

Sometimes the form itself requires you to write your name and address in block letters. But even when the form does not say so, it is safer to use block letters. The same holds good for the PIN code also.

Exercise 1

Bhasha Seekho English courses are available for all levels—Standard, Intermediate, Advanced and Specialized courses for exporters, doctors, scientists, businessmen, children and also those who seek jobs abroad.

'Foreign Language courses in French, German, Arabic, Spanish, Russian, Italian and Japanese also available.'

This is an advertisement. Now choose a language and level (in the case of English) and fill in the blanks in the form given below:

BHASHA SEEKHO LANGUAGES INSTITUTE
G 1416 Chitranjan Park, New Delhi 110036

Please send me Prospectus for ....
(specify language and level)

Name ....

Address ....

Exercise 2 Do you know what eye donation is? Well, read the advertisement that follows:

You can give him sight.

He can feel a flower but he cannot see it.
He has eyes. But he has no sight.

He has his whole life ahead. But his spirit is crushed. By one of the most dreadful inflictions of all. Blindness.

But young Iqbal's case is not without hope. His blindness like many others; is not without cure. There is a remedy that's simple, doesn't cost anything and is effective. Only it needs you.

A simple cornea transplant can restore sight to the blind. The useless cornea, replaced by a healthy one. And the healthy one could be yours.

Eye removal leaves no scar or disfigurement. And once you've pledged to donate, you'll live with the gratifying emotion that your eyes will live much longer than you. And that some blind person will see . . . through them.

If your heart goes out to the blind during your lifetime, let your eyes go out to them after death.
It's the most precious gift you can give them.

To know more about eye donation, and what kinds of blindness can be cured, send us the coupon for a detailed brochure.

Do it today. Remember,
miracles can't cure the blind, You can.

I would like to know more about eye donation and cornea grafting. Send me a detailed brochure.

(Kindly fill in block letters)
Name: Mr/Ms

Address: ....
....
State: ....
Pincode: ....
Age: ....

SiGHT

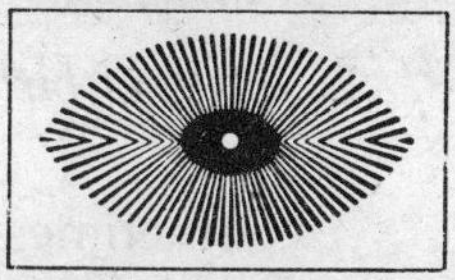

TIMES EYE RESEARCH FOUNDATION
7 Bahadur Shah Zafar Marg, New Delhi 110 002

Sight. A Gift only you can give.

After reading the advertisement you find yourself interested in knowing more about eye donation and cornea grafting. Fill in the blanks in the form given.

Is there any abbreviation in the form that you are not familiar with? Look at the form again. What is 'Ms'? For whom is it used? 'Ms' is a title for a woman who does not wish to call herself either 'Mrs' or 'Miss'. It is pronounced as 'Miz'.

Common terms in forms

There are so many forms that there seems little point in giving *one* model form. Each form is to some extent different from the other. Even so, you should be familiar with some common terms and expressions that you are likely to come across in forms.

1	Name	:	
	Surname or family name	:	
	First name	:	
	Nationality	:	
2	Date of birth (in words)	:	
	(in figures)	:	
	Place of birth	:	Village/Town .... Dist. .... State ....
	Age	:	
	Sex	:	Male/Female
3	Marital status	:	Married/Single
4	Address	:	
	Present address	:	
	Permanent address	:	
5	Qualifications	:	
6	Experience	:	
	Name of institution where employed	:	
	Previous employment	:	
	Names of institutions with dates	:	

Notes: 1 *Name*: If you are asked to write your name only, write the full name in block capitals.

Full name: PRADIP BOSE

But sometimes you are asked to give the surname and the first name/other names separately.

Surname: BOSE *First name/Other name*: PRADIP

2 *Date of birth*: (in words) Twentieth June nineteen sixty-seven
(in figures) 20.6.1967

Sometimes you are asked to indicate your age separately.

Age: 20 years 6 months

3 *Marital status*: Sometimes you are asked to say whether you are married or single.

Married/Single (strike out whichever is not applicable).

4 *Address*: Sometimes you are asked to give your present address and your permanent address separately. *If the two addresses are the same, repeat the full address*. DON'T WRITE—'Same as before' or 'Same as present address'.

5 *Qualifications*: Here mention details of your qualifications, i.e. examinations passed in chronological order. Begin with details of Matriculation examination and go on to the higher degrees.

6 *Experience*: Give details of experience, i.e. institution(s), etc., where you worked with dates and position held, again in chronological order.

Always read the forms carefully before you fill them in. And if it is an application form, keep a copy of what you have filled in with you for future reference.

Activity 2 Forms concerning money

These forms could be deposit slips, withdrawal forms, cheques, money order forms and forms for the issue of demand drafts. While filling them in, you have to be very careful. An error can be costly, or at least cause inconvenience.

Given below is a blank deposit or pay-in-slip. The slip is used to deposit either cash or cheque in your Savings Bank Account.

Your mother has given you Rs 1000/- to be deposited in her Savings Bank Account No. 1421. The money is in denominations of Rs 100/- and Rs 50/-, i.e. (100 × 6) + (50 × 8). Discuss with your partner/group and fill in the slip:

इण्डियन ओवरसीज बैंक
Indian Overseas Bank
_____ [1] _____ शाखा / Branch

तारिख Date _____ [2] _____ 19_____
बचत खाता सं०
SAVINGS A/C No _____ [3] _____
का
of _____ [4] _____

चैक /नकद / Cheque/Cash Rs. [6a]

रुपये / Rupees _____ [5] _____

रोकड़िया / Cashier प्रबन्धक / Manager/लेखापाल / Acctt.

इण्डियन ओवरसीज बैंक / Indian Overseas Bank
_____ [1] _____ शाखा / Branch तारिख Date _____ [2] _____ 19_____
बचत खाता सं०
SAVINGS A/c No. [3]
का / of _____ [4] _____
चैक/ Cheque / नकद/ Cash रु०/ Rs. [6a]
रुपये / Rupees _____ [5] _____
जैसे कि पीछे विस्तृत किया है
As per details furnished overleaf _____

L.F.		In	

[7] जमाकर्ता के हस्ताक्षर (Signature of Depositor)

रोकड़िया/ Cashier प्रबंधक / Manager / लेखापाल / Acctt. पर्ची सं./Slip No.

* उसी शाखा के लिए अलग पर्ची भरी जानी चाहिए/ दूसरी स्थानीय बैक शाखाओं/प्रत्येक राष्ट्रीय समाशोधन केन्द्र (बम्बई, कलकत्ता, मद्रास, नई दिल्ली) तथा दूसरे अस्थानीय चैक ।

*Separate slip should be made out for cheques on the same branch/other local bank branches each National Clearing Centre (Bombay, Calcutta Madras, New Delhi) and other outstation cheques.

After you have filled it in, read the following notes:

1 Here write the name of the Branch.
2 Here give the date, i.e. 20 June 1991.
3 Write Account No. 1421.
4 Write down the name of your mother, i.e. Mrs Abida Khan
5 Here give the amount in words. Say: 'Rupees one thousand only'. Don't forget to use the word 'only' at the end.
6 (*a*) Here cross out the word 'Cheque' and fill in the total amount in figures.
(*b*) On the reverse side of the form indicate the number of notes according to denominations and the total amount.

Write: 100 × 6 = Rs 600/-
50 × 8 = Rs 400/-
Total = Rs 1,000/-

7 Sign your own name. The person who is depositing the money should sign here. Leave all other items blank.

Exercise 1 You have saved Rs 536/- out of your pocket money. Fill in a pay-in-slip to deposit the amount in the Indian Overseas Bank.

Activity 3

You have received a gift cheque no. 2231452, dated 15 May 1991 for Rs 101/- drawn on the State Bank of India, Shahadra, Delhi, from your elder sister. You wish to deposit it in your account in the Indian Overseas Bank. You can use the same pay-in-slip as the one you used for depositing cash in Activity 2, except that in 6(*a*) you must cross out the word 'Cash' and fill in the amount shown in the cheque you wish to deposit. On the reverse of this pay-in-slip, in 6(*c*) you must fill in the name of the bank on which the cheque is drawn, the cheque number and the amount. Leave 6(*b*) blank.

Now discuss with your partner/group and fill in the deposit slip on both sides. Your Savings Bank Account No. is 673. The front and the reverse sides of a pay-in-slip are given below:

इण्डियन ओवरसीज बैंक
Indian Overseas Bank

[1] शाखा / Branch

तारिख Date [2] ______ 19____

बचत खाता सं० SAVINGS A/C No [3]

का of [4]

चैक /नकद / Cheque/Cash Rs. [6a]

रुपये / Rupees [5]

रोकड़िया / Cashier प्रबन्धक / Manager/लेखापाल / Acctt.

इण्डियन ओवरसीज बैंक / Indian Overseas Bank

[1] शाखा / Branch तारिख Date [2] ______ 19____

बचत खाता सं० SAVINGS A/c No. [3]

का / of [4]

चैक/ Cheque / नकद/ Cash रु०/ Rs. [6a]

रुपये / Rupees [5]

जैसे कि पीछे विस्तृत किया है
As per details furnished overleaf

L.F. ____ In ____

रोकड़िया/ Cashier प्रबंधक / Manager / लेखापाल / Acctt. पर्ची सं./Slip No. [7] जमाकर्ता के हस्ताक्षर (Signature of Depositor)

* उसी शाखा के लिए अलग पर्ची भरी जानी चाहिए/ दूसरी स्थानीय बैंक शाखाओं/प्रत्येक राष्ट्रीय समाशोधन केन्द्र (बम्बई, कलकत्ता, मदास, नई दिल्ली) तथा दूसरे अस्थानीय चैक।

*Separate slip should be made out for cheques on the same branch/other local bank branches each National Clearing Centre (Bombay, Calcutta Madras, New Delhi) and other outstation cheques.

नोट/Note	रू. Rs.	पै. P.
X 500	6b	
x 100		
x 50		
x 20		
x 10		
x 5		
x 2		
x 1		
रेजगारी/ Coins		
जोड़/Total		

अदा करने वाले बैंक का नाम Name of the Bank drawn upon	चेक सं. Cheque No	रू. Rs.	पै./ P.
6c			

अदा करने वाले बैंक का नाम Name of the Bank drawn upon	चेक स. Cheque No.	रू. Rs.	पै. P.
6c			
जोड़/Total			

Activity 4

1 You owe your friend Girish Wagle Rs 50/-. You have no ready cash, so you make out a cheque in his favour for the correct amount. Fill in the cheque given on pa͜ge 117 so that Girish can have the amount immediately:
2 What would happen if you were to cross out the words 'OR BEARER'?
3 What should you do if you want the amount to be deposited in Girish's account only? Discuss with your partner/group and find out.

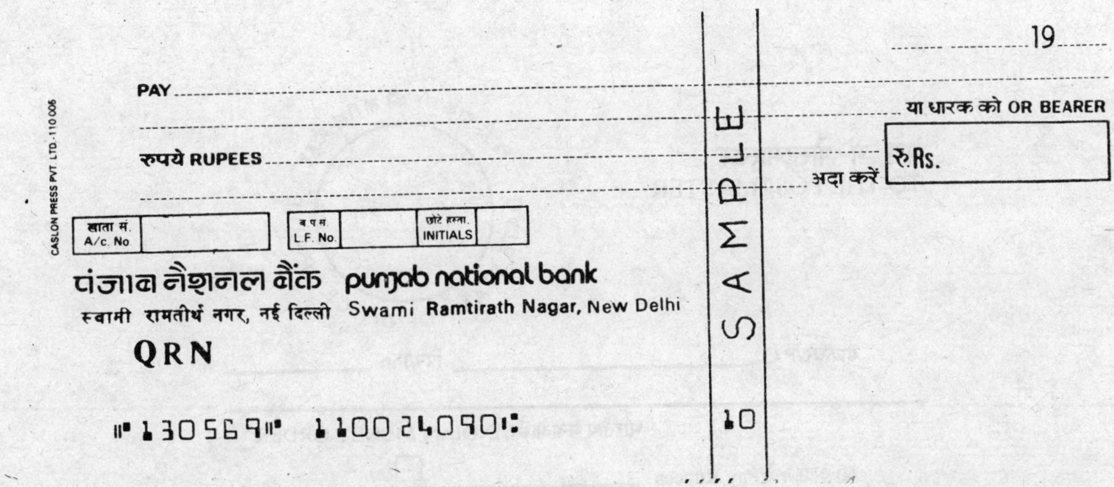

Exercise 1 On page 118 is another form which is very commonly used, namely, the money order form.

Ram Dayal, a peon in your colleage wants you to fill in a money order form for him. He wants to send Rs 657/- to his wife, Shrimati Sita Devi, c/o Shri Gian Prasad, Village Himpur, P.O. Shamnagar, District Patna, Bihar, 800 001. He lives in No. 2 Staff Quarters, S.D.P. College, Maurice Nagar, Delhi 110 007.

Remember, you are to fill in only the seven items marked in the form, not any other blanks.

Discuss with your partner/group and fill in the form.

1 Amount being sent is to be entered here in words: 'Rupees six hundred and fifty-seven only'.
2 Write the amount in figures here. Rs ..../-.
3 Complete name and address of the recipient. Don't forget to write the PIN code as it speeds up the delivery of your money orders and letters.
4 The sender should sign his name here.
5 Indicate the correct date here.
6 The sender's name and address should be written here.
7 The sender can write his message to the recipient here. Naturally the message must be brief and to the point.

Activity 5 Travel forms

A blank reservation form for travel by rail is given on page 119. Now do the following task:

Shri R N Mehta, Smt Sudha Mehta, Raju Mehta and Sumati Mehta want to reach Calcutta on 2 July 1991. You have been requested to make reservations for them. They will travel by 2 Down (Delhi–Calcutta) Kalka Mail starting from Delhi on 1 July 1991. They require 4 berths in a Second Class 3-Tier Sleeper. Shri R N Mehta is 40 years old, his wife Sudha is 36 years old, son Raju is 13 years and daughter Sumati is 8 years old. Their Delhi address is 34/II C Jorbagh, New Delhi 110 003. Their Telephone No. is 612625. You are making the reservations on 14 May 1991 at 3.00 p.m. The applicant is R N Mehta and you are to sign for R N Mehta. Note that the requisition slip (given on page 119) can be used for either reservation, cancellation, return or onward journey. Tick the one applicable here.

Discuss with your partner/group and fill in the reservation form.

सेवा में पोस्टमास्टर
TO THE POSTMASTER

बिक्री डाकघर की तारीख मोहर
DATE STAMP OF OFFICE OF SALE

डाकघर/P.O. ______________ पिन/Pin ________

भारतीय मनीआर्डर/INDIAN MONEY ORDER

रु० अदा करें/Pay Rupees ______________ [1]

सेवा में/To

रु./Rs. ______________ [2]

[3]
____
____
____

पिन
Pin ☐☐☐☐☐☐

दिनांक
Date................ [5]

भेजने वाले के हस्ताक्षर
Sender's Signature................ [4]

भारतीय डाक विभाग/DEPARTMENT OF POSTS
पावती/ACKNOWLEDGEMENT

म० आ० नं०
M.O. No..................

दिनांक
Date..................

प्रेषक डाकघर की नाम–मोहर

Name Stamp of the office of issue

भेजने वाले का नाम व पूरा पता/Sender's Name and Full Address

[6]
____
____

पिन
Pin ☐☐☐☐☐☐

संदेश के लिए स्थान/Space for Communication

[7]

रु०/Rs................

उ.रे./N.R. सी.एम. 257 (संशोधित) (ह.)
C.M. 257 (NR)

आरक्षण/खारिज/वापसी/आगे की यात्रा हेतु अनुरोध पत्र
REQUISITION FOR RESERVATION/CANCELLATION/RETURN OR ONWARD JOURNEY

जिस स्टेशन से Station from........................... जिस स्थान को To....................
यात्रा की तिथि Date of journey........................... ट्रेन नं. Train No...............
श्रेणी Class................................... बर्थ/सीट Berth/Seat...............................

क्रम स. S. No.	नाम Name in Block letters	स्त्री/पु. Sex	आयु Age	कर्मचारी द्वारा भरा जायेगा To be filled in by the staff
1.	....	....	....	टिकट नं. .... Ticket No./PNR No.
2.	....	....	....	कोच नं. .... Coach No.
3.	....	....	....	बर्थ/सीट नं. .... Berth/Seat No.
4.	....	....	....	प्रतीक्षा सूची नं. .... Wait list No.
5.	....	....	....	ह.ई. आर सी. .... Sig. of E.R.C.
6.	....	....	....	

आवेदक का नाम Name of the applicant..
आवेदक के हस्ताक्षर Signature of applicant..
तारीख Date..................................

विशेष अनुरोध
Special Request

(i) कूपा/केबिन/निचली शायिका/मध्यवर्ती शायिका/ऊपरी शायिका
Coupe/Cabin/Lower/Berth/Middle Berth/Upper Berth ☐

(ii) धूम्रपान निषेधयान
Non Smoker Coach ☐

(iii) पसन्द का भोजन (शाकाहारी/मांसाहारी)
Choice of Meals (Veg./N. Veg.) ☐

पसंद दर्शाने के लिए खाने में "√" निशान लगायें ।
Mark "√" in the block to show the choice.

पूरा पता Address in full..
....

दूरभाष Telephone.................................. समय Time..........................

(कृ.पृ.उ./P.T.O.)

Activity 6 Registration as voter

You have completed 18 years of age and you wish to register yourself as a voter. On page 120 is a blank form for registration.

Discuss the details to be filled in with your partner/group and complete the form according to the instructions given.

Before you start filling the form, find out the following information:

1 In which constitutency does your area fall?
2 What is an electoral roll?
3 Who is the claimant?
4 Who will sign for the elector?
5 What is the application fee?

Note: You could contact your Political Science teacher for any clarification.

ELECTION COMMISSION OF INDIA

FORM FOR REGISTRATION AS VOTER

Have you registered yourself as voter if not, then you can get enrolled as voter even now so as to participate in the forthcoming election by filling and submitting the Form 6 in duplicate which is reproduced below for the sake of public convenience.

In addition to printed forms, newspaper cuttings or photostat copies thereof, handwritten, typed or cyclostyled copies (as per the format) of this application form will also be accepted.

Any citizen 18 years and above on 1.1.91. (1.1.90 in case of Assam) may apply for registration as voter.

Application is to be submitted to the Electoral Registration Officer (ERO) of the concerned constituency. Addresses of EROs are available with the District Election Officers (Collector/Deputy Commissioner/District Magistrate) or Chief Electoral Officer of the State. However, in case of Delhi, applications will be accepted by the Chief Electoral Officer, Old St Stephens College Building, Kashmiri Gate, Delhi.

Application is to be accompanied by a fee of 10 paise payable in cash or by means of non-judicial stamps.

FORM 6

[See rules 13(1) and 26]

Claim application for inclusion of name

To

The Electoral Registration Officer,

.... Constituency.

Sir,

I request that my name be included in the electoral roll for the above constituency in Part No........ relating to ....

My name (in full) .... Sex ....

My Father's/Mother's/Husband's name ....

Particulars of my place of residence are:

House No ....

Street/Mohalla ....

Town/Village ....

Post Office ....

Police Station/Tehsil/Taluka/Mouza ....

District ....

I hereby declare that to the best of my knowledge and belief:

(i) I am a citizen of India;

(ii) My age on the first day of January last was .... years and .... months;

(iii) I am ordinarily resident at the address given above;

(iv) I have not applied for the inclusion of my name in the electoral roll for any other constituency;

(v) My name has not been included in the electoral roll for his or any other assembly constituency

or

my name may have been included in the electoral roll in .... State in which I was ordinarily resident earlier at the address mentioned below and, if so, I request that the same may be excluded from that electoral roll.

Place ....

Date ....

....

*Signature or thumb impression of claimant

* To be filled by the applicant.

(contd.)

I am an elector in the electoral roll in which the claimant applied for inclusion and my name is enrolled at Serial No .... in Part No .... of the roll. I support this claim and countersign it.

....
Signature of the elector

Name (in full) ....

NOTE: Any person who makes a statement or declaration which is false and which he either knows or believes to be false or does not believe to be true is punishable under Section 31 of the Representation of the People Act, 1950.

Intimation of action taken

The application in Form 6 of Shri/Shrimati/Kumari ....
address .... has been:

(a) accepted and his/her name has been included in the electoral roll *vide* Serial No .... in Part No ....

(b) rejected for the reason ....
....

Date ....

Electoral Registration Officer
Address ....
....

Receipt of application

Received the application in Form 6 from Shri/Shrimati/Kumari* ....
.... address ....
....

Date ....

Electoral Registration Officer
Address ....
....
....

Activity 7 Job application form

As pointed out in the previous unit, applications for jobs are often required to be sent on prescribed forms. Here is a blank application form:

1 Name of the post applied for ....
....

2 Surname (in block letters): ....
Name: ....

3 Address:
(*a*) Present address: ....
(*b*) Permanent address: ....

4 Date of birth and age: ....

5 Nationality: ....

6 Do you belong to a Scheduled Caste or a Scheduled Tribe? Yes/No
(Cross out what is not applicable)
If so, specify the Caste/Tribe ....

7 Marital status:

8 Educational qualifications:
(beginning with Matriculation)

Exam. passed (1)	*Name of school/ college* (2)	*University/ board* (3)	*Year* (4)	*Division & % of marks* (5)

9 Experience:

Name of organization (1)	*Designation* (2)	*Period of service with dates* (3)

10 References: (Names, designations and addresses of two responsible persons not related to the candidate to whom a reference can be made about him.)

(*a*)
(*b*)

11 Any other information you may wish to add:

I solemnly affirm that the information given above is true to the best of my knowledge and belief.

Date: ....

Place: Signature

Read the form carefully and fill it up. Later exchange the form with your partner for checking.

Further practice

Fill in the following application form for the issue of a passport:

1 Full name (in block letters)
   (*a*) Surname:
   (*b*) Name:
2 Father's name:
3 Date of birth:
   (*a*) in words:
   (*b*) in figures:

4 Age (on the date of application) :
5 Place of birth: Village/Town:
Tehsil:
District: State:
6 Occupation:
7 Height:
8 Any mark of identification:
9 Colour of hair:
10 Marital status (whether married/single
11 Present address:
12 Permanent address:
13 Places where you stayed during the last five years:
14 Countries to be visited:
15 Purpose of Journey: Pleasure:
Study:
Job:
Conference:
Any other:
16 Date of Departure:

I certify that the above particulars are correct to the best of my knowledge and belief.

....

Date: Signature

Fill the first 13 items with reference to yourself. For the rest, use your imagination.

Making Applications and Answering Advertisements

UNIT 1 MAKING APPLICATIONS

We write letters on a variety of occasions and for a variety of purposes. There are broadly two kinds of letters—formal letters and informal or friendly letters.

Formal letters include official letters, business letters and letters to newspapers. Writing applications too comes under this category. Of these, the most important is the application for a job. But there are others that are important too—application for leave, application for a fee concession or a scholarship, application for a telephone connection and other facilities. We also need to apply for a prospectus, for the details of a course and also for an application form. Sometimes on seeing advertisements we write letters to make enquiries about the articles advertised and place orders for them.

Activity 1 Application for a job

Given below are various parts of an application for a job. The parts are jumbled:

I shall be grateful if you could kindly consider my application favourably.

F 2/8 Model Town
Delhi 110 009

I passed my Senior Secondary Examination from Delhi in May last year in the second division with 256/500 marks. I have a typewriting speed of 120 words per minute.

Yours faithfully

25 January 1991

I wish to apply for the post of a typist as advertised in the *Indian Express* of 20 January 1991.

Thanking you

Sir

Encl: Biodata

The Manager
Travel India
21 Ambika Apartments
Janakpuri, New Delhi 110 058

I am enclosing my biodata.

sd/-

(Nandita Muttoo)

1 Read the jumbled letter, discuss with your partner/group and put the various parts of it in the right order.

2 Where will you insert the following?

(*a*) I am learning shorthand also.

(*b*) Sub: Application for the job of a typist.

(*c*) As for experience, I have been doing part-time work as a typist in a chartered accountant's firm for the last two months.

Discuss with your partner/group the best places to add them and rewrite the letter.

Format of an application for a job

Here is an outline model for an application for a job and other official letters. Each major part is identified by a capital letter and its function is explained in the *Notes*. Read them carefully:

12 Mount Road
Madras 600 001 Ⓐ

21 May 1991 Ⓑ

Ⓒ The Personnel Manager
Ashoka Hotel
50 B Chanakyapuri
New Delhi 110 021

Sub: Application for the post of a Steward Ⓓ

Ⓔ Sir

Ⓕ I wish to apply for the post of a steward as advertised in ....

....

....

....

Ⓖ Thanking you

Yours faithfully

Ⓗ sd/

(P. Srinivasan)

Ⓘ Encl: As above.

Notes: A The address of the sender is written at the top right-hand corner. Do not put your address at the bottom of the letter. Also, do not write your name above your address. And take care to write the complete address including the PIN code.

B The date goes under the address. The acceptable way of writing it is either 21 May 1991 or 21.5.1991.

C The name, official designation and address of the recipient is written on the left, a little below the date. Often the application is addressed to an official by designation. But if you know the name of the official use it. Your letter will then receive prompt attention.

D Mention the subject briefly.

E The salutation comes below the address of the recipient. For an application, the normal salutation is 'Sir/Madam'. But for other official letters you could use 'Dear Sir/Madam'. If you have written the name of the official in ©, e.g. Mr Hemant Saikia, Senior Editor, Sahitya Publishers, then for the salutation you should use the surname, e.g. 'Dear Mr Saikia'.

F The main body of the letter can be divided into suitable paragraphs. In typed letters, the current practice is to start the main body of the letter at the beginning of the line and to leave one line space between paragraphs. In handwritten letters, the first line of the letter usually begins below the end of the salutation and the first line of paragraphs is indented.

G These are words of leave taking. If you have used 'Sir/Madam' or 'Dear Sir/Madam' in your salutation, then leave taking should be 'Thanking you'. However, if you have used 'Dear Mr/Mrs/Ms' then leave taking should either be 'With best wishes' or 'With regards'.

H Words used in this position are called the subscription or the complimentary close. The usual form for official letters is either 'Yours faithfully' or 'Yours truly' only if in your salutation you have used 'Sir/Madam' or 'Dear Sir/Madam'. However, if you have used the name of the official, then the subscription used is 'Yours sincerely'. In typed letters, the practice these days is to have the subscription at the beginning of a line. In handwritten letters it comes almost to the right edge of the lines.

I Below the signature comes your name in full. The person who gets your letter or application should know who you are.

J Encl. is the short form for enclosure(s). If you send copies of your certificates, say so in the body of the letter, e.g. 'I am enclosing copies of my Matriculation and Senior Secondary certificates'. And draw attention to this fact at the end of the application or the official letter, thus: Encl.: 2.

The modern practice is not to use any punctuation at the end of the line in addresses, dates, salutations, leave taking and subscription.

Useful vocabulary

permanent	scholarship
temporary	biodata
part-time	curriculum vitae
demand draft	diploma
postal order	certificate
by money order	degree
course	commercial
full details	official
full particulars	Does not apply/Not applicable
complete information about	application
enclose a	apply for
am enclosing	I wish to apply for
available	I would like to apply for
audio cassette	job/post/position
video cassette	I have had experience of
salary	I have been ill for the past
grade	I have been ill since

Exercise 1 Read the following advertisement that appeared in *The Times of India* of 22 December 1990:

> Wanted smart and experienced male/female office assistants, commercial artists. Salary Rs 2,000/- per month, negotiable. Apply within fifteen days: Manager, Indian Advertising Co, 27 Nehru Place, New Delhi 110 003.

Write an application for the job of either an office assistant or a commercial artist.

Hints: (*a*) *For Office Assistant*:

(*i*) Say that you possess a Diploma in Office Management from the Commercial Training Institute, Kashmiri Gate, Delhi.

(*ii*) Also mention experience of working in an office. Specify the period.

(*b*) *For Commercial Artist*:

(*i*) Say you possess a Diploma in Commercial Art from the Govt. Polytechnic/Women's Polytechnic, South Extension, New Delhi.

(*ii*) Also say that you possess two years' experience of designing commercial posters for an advertising company.

(*iii*) Enclose copies of the posters designed by you and say so in the body of the application.

Discuss with your partner/group the best way to use the hints given above and write the application.

Activity 2

In the application in Activity 1 Nandita Muttoo had said she was enclosing her biodata with her application. Do you know what 'biodata' is? A biodata contains facts about a person's life and career. It is also called 'curriculum vitae', which is a short written account of one's career and qualifications enclosed with the letter of application.

Here is an outline of a biodata:

1 Full name (in block capitals) : ....

2 Date of birth : ....

3 Permanent address : ....

4 Educational qualifications : ....

Examination(s) passed	*Name of board/ university*	*Year of passing*	*Division with marks*	*School/college attended*

5 Experience

Name of company/firm	*Position held*	*Period of employment with dates*

6 Present employment

Name of company/firm	*Position held*	*Date of joining*

7 References (*a*) : (Names of two/three persons holding responsible positions to
(*b*) : whom reference could be made about you. Furnish name and
(*c*) : full address of these persons.)

This outline could of course be modified according to one's need. Now read Nandita Muttoo's application, discuss it with your partner/group and write a suitable biodata that could be attached to her application.

Note: The biodata should highlight those facts that you consider important and that increase your chances of getting the job.

Exercise 1 Write your own biodata for the job of an office assistant or a commercial artist for which you have drafted an application in Exercise 1 of Activity 1 of this unit. Invent details, if necessary.

Activity 3

Given below are some phrases and sentences that one might use in writing letters. Tick off those that you consider acceptable and appropriate for writing an application for a job:

1 I look forward to hearing from you.
2 Hope to hear from you.
3 I saw your ad in today's *Hindustan Times.*
4 I shall leave no stone unturned to satisfy you.
5 I need this job very badly.
6 Yours sincerely.
7 Dear Sir.
8 Yours truly.
9 I would be most grateful if you could ....
10 With reference to your advertisement in today's *Hindustan Times,* I wish to apply for the job of a ....

Discuss with your partner/group and provide reasons for your choice. Say why the others are not suitable.

Application on printed forms

Often large organizations ask for applications on printed forms. In such cases you have to fill in the application form carefully. Remember you are not to leave any blanks. If a column asks for information that does not apply to you, don't leave it blank or use a dash. Instead write 'No', or 'Does not apply', or 'Not applicable'. Let's take an example. Suppose the following question is asked:

'Do you belong to a Scheduled Caste?'

If you do, there is no problem. Just say: 'Yes'. But if you don't, *don't leave the blank as it is*. Nor should you use a dash in the space provided. Instead, say: 'No'. Suppose the next column says:

'If you do, specify the Caste:'

Your answer should be: 'Does not apply', or 'Not applicable'.

Even for applications made on printed forms, you are still required to write a forwarding letter.

Activity 4

Here is an advertisement for the post of a trained graduate teacher that appeared in the *Hindustan Times* of 5 April 1991:

> Wanted trained graduate teachers for various subjects with 3 years' teaching experience. Grades govt. approved. Apply on prescribed forms available from the Manager, D.A.V. Senior Secondary School, Hissar (Haryana), along with copies of certificates and a crossed postal order of Rs 5/- by 30 May 1991.

What to do

1 First write a letter to the Manager of the School asking for an application form.
2 Suppose you have got the application form from the School and have filled it in. Send a covering letter with your application form and the postal order of Rs 5/-.

Given below are the outlines of the letters with blanks. Fill in the blanks:

Request for an application form

C 3/297 Janakpuri
....
.... 1991

The ....
....
Hissar (Haryana)

Sub:

....

Kindly r.......................... to your ad.......................... in the .... of 5 .... for the .... of trained .... in your .... I shall be g.......................... if you could kindly .... me an .... for the post at the .... given above.

....

Yours ....

(Amrita Singh)

Covering letter accompanying application form

....

....

....

....

....

....

....

....

Sub:

....

I am enclosing my .... on the printed form for the post of.. . Attested .... of my certificates and a crossed .... order no. .... dated .... for Rs .... are also ....

Thanking you

Yours ....

....

(......................................)

Encl: ....

....

Application for leave

If you have a job, you may want to apply for leave. There are various kinds of leave due to an employee, but the format of a leave application remains the same.

Activity 5

Your are a teacher in the Government Boys Senior Secondary School, Sarojini Nagar, New Delhi. You have to take your mother to the hospital for a medical check-up and cannot attend school. Write an application for casual leave for a day.

Here is an outline of an application. Discuss it with your partner/group and fill in the blanks:

Address: ....

....

Date: ....

To

....

....

....

....

I have to take my mother to the .... for a .... on 25 June 1991 and shall not be able to attend ....

I shall be .... if you .... g.................. me .... for 25 ....

....

....

....

(A C George)

Exercise 3 You are down with malaria and have to take medical leave. Write an application enclosing a medical certificate from your doctor.

Activity 6

Sometimes it becomes necessary to apply for a fee concession or scholarship available in college.

Some fee concessions are available to students whose parents earn not more than Rs 1,000/- per month and also to students for excellence in studies or in sports.

Write an application to the Principal for fee concession, either because your parents' income is Rs 1000/- or because you have done very well in studies or in sports.

Hints: In both cases you will need to support your claim with documentary proof. In one case you will need to give a proof of the fact that the monthly income of your father is not more than Rs 1000/- per month. In the other you will have to produce a certificate saying that you have done very well in your studies, or in some game.

Answering advertisements

Application for jobs are sent in response to advertisements in newspapers and magazines. We have done these earlier. But there are other advertisements also, e.g. advertisements for educational courses, for books and other articles, and we may want to write letters of enquiry or place an order.

Activity 7

Here is an advertisement for a course in speaking English.

You are interested in the course. Write a letter asking for details. Here is an outline to help you. Fill in the blanks:

> Learn to speak ENGLISH faster!
>
> *Write for details:*
>
> **SPEAKWELL**
> B2/56 Ashok Vihar
> Delhi 110 054

....

....

....

The Director
Speakwell
....
....

Dear Sir

Please ....

....

if you could kindly send me .... of your .... at the ....

Thanking you

Yours ....

(   )

Exercise 1 Read the following advertisement and ask for the prospectus and full details of the course:

> **Learn URDU through correspondence in 20 easy lessons!!**
>
> Apply for prospectus, form, etc., with stamps of Rs 3/- to
> Director, Urdu Correspondence Course
> Urdu Academy, Jamia Millia, Jamia Nagar
> New Delhi 110 025

Activity 8 Placing an order

Read the following advertisement and place an order with the General Manager for the two commemorative coins issued by the Indian Government Mint:

> **SPECIAL COMMEMORATIVE COINS IN TWO DENOMINATIONS:**
>
> 100 rupees single coin and 20 rupees single coin
> Available from
> The General Manager
> Indian Government Mint, Fort
> Bombay 400 023
>
> **SEND MONEY BY DEMAND DRAFT OR CROSSED POSTAL ORDER**

Hint: Take care to write such letters in a legible hand. Also write your name and complete address in BLOCK CAPITALS. And don't forget to write full details of the Demand Draft, i.e. name of the bank on which drawn, number of the Draft, amount, date of issue, etc., or in the case of Postal Order, number of the Order, date of issue, amount, etc.

Exercise 1 Read the following advertisement and place an order for either the book or the audio-cassettes or both:

> **Just Released**
>
> 1 *Ramayana for Children* by Ashok Kumar. Profusely illustrated. Rs 20/-
> 2 *Ramacharitamanas* (a selection) sung by the famous Jain Bandhu
> A set of 10 cassettes for Rs 300/-
>
> *Packing, postage free for orders worth Rs 300/- or more. No VPP. Write to:*
>
> Amar Mitra Publishers, 10 Canal Road, Chandigarh 160 017

Further practice

1 The entire family is planning a holiday in Himachal Pradesh. Read advertisement no. 1 on page 134 and write a letter asking for the booklet containing information on the tourist spots in the State and also rates of hotel accommodation available there.

2 Read advertisement no. 2 on page 134. Place an order for 50 greeting cards which the entire family has decided to send this year. Calculate the cost @ Rs 2.50 per card.

3 You are the head of a small firm called Mehta & Sons, Booksellers, 24 Vikas Building, M G Road, New Delhi 110 003. Place an order with the Spastics Society of Northern India for 500 greeting cards.

4 You are interested in taking up a course in dress designing during your summer holidays. Read advertisement no. 3 on page 134 and ask for full details of the course.

BOOK III

Workbook

Gopal Krishan
S C Sood
Vinod Srivastava

Oral Communication

UNIT 1 GUESSING GAMES

To the teacher:

1 Divide the class into pairs/groups as necessary.
2 Ask the students to read the exercise. Make sure that they have understood the instructions before they begin and that they use the target language.
3 Change roles frequently to keep the game going.

Exercise 1 This is a guessing game. It has to be played with a partner.

How to play

First you will be the 'knower' and your partner the 'guesser'. You think of something. It can be anything, e.g. a table, a celebrity, or a part of the body. You write it on a piece of paper and put it face down under a paper weight so that your partner cannot see what is written on it. Your partner has to guess what you have written. S/he can put to you as many questions as s/he likes. But you will answer with only 'Yes' or 'No'. To begin with, you can stimulate the guessing by offering some hint, e.g. the first letter of the object's name, its function, etc. When your partner has guessed, it is her/his turn to be the knower and your turn to be the guesser. Thus, the game goes on in turns between you and your partner.

Suggested topics

1 Concrete things: classroom furniture, stationery items, household goods, means of transport
2 Celebrities (living or dead), professionals
3 Animals, birds
4 Abstract qualities: virtue, reputation, etc., should be taken up after the students have got some practice in the guessing game.

Variations of the game

It can also be played in small groups:

1 A group of knowers on the one hand and just one guesser on the other. When s/he has guessed s/he joins the group of the knowers and one of them becomes the guesser.
2 One knower and a group of students as guessers. When what the knower has written has been guessed, he joins the group of guessers and another student is appointed as the knower.
3 One group of knowers and one group of guessers.

Exercise 2 (Group work) This is also a guessing game and can be played in a small group. Many variations can be devised of this basic guessing game. Some ideas are suggested in this exercise and the teacher can use her/his imagination to suit the class.

How to play

One of you is the guesser and the others in the group are the knowers. They sit on one side of the table, with you on the other, so that you cannot hear what they say among themselves or see what they write.

As in Exercise 1, the knowers consult each other and think of something. They write it on a piece of paper and put it face down so that you cannot see what is written on it.

You have to guess what is written on the piece of paper. But this time you do not ask any questions. It is your classmates who will make statements about what they have thought of. They will throw hint after hint about the solution, in the form of simple positive or negative statements.

The number of guesses you can make is limited to three. So make your guesses only when you are sure you are right.

Example: If your classmates have thought of 'elephant', then the hints might be: (*a*) it's an animal, (*b*) it has four legs, (*c*) it's the largest animal, etc.

When you have guessed, you join the group of the knowers and one of them becomes the guesser. The game is repeated with new things to be guessed.

Variations of the game

It can also be played between:

1 Two groups—one knowers and the other guessers.
2 Pairs.
3 One knower and a group of students as guessers.

UNIT 2 FILLING IN MISSING INFORMATION

To the teacher:

1 Form pairs—Student A and Student B.
2 Name Student A and Student B.
3 Ask them to open their respective pages and read the instructions.
4 Make sure that Student A does not see Student B's page and vice versa.
5 Make sure that the students have understood the instructions before the activity is begun. If necessary, repeat the instructions in the learner's mother tongue.
6 Keep moving among the pairs when the activity is on and make sure that they hold their discussions in the target language.
7 Change the roles of the students in the next exercise so that Student A becomes Student B and Student B becomes Student A.

Exercise 1(*a*) Fill in the missing information (*for Student A*):

On page 139 is given the Monday timetable of a particular college. Some of the information in this table is missing. Student B can supply you with this information. But in her/his table, too, there are some blank columns. These s/he can complete with the information given in your table. Both of you have to complete the missing information in your tables with each other's help through *speech alone*. Do not look at each other's tables.

Compare your tables when you have finished. You can ask questions such as these:

Which class does Mr Sharma teach in the second period?
What subject does he teach?

Name of the college: PGDAV College (University of Delhi)

Teacher	*Subject*	*Class*	*Period*
Ms Kumar	....	III Yr	I
Mr Sharma	....	....	II
....	Hindi	....	III
....	History	....	IV
....	Accountancy	III Yr (Hons)	V
Mr Malik	....	II Yr (Hons)	VI
....	Pol. Science	....	VII

Exercise 1(*b*) Fill in the missing information (*for Student B*):

Given below is the timetable of a particular college. Some of the information in this table is missing. Student A can supply you with this information. But in her/his table, too, there are some blank columns. These s/he can complete with the information given in your table. Both of you have to complete the missing information in your tables with each other's help through speech alone. Do not look at each other's table.

Compare your tables when you have finished. You can ask questions such as these:

Who teaches English in the first period?
What does Mr Malhotra teach in the third period?

Name of the college: ....

Teacher	*Subject*	*Class*	*Period*
....	English	....	I
....	Sanskrit	II Yr	II
Mr Malhotra	....	I Yr	III
Mr Dhawan	....	III Yr	IV
Mr Aggarwal	....	....	V
....	Math.	....	VI
Mrs Sharma	....	I Yr (Hons)	VII

Exercise 2(*a*) Fill in the missing information (*for Student A*):

Here is an application form of a candidate partly filled in. Some of the information about this candidate is with your partner and some with you. S/he will help you in completing the missing information. You will also help her/him in completing the information missing in her/his sheet.

You can ask questions like:

Is he married or single?
Which examination did he pass from Delhi College of Engineering?

Application for the job of: ....

Name: ....

Father's/Husband's name: *Mr. Sham Nath*..

Date of birth: *3 January 1965*..

Marital status: *(Married/Single)*..

Religion: ....

Nationality: *Indian*..

State to which you belong: ....

Local address: ....

Permanent address: *C 5 Gali Ram Kali, Sonepat, Haryana*..

Academic qualifications:

Examinations passed	*University/Board*	*Marks/Division*
SSC	....	250/II
....	Delhi College of Engineering	....
Any other	....	....

Present employment: *M/s Escorts Ltd*..

Present salary: ....

Salary expected: ....

Exercise 2(*b*) Fill in the missing information (*for Student B*):

Here is a passage giving the particulars of a candidate. Some of the information in this passage is missing. This missing information is available with your partner. S/he will help you complete this passage. Your partner will also ask you for some information about this candidate.

You can ask questions like:

What is his father's name?
How many marks did he secure in the SSC?

Application for the job of an engineer

Mr Ram Lal, s/o of Mr ...., has applied for the job of an engineer. He is 26 years old, his date of birth being .... He is not married. He is a Hindu and his nationality is .... He was born in the state of Haryana, and he is now residing at D 305 Inderpuri, New Delhi. His permanent address is .... Regarding his academic qualification, it can be said that he has been an average student. He passed his SSC from CBSE with .... marks. Then he did his BE (Civil) from .... with 400 marks in the II division.

He is presently employed with .... getting a salary of Rs 2000/- per month. He now expects Rs 2500/- per month.

UNIT 3 ASKING FOR AND GIVING INSTRUCTIONS

To the teacher:

Arrange students as in Unit 2.

Exercise 1(*a*) Complete the drawing (*for Student A*):

Here is a drawing of a kitchen. Student B also has a drawing but it is incomplete. Help her/him to complete it by telling her/him where the various things go. The missing objects are shown in the drawing below the kitchen. These objects are to be put into the kitchen as shown in your drawing. Student B is allowed to ask you questions, but s/he *must not see* your drawing.

When you have finished, compare your drawings. When you tell Student B where to draw the various things, you can use sentences like these:

> There are two cupboards fixed to the wall. There is a fridge and a cooking range in the kitchen. The fridge is on the right of the sink and the cooking range is on the left.

Exercise 1(b) Complete the drawing (*for Student B*):

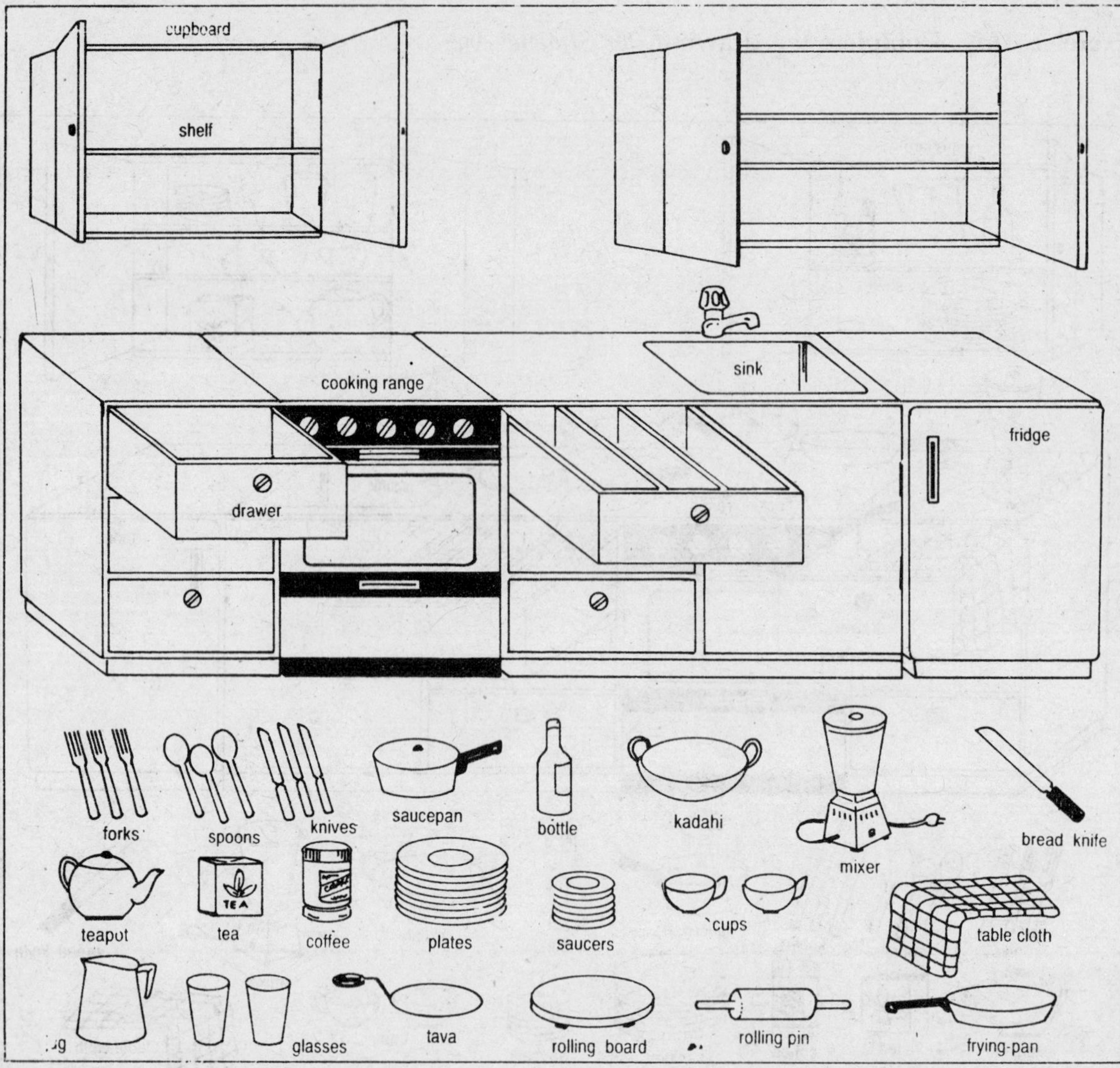

Here is a drawing of a kitchen. The drawing shows a number of things which are found in a kitchen. Student A is going to tell you what to put where. When s/he tells you, draw the object(s) in the correct place. You are allowed to ask questions but you *must not look* at Student A's drawing. Just write the names of the objects if you cannot draw.

When you have finished compare your drawings. You can ask questions like:

> Where does the table cloth go?
> Where do I put the cups?

You may ask her/him to repeat the instructions, e.g.

Sorry, I didn't follow that. Could you repeat it, please?

Exercise 2 (*a*) Complete the drawing (*for Student B*):

Here is a drawing of a living-room complete with a television set, a radio, a clock, etc. Student A also has a drawing of a living-room, but her/his drawing is incomplete. Help her/him to complete it by telling her/him where the various things go. The missing objects are shown in the drawing below the living-room. Student A is allowed to ask you questions, but s/he *must not see* your drawing.

When you have finished, compare your drawings. When you tell Student A where to put the various things, you can use phrases like these:

The coffee table is between the armchair and the sofa. The ashtray is on the coffee table.

Exercise 2(*b*) Complete the drawing (*for Student A*):

Here is a drawing of a living-room. The drawing shows a number of things which are to be put in this room. Student B is going to tell you exactly where they are to go. When he tells you, draw them in the correct places. You are allowed to ask questions but you *must not look* at Student B's drawing. Write only the names of the objects if you cannot draw them.

When you have finished, compare your drawings. You can ask questions like:

Where is the television set?
Where do I put the poster?

You can ask him to repeat if you do not follow his instructions, e.g.

I didn't understand that. Could you say it again, please? Do you mean on the wall or on the shelf?
Which table? The coffee table or the small table next to the sofa?

UNIT 4 ASKING FOR AND GIVING INFORMATION

To the teacher:

Arrange students as in Unit 2.

Exercise 1(*a*) Asking and answering questions (*for Student A*):

You want to sell a scooter you bought some time ago. You put the following advertisement in a newspaper:

FOR SALE
A scooter.
1989 model, *low mileage.*
Reasonable price. Phone: 617 658

Student B phones you and later comes to meet you at your shop.

He will ask you a few questions about the vehicle. Before you start, look at the following information so that you can answer his questions:

Manufacturer	Bajaj
Make and model	CUB/1989
Engine capacity or Horsepower (hp)	100 cc
Mileage done	10,002 km
Petrol consumption	50 km/litre
Price	Rs 7,000/-
Accessories	Spare wheel, tool kit, seat covers, mirrors, foot rests
Insurance	Comprehensive insurance
Paint	Original
Tyres	New
Can be inspected at	A 82 Defence Colony between 4 and 6 p.m. on Saturday/Sunday with prior appointment

Exercise 1(*b*) Asking and answering questions (*for Student B*):

You want to buy a second-hand scooter/motor cycle. You read the following advertisement in the newspaper:

FOR SALE
A scooter. 1989 model, *low mileage.* Reasonable price. Phone: 617 658

You phone 617 658. Student A is the person who is selling the vehicle. As arranged, you later meet him at his shop. Introduce yourself and state the purpose of your visit. Now get the following information about the scooter:

Its make and model
Its engine capacity (horsepower)
Year of purchase
Is it insured?
Petrol consumption
Mileage done
Is an inspection possible? If so where and when?
Is a spare wheel available?
Is a tool kit available?
Has it been repainted/are the tyres worn out or in good condition?
Has the engine been rebored?

End your conversation saying you are interested in buying the vehicle. Fix a place and time for the inspection of the vehicle.

UNIT 5 COMPLETING A DIALOGUE

1 Given below is a dialogue in which the responses of one of the speakers have been left out. These are listed separately in a jumbled order. Study the dialogue carefully and fill in the blanks with the appropriate responses from the list.

List

'I earn a hundred and fifty francs a month.'
'I really couldn't say.'
'I know Margot's age.'
'My brother sends it to me.'
'He will sell them later. They will bring him in many times as much as they would now.'
'Thirty-one.'
'No. He pays me a monthly salary. In return he gets everything I paint.'

Dialogue

'How old are you, Mr Van Gogh?'

....

'Has Margot told you that she is older than you?'

....

'May I ask you how much money you earn?'

....

'What is the source of that income?'

....

'You mean your brother supports you?'

....

'How many of them does he sell?'

....

'Well, I can. Your father tells me he has never sold one of your pictures yet.'

....

'That is problematical, to say the least. Suppose we discuss the facts.'

Vincent studied the hard, unbeautiful face of the elder sister. He could expect no sympathy from her.

'If you don't earn anything,' she continued, 'may one be allowed to ask how you expect to support a wife?'

(Adapted from *Lust for Life* by Irving Stone, Washington Square Press, 1967, p. 247)

2 Now fill in the blanks:

Vincent is a .... He wants to marry .... He is talking to the .... of Margot. She enquires about his .... Vincent's brother sends him 150 francs every ....

3 Answer the following questions about yourself:

(*a*) How old are you?
(*b*) Do you have a job? If so, what is your monthly salary?
(*c*) If you do not have a job, who supports you?

UNIT 1 VOCABULARY

Exercise 1 A crossword puzzle

```
N I N U N E M P L O Y M E N T T S L U M S E
O V I O L E N C E X P L O I T A T I O N R N
I D E S P A I R A M A L N U T R I T I O N T
T N E G L E C T I D R O U G H T G R E E D O
A O P N A L H U N G E R Y G E R M S V C M O
P I O S S E L F I S H N E S S A U T O A S H
I T H N D S I L L I T E R A C Y Y E L E I A
C A R O N E F A M I N E I R A C I S M P L N
I E I I E C 9 I G N O R A N C E 9 W A R A 5
T R A T I I N G D U I N E Q U A L I T Y N G
R C N A R V H N N S T D I S E A S E S N O N
A E O N F R T I O T A T S S S T E N T O I I
P R I D S E I D I R R N E P L N C I R I T N
Y A T E R S A E T A D E I U O E I S O T A I
T C A T E L F E A H Y M L O O M T R P A N A
I H T I E A E F Z C H T I R H P S E S R R R
N T I N T I C T I H E I M G C O U H E E E T
U L N U N C I S N T R M A H S L J C M P T V
M A A E U O N A U W L M F T R E S A A O N A
M E S L L S U E M O A O C U H V I E G O I U
O H L D O R E R M R R C P O V E R T Y C N O
C ' S D V A Y B I G O T R Y ! D B O M B S Y
```

1 There are many things that make it difficult for children to grow up and lead productive lives. The above crossword puzzle contains 22 words/phrases, running across the page from left to right, which describe these negative things.

The puzzle also contains 31 words/phrases which describe things that can have a positive impact on children's welfare. These move upwards from the bottom of the page to the top.

How many can you find? *Warning*: some are deceptive—they overlap. As you find each word/phrase, cross out the letters in it. When you have finished, circle everything that is left, and you will have found two bonus words. If you are unable to find all 53 words/phrases, don't get cross!

2 Discuss with others in the group how these words/phrases (a) make it difficult for children to lead productive lives, and (b) contribute to children's welfare.

3 Use these words/phrases in your own sentences to show that you understand their meaning.

Exercise 2 Observe the word 'unemployment' which occurs in Exercise 1. You will notice that this word is made up of three parts. These are 'un', 'employ' and 'ment'. What names do we give to these? Ask your teacher.

From this word 'unemployment' you can see that words conveying opposite meanings (*antonyms*) can be formed by adding 'un', etc., before the word. We can also form negatives by adding something after the word.

You will also observe that we can change the grammatical category of a word by adding something before or after the word. In the word 'employment', 'ment' has been added to form a noun from the verb 'employ'.

Questions

1 In Exercise 1 you have some words that have *prefixes/suffixes* attached to them. Rewrite these words showing the prefix, root and the suffix. Then make as many words as you can from the roots. Compare your list with that of the others in your group.

Example: *mismanagement* = mis + manage + ment
manage: manager, managerial, manageable, unmanageable

2 Which of these prefixes/suffixes are used to:

(*a*) make a word negative? Can you make a list of other prefixes/suffixes which are used for this purpose?

(*b*) make a verb from a noun? Can you list a few more prefixes/suffixes used to make verbs from nouns?

Compare the list you have made with that of the others in your group.

3 Complete the following table:

go	went	gone
stay	....	....
....	frightened	....
....	....	had
come	....	....
....	did	....
....	....	been
tell	....	....
....	spent	....

Exercise 3 Fill in the blanks with the appropriate forms of the words given in brackets:

Earlier in the century the United States experienced a long era of sustained growth in many aspects. There was a steady increase in the level of .... (educate), life .... (expect), and standard of living. .... (Grow) of all kinds was welcomed, including .... (industry) expansion and .... (populate) increase. A feeling of progress,

(*contd.*)

of .... (achieve), of well-being was everywhere. As a corollary, a striving for .... (excellent) and the search for understanding were .... (wide) admired. Today the mood is one of less .... (certain). There are those who are .... (pessimist) because of sudden .... (curtail) of growth in the use of energy in the form of oil. They believe that the part of the standard of living which is based on large-scale .... (consume) of energy is not .... (like) to improve during this century. They conclude that the kind of .... (economy) growth experienced in the 1950s and 1960s will not occur again.

(From 'The Electronics Revolution' by Philip H Abelson & Allen L Hammond, *Span*, New Delhi, July 1979, p. 30)

Exercise 4 Make a list of the prefixes and suffixes that are used to change the grammatical category of a word. Compare your list with that of the others in the group.

Exercise 5 Read the following passage carefully and then answer the questions that follow:

The horse and the colt

Once upon a time there lived a horse and his offspring, a colt. They grazed together in a meadow, where the streams, the flowers, and the cool shade, offered all that happiness required. Abusing these enjoyments, as is customary with young people, the colt stuffed himself every day with clover, whiled away the time on the flowery plain, galloped about without reason, bathed without requiring it, and rested himself without being tired.

Lazy and fat, the young colt grew weary, and became tired of having all that he wanted. Disgust soon followed, and seeking his father he complained: 'For some time I have been unwell. This grass is unwholesome and dry; the clover is without taste. The water is muddy and the air we breathe here attacks my lungs. I am sure I shall die unless we leave.'

'Since it concerns your life, my dear son', replied his father, 'we will find another home at once.' No sooner said than done, and the two immediately set off in search of a new meadow.

The young traveller neighed for joy; the old one, less merry, went at a sedate pace and taking the lead, made the colt clamber up steep and rocky mountains where there was not so much as a blade of grass. Evening came, but there was still no pasture, and our travellers had to go to bed without any supper. The next day, nearly exhausted by hunger, they were glad of a few stunted briars. This time the colt had no more energy to gallop. After two more days, he scarcely had the strength to drag one leg after the other.

Considering the lesson well learned, the father returned by a road unknown to his son, and led him to their old meadow in the middle of the night. As soon as our young colt discovered a little fresh grass, he attacked it greedily. 'Oh! What a delicious feast! What beautiful grass!' he exclaimed. 'Was there ever anything so sweet and tender? My father, we will seek no further; let us settle forever in this lovely spot. What other place could equal this?'

(*contd.*)

> As he thus spoke, day began to break and the colt, recognizing the meadow he had so lately left, cast down his eyes in the greatest confusion.
>
> His father said to him mildly: 'My dear son, in future remember this: he who enjoys too much is soon disgusted with his good fortune. To be happy, one must be moderate.'
>
> (From *Aesop's Fables*, Ward Lock and Co Ltd, London, 1962, pp. 120–1)

(*a*) Underline all the words in the text which have a prefix or suffix in them. Rewrite these words showing the prefix/suffix and the root separately.

(*b*) Which of these prefixes are used to make a word negative? Look at the word 'justice'. What does this word mean to you? Ask your teacher for help. Adding the prefix 'in' to justice, you get the word 'injustice'. What happens to the meaning of the word 'justice' when it is prefixed with 'in'. Does it remain the same as before? You are right if you think the meaning has changed. From the positive meaning of justice we get the negative word 'injustice'. Which other prefixes are used to make a word negative?

(*c*) Add an appropriate prefix to the following words to make them negative. The first one has been done for you.

active	—	*in*active
predictable	—	.........predictable
organized	—	.........organized
ability	—	.........ability
possible	—	.........possible
legible	—	.........legible
stabilize	—	.........stabilize
responsible	—	.........responsible
contented	—	.........contented

UNIT 2 LINKING DEVICES

Look at the following:

1 Murad wanted to give a gift to Salma, his wife, on Salma's birthday.
2 Murad bought some perfume for Salma.
3 Murad put some perfume in the pocket of Murad's briefcase.
4 Murad forgot about some perfume.

These sentences can be rewritten as follows:

Murad wanted to give a gift to Salma, his wife, on her birthday. One day, he bought some perfume for her. However, he put it in the pocket of his briefcase and forgot about it.

What we have done in rewriting these sentences is that we have replaced nouns with pronouns and added or deleted a few words, here and there. These changes have been made to make the text coherent so as to read natural.

A writer may use such devices in his text to:

1. signal the sequence of events reported (such as first, next, etc.).
2. organize his text (such as in conclusion, that is to say, in this connection, in short, for example, to resume, to sum up, etc.).
3. indicate his own view of the facts (such as moreover, similarly, incidentally, however, as a matter of fact, in any case, therefore, in order to, although, etc.).

We call these *linking devices.*

Exercise 1 Read the following story and then circle all the pronouns and say what/who they refer to (as shown in line 1 of the given text). You can use different colours for different references:

> A simple farmer was so happy with his first crop of mangoes that he thought it well to bring a basket of them to the King.
>
> When he arrived at the palace he asked the servants to tell him how he could meet the Raja and make a present of the juicy fruit.
>
> 'Well, I'll take you to him', said one of the servants, 'but only if you promise to give me half of whatever he gives you.'
>
> The farmer promised and the servant took him to the King.
>
> The King gratefully accepted the mangoes and asked the villager what he could give him as a reward.
>
> 'Please give me a hundred strokes of the lash, that's the only reward I desire. And since your servant and I have agreed to divide the reward equally, fifty are for him.'
>
> The Raja laughed at the ingenuity of the man. He gave him a thousand rupees and dismissed the servant.
>
> (From *The Wisdom Stories* by J Maurus, St Paul Publications, Allahabad, 1976, p. 83)

Exercise 2 Fill in the blanks with suitable pronouns in the following story:

> A hunter found a human skull in the forest. Surprised, ... asked ...., 'What brought .... here?' The skull answered 'Talking brought .... here.' Amazed, the hunter ran to the King and reported to ...., '............ have found a skull in the forest .... talks.' Neither the King nor .... courtiers would believe such a thing. So the King along with the hunter and .... guards set out to find the truth.
>
> When .... came to the skull, the hunter asked as before, 'What brought .... here?' There was no answer, for the skull remained silent. The angry King called the hunter a liar and ordered .... guards to cut off .... head and leave it in the forest as a prey for the ants.
>
> When everybody had left, the skull spoke again and .... asked the head of the hunter, 'What brought .... here?'
>
> And the head of the hunter gave the answer: 'Talking brought .... here.'
>
> (From *The Wisdom Stories* by J Maurus, St Paul Publications, Allahabad, 1976, p. 16)

Let us look at some other linking devices. Read the following passage carefully:

> Our tour begins at the Purana Qila, legendary site of the city of Indraprastha, home of the heroic Pandavas in the epic the *Mahabharata*.(1) Though some people might dismiss this for the lack of any concrete evidence, *on the other hand* there are others who believe that the archaeological finds during the recent excavations at Purana Qila are proof of a continuous settlement here from the third century BC to the late Mughal period.(2) The fort as it stands today is the work of both the Mughal Emperor Humayun *and* the Afghan ruler Sher Shah.(3) The massive wall and gateways were built by Humayun who called the fort Dinpanah.(4) *But*, when Sher Shah took possession of it, he renamed it Shergarh.(5) He also strengthened the fortifications, built the Qila-i-Kuhna Masjid and the Sher Mandal which *in fact*, was used as a library by Humayun.(6)
>
> The Purana Qila *or* Dinpanah continues to be one of Delhi's most spectacular monuments *whether* we accept the Pandavas' association with it *or* not.(7) *Besides* its glory is much more than historical, it is architectural.(8)

Now look at the functions that the words 'and', 'or', 'whether' perform in sentences 3 and 7:

'Whether' is a connecting device within the sentence.

'And' and 'or' introduce new ideas in sentences 3 and 7. Thus, they too are connecting devices within the sentence.

You will notice that 'whether', 'and', 'or' are conjunctions and are generally used as connecting devices within sentences. Now study the function of the italicized words or phrases in sentences 2, 5, 6 and 8.

One of them expresses the writer's opinions. The others are sentence connectors and indicate the relationship between sentences, i.e. by looking at the sentence connector you can even guess what kind of statement is likely to follow.

Now match the two columns given below:

Linking Devices	*Functions*
Besides	expresses the writer's opinion
On the other hand	gives additional information
In fact	gives information contrary to what is expected
But	contrasts

Sentence connectors are also known as *linking devices*. Given below is a list of some linking devices:

they, even, and yet, that, he, and in fact, for, now

Choose the appropriate ones from the above list to fill in the blanks in the passage that follows:

> .... at first sight it might seem as if modern human beings who spend so much time getting help from machines are very lazy. .... what are the machines for but to save trouble? .... are extra limbs which men
>
> (*contd.*)

have made outside themselves to do their work for them. Cranes and lifts are extra arms to do the job of lifting, trains and motors extra legs to do the job of walking and running. Typewriters and printing-machines are extra brains to save us the trouble of remembering. We have .... invented for ourselves new kinds of limbs, and make aeroplanes to take the place of the wings we have not got. .... it is difficult to suppose that men would have gone to all the bother of inventing these complicated machines to serve as their extra limbs merely because they were lazy; .... they would have taken all this trouble merely to save themselves trouble. .... man is not at all lazy; .... is the most restless and energetic of all living creature.

(From *Our Civilization* by C E M Joad, Adam and Charles Black, London)

Exercise 3 In the passage that follows fill in the blanks with suitable link-words listed below:

yet, or, that, owing to, and, but, also, although, that is why

King gold

I am considered a sacred metal, the Sun God's metal. I am one of the heaviest metals known. .... a gold nugget no larger than a matchhead can be drawn out into a wire more than three kilometres long .... can be beaten into a transparent bluish-green leaf 50 sq m in size. I am so soft and pliant .... you can leave a scratch on me with your nail! .... when jewellers use me, they usually make additions of copper, silver, nickel, cadmium, palladium and other metals to make me stronger.

Only a small amount of gold is used by dentists and jewellers, ... still less is used for technical purposes. Electronic goods are beginning to consume more and more of me, for transistors and diodes. .... my exceptional chemical resistance, gold-platinum alloys go into the construction of equipment for synthetic fibre plants. Made from me are packing rings of vital units of accelerators of charged particles. Various joints in accelerator cavities and tubes are coated with me.

.... I am the most celebrated metal of any times, I am .... the saddest of all. I am often described as the 'King of Metals', highly glorified, highly valued and worshipped. .... my fate is not to be envied. I am an eternal prisoner. Just think! The minute I am freed from the Earth's depth, I am imprisoned again in unassailable safes, armour-plated vaults .... concrete-lined underground dungeons.

(From *Target*, New Delhi, 11 Nov 1990)

Exercise 4 Choose the correct alternatives out of each of the three given in italics which fit in the context:

Even though/However/Consequently the country is passing through a difficult period *because/ indeed/somehow* there is no stable government at the centre, we hope that there will not be need for another election before the term of this Lok Sabha expires. *On the whole/For instance/Still* if the present arrangement collapses there may be no option *but/except/finally* to go to the polls.

Exercise 5 The sentences given below have been broken into two parts such that the first part is on the left and the second part on the right. Try to match the two parts to form a single sentence. Compare your answer with that of other pairs/groups. What helps you in joining these sentences?

SNAKEBITE

	List A		*List B*
1	Snakebite is a complex issue;	(*a*)	but also to various other creatures.
2	Instead of screaming and running about,	(*b*)	and bite people only when trapped or provoked.
3	Snakes are vulnerable not only to man	(*c*)	the victim must stay calm and rush to the nearest hospital immediately.
4	Snakes are basically shy by nature,	(*d*)	since they help control the immense rodent population.
5	Snakes need to be protected	(*e*)	yet it must be made simple enough for illiterate people to understand it.

UNIT 3 REORDERING

Exercise 1 Given below are a few jumbled up sentences. Rewrite them in proper order. Then close the book and narrate the story to your partner in your own words. Your partner also has a story to tell. Listen to his story and rewrite it.

1 'I learnt it from the ass', replied the fox simply.
2 The lion, the fox and the ass entered into an agreement to help each other.
3 Then he requested the fox to make a proper division.
4 When they had made their kill, the lion begged the ass to allot the portion due to each of them.
5 The lion burst into a great rage and killed him with a single stroke of his paw.
6 The ass carefully divided the spoils into three equal shares, and modestly asked the other two to make the first choice.
7 The lion said, 'Who has taught you, my very excellent fellow, the art of division? You are perfect to a fraction.'
8 The fox piled all that they had killed into one large heap, leaving for himself the smallest possible morsel of flesh.

....

....

....

....

....

....

....

....

....

....

....

....

....

(From 'The Lion, the Fox and the Ass',
Aesop's Fables, Ward Lock and Co Ltd, London, 1962, p. 46)

What helps you in rewriting these sentences in their proper order: lexical items? sentence structures? lexical and grammatical cohesion? linking devices? thematic development? Discuss with others in your group.

Exercise 2 The following sentences are jumbled up. Rewrite them in proper order. Then shut your book and narrate the story to your partner in your own words. Your partner also has a story to tell. Listen to his story and rewrite it.

1 The cook stole a leg from a beautiful roast stork just before it was served to the King.
2 'But, Your Majesty, you didn't clap last night.'
3 The King clapped his hands and the birds flew off. 'There,' he said, 'you see, they all have two legs the moment I clap.'
4 The King asked him angrily why the bird had only one leg.
5 Next morning the King and the cook went down to the river and saw the storks all standing on one leg.
6 The cook replied, 'Storks have only one leg—come to the river with me tomorrow and I will show you, Your Majesty.'

....

....

....

....

....

....

....

....

....

....

....

....

(From *Challenge to Think* by Christine Frank, Mario Rinvolucri and
Marge Berer, OUP, Oxford, 1982)

What helps you in rewriting these sentences in their proper order: lexical items? sentence structures? lexical and grammatical cohesion? linking devices? thematic development? Discuss with others in the group.

Exercise 3 Join the following parts of sentences so as to make complete sentences and thus a coherent story:

1 A man after fourteen years' penance in a solitary forest
2 and said, 'Master, master, I have acquired the
3 The master rebuked him and replied,
4 'Verily you have obtained only that
5 ordinary men do by paying
6 a penny to the boatman.'
7 after fourteen years' arduous labour,
8 which is worth a penny;
9 of your fourteen years' labour?'
10 power of walking on water.'
11 Overjoyed at this, he went to his guru
12 obtained at last the power of walking on water.
13 'Fie, o child! is this the result
14 for what you have accomplished

(From *The Wisdom Stories* by J Maurus, St Paul Publications, Allahabad, 1976)

What helps you in joining these parts of sentences so as to make a coherent story? Discuss with others in the group.

Exercise 4 Read the following story and answer the questions that follow:

A certain Ameer was on a voyage in his ship when a great storm arose. One of the slaves on board, who had never been to sea, began to wail and cry out in fear. This went on for some time and no one could silence him.

In anger the Ameer asked, 'Is there no one here who can silence this wretched coward?'

A philosopher, who happened to be a passenger, said, 'I think I can quiet this man, Sir, if you give me full permission to do as I please with him.'

'Go ahead,' said the Ameer, 'you have my permission.'

The philosopher called some sailors and ordered them to throw the slave into the sea. This they did. In desperation the poor man screamed with fear and thrashed out wildly with his arms and legs. But in a few seconds the philosopher ordered them to haul him up on board again. Back on deck the slave lay exhausted and frightened, but absolutely silent. The Ameer marvelled at the sudden change in the slave and asked for an explanation.

Said the philosopher: 'We never realize how well off we are in any situation until we fall into a worse one.'

(From *The Wisdom Stories* by J Maurus, St. Paul Publications, Allahabad, 1976, p. 81)

1 Match the subjects and their verbs in the following as used in the passage:

(*a*)	A great storm	(*i*)	began to wail and cry out
(*b*)	One of the slaves	(*ii*)	ordered them

(*c*)	The philosopher	(*iii*)	arose
(*d*)	The poor man	(*iv*)	asked
(*e*)	The Ameer	(*v*)	screamed

2 Complete the following:

(*a*) 'who' in line 2 stands for ....

(*b*) 'This' in line 3 stands for ....

(*c*) 'who' in line 6 stands for ....

(*d*) 'This' in line 10 stands for ....

(*e*) 'they' in line 10 stands for ....

3 Reorder the following sentences in the light of this story:

(*a*) An Ameer was on a voyage with one of his slaves.
(*b*) A philosopher came forward to silence the slave.
(*c*) The slave had never been to sea before.
(*d*) 'Is there no one who can silence the man', asked the Ameer?
(*e*) The philosopher ordered some sailors to throw the slave into the sea.
(*f*) So he began to cry in fear.
(*g*) The Ameer was surprised at the sudden change in his slave.
(*h*) The philosopher ordered them to haul him up on board again.
(*i*) The slave screamed with fear.
(*j*) Back on deck he lay absolutely silent.

4 Now shut your book and rewrite this story in your own words.

Exercise 5 You are given below three paragraphs which have been jumbled up. Decide on the appropriate order of these paragraphs. Discuss your choice with your partner(s) and justify it.

It's a fascinating world—and as the story of its evolution, its present, its many hues, unfolds exhibit after exhibit, you are left marveling both at the world and at the museum.

Even without that reminder, the museum makes you reflect—on nature, on man, on the interrelationship between the two and on the callousness of one toward the other. Do we realize, the museum provokes us to ask, that in destroying nature we are slowly destroying ourselves?

As you leave the mammal section of the National Museum of Natural History (NMNH) in New Delhi your face stares back at you from a mirror placed at the exit. So does a poster: 'YOU ARE LOOKING AT THE ONLY ANIMAL THAT CAN PROTECT THE NATURAL ENVIRONMENT.' That's you.

(From 'A Living Museum Needs To Grow' by Manini Chatterjee, *Span*, New Delhi, Nov 1983, p. 45)

UNIT 4 MATCHING ACTIVITIES

Exercise 1 Where do you find the following signs/phrases/single sentences?

1 Keep off the grass
2 Bill stickers will be prosecuted/Stick no bills
3 Beware of the dog

4 IN/OUT
5 Dangerous curve ahead
6 In case of fire, use the staircase
7 Please be seated, the doctor is in

Exercise 2 Match the following signs with their locations. Note that more than one location is possible for certain signs:

Signs	*Location*
SILENCE PLEASE	Hotel
NO PARKING	Library
NO SMOKING	National Highway
ENTRY	Airport
SORRY. NO CHEQUES OR CREDIT CARDS.	Office
IN CASE OF FIRE, BREAK GLASS.	Toilet
LADIES	Passport office
FRAGILE. HANDLE WITH CARE	College compound
INQUIRY	Carton box
NH1	City bus

Exercise 3 Compare your answers with your partner's. Discuss and justify your choice if it differs from her/his.

Exercise 4 Can you think of a few more single sentences/phrases of this type? Make a list of these and say where you find them. Compare your list with that of your companion.

Exercise 5 The table given below contains a list of headlines and a list of functions. Match each headline with the function it seeks to perform. Compare and discuss your answers with your partner/other members of the group. Please note that more than one answer is possible.

Headlines	*Functions*
DONATE EYES	warning
DANGEROUS CURVE AHEAD	giving information
GET YOUR CHILD VACCINATED	invitation
WEAR HELMET	request
A SMALL FAMILY IS A HAPPY FAMILY	seeking information
USE DIPPER AT NIGHT	persuasion
NEED HELP?	
LEPROSY IS CURABLE	

Exercise 6 Match the headlines (*a*) to (*f*) with the news items 1 to 6.

(*a*) Superman springs into action
(*b*) Degree for pedigree

(*c*) Pak manager lashes out at umpire Constant
(*d*) Bomb scare at IGI airport
(*e*) Snatched car found abandoned
(*f*) Gang selling fake degree busted

1 LONDON, 12 August (Reuter): Pakistan manager Haseeb Ahsan launched another salvo in his feud with umpire David Constant by lashing out at the official over an incident during the last day of the final Test at the Oval yesterday.

'I think he misbehaved badly and I am afraid this proves what we have been saying all along—that he is a disgraceful person,' Haseeb said.

2 NEW DELHI, 12 August: A briefcase stuffed with foreign currency worth over Rs. 12 lakh caused a 'bomb scare' at the Indira Gandhi International Airport here.

The police said the unattended briefcase was found at the 'arrival hall' of the airport last evening. Policemen fearing that it was a booby-trap bomb, put the briefcase through an X-ray machine.

3 A thief in New York probably received the shock of his life when he tried to make off with a stolen bicycle.

The bicycle's owner chased the would-be thief and caught up with him after a few minutes, media reports said yesterday, reports DPA from Washington.

Realizing who had caught him, the thief called out 'Superman' and let go his booty.

The bicycle's owner turned out to be actor Christopher Reeves, who in four Superman films has had the opportunity to display with petty criminals.

4 A woman had a horse she thought very smart, but her friends thought the beast stupid. To prove her point she wrote to several universities and offered $50,000 to the university that would confer an honorary degree on the horse. One university accepted, and at the commencement exercises the horse was provided with cap and gown and led to the platform to receive the honorary degree—which was presented by the university president, who said: 'This is the first time in the university's entire history that a degree has been conferred on a whole *horse*.'

5 NEW DELHI, 12 August: The entire police force reeling under repeated 'red alerts' was put on its heel when three youths forcibly snatched away a white Fiat (DHE 3294) from its driver near Masjid Moth in broad daylight around 4 p.m. today.

The car belonging to a resident of Greater Kailash was found abandoned within half-an-hour near a cluster of jhuggis in Okhla-II in the Gobindpuri area.

6 NEW DELHI, 12 August: With the arrest of two persons, the north district police today claimed to have smashed an organized gang of forgers who were selling fake university degrees.

Exercise 7 If you had to pick out just one sentence in the following passage to sum up the main idea, which one would you choose? Compare your answer with that of your partner/others in the group and justify it:

Title: ....

Australia is a land of contrasts. It is geologically one of the oldest of land masses, yet it ranks as one of the youngest of nations. It is half a world away from Europe, but its people are largely of European descent and they follow a Western lifestyle. One of the most sparsely populated of nations, it is also one of the most highly urbanized with 85 per cent of its people living in cities.

....

....

....

....

Exercise 8 What helps you in making your choice? Does it give you any idea about the writing/reading process? Discuss with others.

Exercise 9 Give a suitable title to this passage. How do we select a suitable title for a passage? Discuss with others.

Exercise 10 You are given below three passages and three sentences listed separately. Each of these three sentences is the first sentence of a paragraph. Decide which one is the first sentence of which paragraph. Discuss your answer with your partner(s) and justify it.

(*a*) However, those who prefer optimism have reason for hope.
(*b*) Today the mood is one of less certainty.
(*c*) Earlier in the century the United States experienced a long era of sustained growth in many aspects.

There was a steady increase in the level of education, life expectancy, and standard of living. Growth of all kinds was welcomed, including industrial expansion and population increase. A feeling of progress, of achievement, of well-being was everywhere. As a corollary, a striving for excellence and the search for understanding were widely admired.

There are those who are pessimistic because of the sudden curtailment of growth in the use of energy in the form of oil. They believe that the part of the standard of living which is based on large-scale consumption of energy is not likely to improve during this century. They conclude that the kind of economic growth experienced in the 1950s and 1960s will not occur again.

Human ingenuity in solving problems is great. And native intelligence has been amplified enormously by the use of knowledge accumulated through research. An important product of research and a basis for hoping for a bright new future is the vitality of the electronics revolution. This revolution has been in progress for about 60 years. Lately its tempo has increased greatly. Until recently its importance was overshadowed by changes due to the large-scale expansion in the use of energy. But it promises to be more important, of more enduring consequence, than the earlier industrial revolution.

(From 'The Electronics Revolution' by Philip H Abelson & Allen L Hammond, *Span*, New Delhi, July 1979, pp. 30–5)

Exercise 11 Does this exercise help you to understand the continuity of theme between the focal sentence and the paragraph?

UNIT 5 THINKING AND PLANNING

Exercise 1 You do this activity in pairs/groups. You propose a word or an expression. The other team is required to list concepts that are associated with it in some way. For example, you would associate the word 'paper' with writing, ink, pen, book, etc. The list can go on. If a pair/group lists items for which you fail to find any connection, you may ask that pair/group to justify and explain the words or expressions. For example, if they list 'kite', they may explain, 'You can use paper to make kites for children'. The winner is the team that gets the most associations in the shortest possible time.

Exercise 2 You or your group is supplied with an object. List as many imaginative uses for it as you can think of. For example, for 'umbrella' you may list the following uses:

1 to provide shelter from sun;
2 to provide shelter from rain;
3 to hide one's face from others;
4 to hit your enemy;
5 to play hockey/billiards.

You can think of objects like tooth-brush, newspaper, pencil, hockey-stick, etc.

Exercise 3 Make a list of the characteristics of a good parent.

Note: Before you start writing, discuss among yourselves (in pairs/group) the characteristics and draw up a list of these. Then list the characteristics in order of priority.

Exercise 4 Following the procedure mentioned in Exercise 3, make a list of the characteristics of the following:

1 A good teacher
2 A good friend
3 A good neighbour

Exercise 5 Write suitable captions for the pictures given below and on pages 163-4. Compare your answer with that of your partner/others in the group and justify your captions.

PHOTOS: SONDEEP SHANKAR

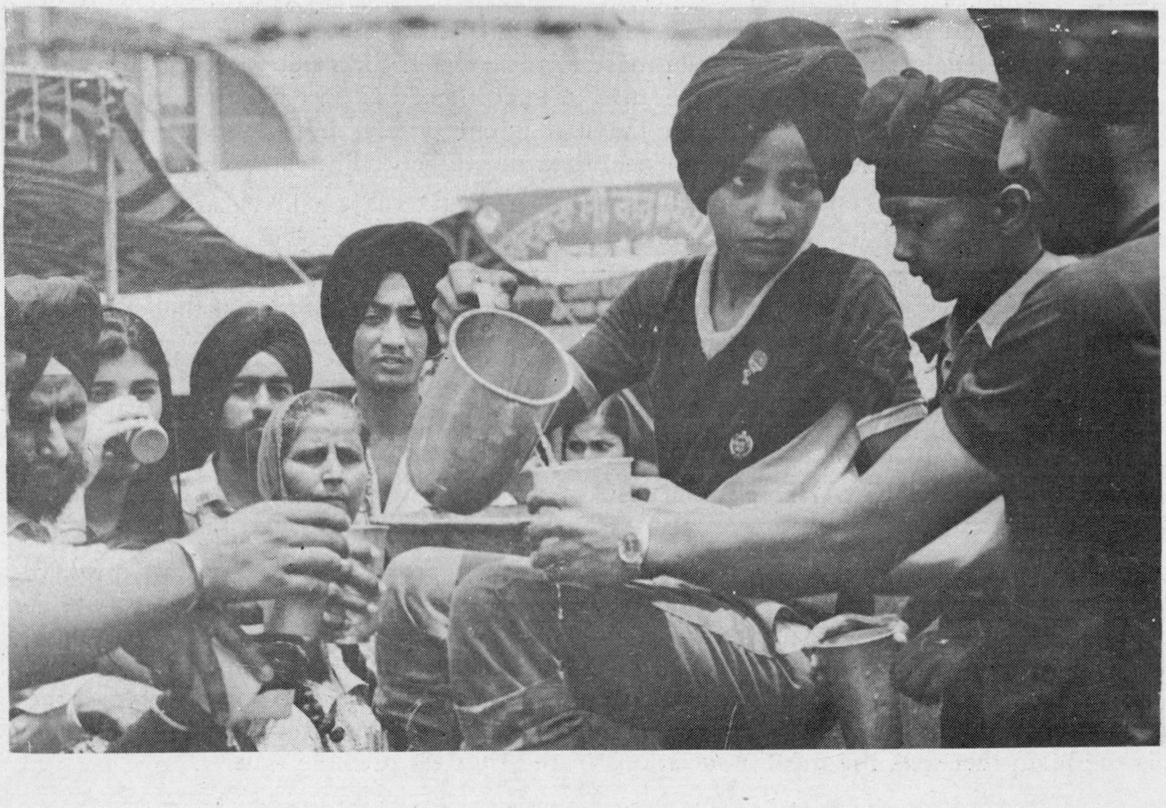

Exercise 6 Discuss with your partner/others in the group the possible contexts of the pictures. On the basis of this discussion write a dialogue/story to match the pictures. You can invent one of your own.

Exercise 7 Your group has been appointed as a committee to start a new computer course in the college. Make a list of the jobs to be done and the equipment needed for this purpose. The reporter of the group will collect ideas from all the participants in the group and discuss the order in which these are to be listed.

Topics for practice:

1 A students' trip to a historical site
2 A hiking trip
3 A social service camp
4 A football match between the staff and the students
5 A blood donation camp

Note: For follow-up work the teacher can ask the students to draft a notice for the notice board or write letters to arrange transport and accommodation, etc.

The king and the two shepherds

JEAN PIERRE CLARIS DE FLORIAN

A certain *mon*............... (*a*) was one day regretting the *misf*........... (*b*) of being king. 'What a weari-some occupation!' he complained. 'Is there any *mort*........... (*c*) on the earth more *wor*..................... (*d*) than I am? I wish to live in peace, and am forced to go to .... (*e*). I cherish my *sub*................ (*f*) and impose few taxes on them; I am a .... (*g*) of truth, and yet I am *conti*................. (*h*) deceived. My people are *oppre*.................. (*i*) with ills, and I am consumed with *gri*............... (*j*). I seek advice everywhere by every means, but my trouble is only thrown away. The more I *exe*............... (*k*) myself, the less I *ach*...................... (*l*).

At this moment a flock of lean sheep caught his eye in the plain. They were almost without any fleece; the ewes without lambs, the lambs without their mothers; dispersed, bleating and scattered; and the sickly looking rams wandering among the bushes. Their shepherd was running here and there, now after this sheep which was at the verge of the forest, now after another which was lagging behind, and then after his lambs. While he was in one quarter, a wolf seized one of the flock and made off with it. Away ran the shepherd, and another wolf carried off the lamb he had just left. The shepherd stopped, out of breath, and tore his hair, not knowing which way to turn. Frantically he called on death for relief.

'Here is a faithful picture of me,' cried the King; 'these poor shepherds endure a slavery no less than we kings. That's some consolation.'

As he uttered these words he saw in a meadow another flock of sheep, all fat and scarcely able to walk from the weight of their fleece. The rams strutted proudly, and the ewes with their dugs full made the bounding lambs hasten to share the sweet nourishment. Their shepherd, stretched luxuriously beneath a hedge, was composing verses in praise of his love, singing them sweetly to the listening echoes; and then repeating the plaintive tune on his flute.

The King was astonished, and said, 'This beautiful flock will soon be destroyed. The wolves will scarcely be afraid of an amorous swain singing to his shepherdess. A flute is a useless weapon against a hungry wolf. Oh! how I should laugh!' At that moment, as if in answer to his words, a wolf came in sight; but scarcely had he appeared than a watchful sheep dog sprang out and throttled him. Two sheep, frightened at the noise of the fight, left the flock and ran about the plain. Another dog set off, brought them back, and order was restored in an instant. Sitting by his hedge, the shepherd watched all this without stopping his tune for a moment.

Thereupon the King said to him half angrily, 'How do you manage? The woods are filled with wolves. Your sheep, fat and beautiful, are almost countless; and with the utmost calmness you take care of the whole flock yourself!' 'Sir', replied the shepherd, 'the whole thing is perfectly easy; my whole secret consists in choosing good dogs.'

(From *Aesop's Fables*, Ward Lock and Co Ltd, London, 1962, pp. 112–14)

Read the story given on the previous page and answer the following questions:

Exercise 1 Fill in the blanks in paragraph 1 with the help of the clues given below:

(*a*) a word which means 'king'.
(*b*) a word for 'bad luck'.
(*c*) that which must die.
(*d*) a word which means 'full of cares'.
(*e*) give the antonym of 'peace'.
(*f*) this word means 'people' over whom the king rules.
(*g*) one who loves.
(*h*) a word which means 'again and again'.
(*i*) a word which means greatly 'troubled'.
(*j*) use the opposite of 'happiness'.
(*k*) to make an effort.
(*l*) the opposite of 'fail'.

Exercise 2 In paragraph 2 there are four words which refer to the same animal:

sheep	a neutral word	(common gender)
ewe	a female sheep	(feminine gender)
ram	a male sheep	(masculine gender)
lamb	a young one of sheep	(common gender)

Find similar related words for the following:

Common gender	*Feminine*	*Masculine*	*Young one (Common gender)*
horse	....	....	....
deer	....	....	....
cat	....	....	....
fowl	....	....	....
pig	....	....	....

Exercise 3 We say 'a flock of sheep' for a group of sheep. Find words to complete the following:

a *flock* of sheep	a .... of birds	a litter of ....
a .... of keys	a .... of tools	a horde of ....
a .... of sticks	a .... of arrows	a host of ....
a .... of sweets	a .... of lions	a herd of ....
a .... of poems	a .... of policemen	a gang of ....
a .... of bees	a .... of islands	a fleet of ....
a .... of soldiers	a pack of	

Exercise 4 The sound sheep make is called 'bleating'. Describe the sounds of the following:

a sheep *bleats*	a dog ....
a lion	a horse ....
an elephant	a crow ....
a bee	a frog ....

Compare your list with that of your partner(s). Can you think of a few more similar expressions? Make a list.

Exercise 5 The singular and the plural of 'sheep' is the same. Can you list some other nouns in which the singular and the plural have the same forms? Compare your list with that of your partner(s).

Exercise 6 In paragraph 3 the King says, 'Here is a faithful picture of me.' What are the points of comparison between the King and the shepherd?

Exercise 7 The scene in paragraph 4 presents a sharp contrast with that in paragraph 2. Write down the points of contrast in your own sentences. Compare your answer with that of your partner(s).

Exercise 8 From your reading of this story, write in about 10 sentences the qualities of a good shepherd/king.

Pre-reading exercises

1 When did the modern Olympic Games start?
2 Where were the first Olympic Games held?
3 After an interval of how many years are these Games held?
4 Where were the latest Olympic Games organized?
5 Where are the next Olympic Games scheduled to be held?
6 When did India first participate in these Games?
7 Who is the father of the modern Olympic Games?
8 Discuss with your partner(s) the meaning of the following quotation and then present before the class your arguments either for, or against, the statement:

The important thing in the Olympic Games is not winning but taking part. The essential thing in life is not conquering but fighting well.

My greatest Olympic prize

JESSE OWENS

1 It was the summer of 1936. The Olympic Games were being held in Berlin. Since Adolf Hitler had proclaimed that his performers were members of a 'master race', nationalistic feelings were running high.

2 I wasn't too worried about all this. I'd trained, sweated and disciplined myself for six years with the Games in mind. While I was going over on the boat, all I could think about was taking home one or two of those gold medals. I had my eye especially on the long jump. A year before I'd set the world record of 26 feet 8½ inches. Everyone expected me to win that Olympic event hands down.

3 I was in for a surprise. When the time came for the long-jump trials, I was startled

(contd.)

to see a tall boy hitting the pit at almost 26 feet on his practice leaps. He turned out to be a German named Luz Long. I was told that Hitler had kept him hidden away, evidently hoping he would win the jump.

4 I supposed that if Long won, it would add some new support to the Nazis' Aryan-superiority theory. After all, I am a Negro. A little hot under the collar about Hitler's ways, I determined to go out there and really show *Der Fuhrer* and his master race who was superior and who wasn't.

5 An angry athlete is an athlete who will make mistakes, as any coach will tell you. I was no exception. On the first of my three qualifying jumps, I leaped from several inches beyond the take-off board for a no-jump. On the second jump, I was even worse. 'Did I come 3,000 miles for this?' I thought bitterly. 'To fail in the trials and make a fool of myself?'

6 Walking a few yards from the pit, I kicked disgustedly at the ground. Suddenly I felt a hand on my shoulder. I turned to look into the friendly blue eyes of the tall German long jumper. He had easily qualified for the finals on his first attempt. He offered me a firm handshake.

7 'Jesse Owens, I'm Luz Long. I don't think we've met.' He spoke English well, though with a German twist to it.

'Glad to meet you', I said. Then, trying to hide my nervousness, I added, 'How are you?'

'I'm fine. The question is: How are you?'

'What do you mean?' I asked.

'Something must be eating you', he said — proud the way foreigners are when they've mastered a bit of slang. 'You should be able to qualify with your eyes shut.'

'Believe me, I know it', I told him — and it felt good to say that to someone.

8 For the next few minutes we talked together. I didn't tell Long what was 'eating' me, but he seemed to understand my anger, and he took pains to reassure me. Although he'd been schooled in the Nazi youth movement, he didn't believe in the Aryan supremacy business any more than I did. We laughed over the fact that he really looked the part, though. An inch taller than I, he had a lean muscular frame, clear blue eyes, fair hair and a strikingly handsome face. Finally, seeing I had calmed down, he pointed to the take-off board.

9 'Look', he said, 'why don't you draw a line a few inches behind the board and aim at making your take-off from there? You'll be sure not to foul, and you certainly ought to jump far enough to qualify. What does it matter if you're not first in the trials? Tomorrow is what counts.'

10 Suddenly all the tension seemed to ebb out of my body as the truth of what he said hit me. Confidently, I drew a line a full foot behind the board and jumped from there. I qualified with almost a foot to spare.

11 That night I walked over to Luz Long's room in the Olympic village to thank him. I knew that if it hadn't been for him I probably wouldn't be jumping in the finals the following day. We sat in his quarters and talked for two hours — about athletics, ourselves, the world situation, a dozen other things.

12 When I finally got up to leave, we both knew that a real friendship had been formed. Luz would go out to the stadium the next day trying to beat me if he could. But I knew that he wanted me to do my best — even if that meant my winning.

13 As it turned out, Luz broke his own past record. In doing so, he pushed me on

(*contd.*)

to a peak performance. I remember that at the instant I landed from my final jump—the one which set the Olympic record of 26 feet $5\frac{5}{10}$ inches—he was at my side, congratulating me. Despite the fact that Hitler glared at us from the stands not a hundred yards away, Luz shook my hand hard—and it wasn't a fake 'smile with a broken heart' sort of grip, either.

14 You could melt down all the gold medals and cups I have, and they wouldn't be a plating on the 24 carat friendship I felt for Luz Long at that moment.

15 I realized then, too, that Luz was the epitome of what, Pierre de Coubertin, founder of the modern Olympic Games, must have had in mind when he said, 'The important thing in the Olympic Games is not winning but taking part. The essential thing in life is not conquering but fighting well.'

Exercise 1 Answer the following questions:

(*a*) In which city were the 1936 Olympic Games held? (para 1)
(*b*) Which particular Olympic event did everyone expect Jesse Owens to win easily? (para 2)
(*c*) Name the nationality of Luz Long. (para 3)
(*d*) How many trial attempts are allowed to qualify for an Olympic event? (para 5)
(*e*) How much did Jesse Owens jump in the final attempt? (para 13)

Exercise 2 Name the paragraph in which you find the following information:

(*a*) Jesse Owens is surprised to see an unknown competitor.
(*b*) Jesse Owens loses his temper.
(*c*) Jesse Owens fails to qualify on his first two attempts.
(*d*) Luz Long comes to meet Jesse Owens.
(*e*) Luz Long does not believe in the Nazis' Aryan supremacy theory.
(*f*) Luz gives Jesse an idea how to qualify for the long jump event.
(*g*) Jesse goes to meet Luz in his room in order to thank him for his help.
(*h*) Luz Long congratulates Jesse on his success.
(*i*) The name of the founder of the modern Olympic Games.

Exercise 3

(*a*) Which word in paragraph 1 means 'announced'?
(*b*) Look in paragraph 3 for a word which means 'surprised'?
(*c*) Which word in paragraph 4 means 'decided firmly'?
(*d*) In paragraph 6, underline the word which means 'with dislike'.
(*e*) In paragraph 8, find the word which means 'remove the fears or doubts'.
(*f*) In paragraph 13, underline the word that means 'angry or fierce look.'
(*g*) In this same paragraph, look for the word which means 'hold firmly'.
(*h*) In paragraph 14, find a word which means 'a thin coating of gold, silver, etc'.

Exercise 4 Fill in the blanks in the following table:

(*a*)	calm	calmness	calmly
(*b*)	angry	....	angrily
(*c*)	bitter	....	....
(*d*)	....	ease	easily
(*e*)	proud	....	....
(*f*)	....	certainty	....

Exercise 5 Describe in your own words a thrilling match that you may have watched on the television/field.

or

Write a short paragraph on your participation in a sports competition.

My financial career

STEPHEN LEACOCK

When I go into a bank I get rattled. The clerks rattle me; the wickets rattle me; the sight of the money rattles me; everything rattles me.

The moment I cross the threshold of a bank and attempt to transact business there, I become an irresponsible idiot.

I knew this beforehand, but my salary had been raised to fifty dollars a month and I felt that the bank was the only place for it.

So I shambled in and looked timidily round at the clerks. I had an idea that a person about to open an account must needs consult the manager.

I went up to a wicket marked 'Accountant'. The accountant was a tall, cool devil. The very sight of him rattled me. My voice was sepulchral.

'Can I see the manager?' I said, and added solemnly, 'alone'. I don't know why I said 'alone'.

'Certainly', said the accountant, and fetched him.

The manager was a grave, calm man. I held my fifty-six dollars clutched in a crumpled ball in my pocket.

'Are you the manager?' I said. God knows I didn't doubt it.

'Yes', he said.

'Can I see you', I asked, 'alone?' I didn't want to say 'alone' again, but without it the thing seemed self-evident.

The manager looked at me in some alarm. He felt that I had an awful secret to reveal.

'Come in here', he said, and led the way to a private room. He turned the key in the lock.

'We are safe from interruption here', he said; 'sit down.'

We both sat down and looked at each other. I found no voice to speak.

'You are one of Pinkerton's men, I presume', he said.

He had gathered from my mysterious manner that I was a detective. I knew what he was thinking and it made me worse.

'No, not from Pinkerton's', I said, seeming to imply that I came from a rival agency.

'To tell the truth', I went on, as if I had been prompted to lie about it, 'I am not a detective at all. I have come to open an account. I intend to keep all my money in this bank.'

The manager looked relieved but still serious; he concluded now that I was a son of Baron Rothschild or a young Gould.

'A large account, I suppose', he said.

(*contd.*)

'Fairly large', I whispered. 'I propose to deposit fifty-six dollars now and fifty dollars a month regularly.'

The manager got up and opened the door. He called to the accountant.

'Mr Montgomery', he said unkindly loud, 'this gentleman is opening an account. He will deposit fifty-six dollars. Good morning.'

I rose.

A big iron door stood open at the side of the room.

'Good morning', I said, and stepped into the safe.

'Come out', said the manager coldly, and showed me the other way.

I went up to the accountant's wicket and poked the ball of money at him with a quick convulsive movement as if I were doing a conjuring trick.

My face was ghastly pale.

'Here', I said, 'deposit it.' The tone of the words seemed to mean, 'Let us do this painful thing while the fit is on us.'

He took the money and gave it to another clerk.

He made me write the sum on a slip and sign my name in a book. I no longer knew what I was doing. The bank swam before my eyes.

'Is it deposited?' I asked in a hollow, vibrating voice.

'It is', said the accountant.

'Then I want to draw a cheque.'

My idea was to draw out six dollars of it for present use. Someone gave me a cheque-book through a wicket and someone else began telling me how to write it out. The people in the bank had the impression that I was an invalid millionaire. I wrote something on the cheque and thrust it in at the clerk. He looked at it.

'What! are you drawing it all out again?' he asked in surprise. Then I realized that I had written fifty-six instead of six. I was too far gone to reason now. I had a feeling that it was impossible to explain the thing. All the clerks had stopped writing to look at me.

Reckless with misery, I made a plunge.

'Yes, the whole thing.'

'You withdraw your money from the bank?'

'Every cent of it.'

'Are you not going to deposit any more?' said the clerk, astonished.

'Never.'

An idiot hope struck me that they might think something had insulted me while I was writing the cheque and that I had changed my mind. I made a wretched attempt to look like a man with a fearfully quick temper.

The clerk prepared to pay the money.

'How will you have it?' he said.

'What?'

'How will you have it?'

'Oh'–I caught his meaning and answered without even trying to think–'in fifties'.

He gave me a fifty-dollar bill.

'And the six?' he asked dryly.

'In sixes', I said.

He gave it me and I rushed out.

(contd.)

As the big door swung behind me I caught the echo of a roar of laughter that went up to the ceiling of the bank. Since then I bank no more. I keep my money in cash in my trousers pocket and my savings in silver dollars in a sock.

(From *Literary Lapses* by Stephen Leacock, Penguin, rpt 1939, pp. 7–10)

Exercise 1 What are the things that make the writer nervous upon entering a bank?

Exercise 2 What are the expressions in paragraph 4 that indicate loss of confidence and an unwillingness to enter the bank?

Exercise 3 In the first and second paragraphs there are two expressions that have the same meaning. One of them is 'When I go into a bank . . . '. Find the other expression.

Exercise 4 Note how the writer describes the way he speaks. At one time he 'found no voice to speak'. At other times he describes his voice as 'sepulchral' and 'hollow, vibrating'. Indicate whether this shows:

confidence ☐ anger ☐ nervousness ☐ aggression ☐

Exercise 5 Compare the expressions: 'Can I see you?' and 'Can I see you, alone?' Which word spoken by the writer made the bank manager conclude that he had a terrible secret to reveal?

Exercise 6 What is Pinkerton's? State whether it is:

a bank ☐ a shop ☐ a detective agency ☐ an office ☐

Exercise 7 When the writer said, 'I have come to open an account. I intend to keep all my money in this bank', the bank manager concluded that he was the son of Baron Rothschild or a young Gould. Even if you have never heard of Baron Rothschild or Gould you can still guess why these persons have been mentioned here.

Try and guess whether these persons are:

extremely rich ☐ poor ☐ neither rich nor poor ☐

Exercise 8 Montgomery is the name of:

the bank manager ☐ the accountant ☐ the writer ☐

Exercise 9 Given below are some jumbled up sentences. Arrange them in proper sequence by following the order of events as narrated in the story:

— This strange behaviour made the manager think that he was a detective.
— The writer deposited the amount and then, by mistake, wrote out a cheque drawing out the whole amount.
— Since then he does not bank any more.
— Later he thought that he was a millionaire.
— As he walked out of the bank he could hear the bank people laughing at him.
— Banks made the writer very nervous.
— When he came to know that the writer had only fifty-six dollars he became very cold towards him and sent him to the accountant.
— The writer wanted to open an account and asked to see the manager alone.

Bus commuters: an endangered species

1 I have just returned from the chautha ceremony of my friend's father. He did not die of old age. He fell off a bus and got crushed under its wheels. He was the victim of criminal negligence, almost a conspiracy, a conspiracy which we all have helped hatch together.

2 Trauma researchers around the world have been saying for years that 'accidents' don't just happen. They are very often the result of bad or defective equipment and poor environmental design. When those in authority are insensitive to the issues of safety, the people suffer for no fault of theirs.

3 Painstaking research done by scores of dedicated scientists over the past few decades has clearly established the following general principles: human error is only the final action in a sequence of many causative factors that result in an 'accident' and the error cannot be isolated as a cause. The error itself is very often the result of bad design, bad working conditions and even lack of choice.

4 One important consequence of this new understanding is that we now know that improvement in vehicle design and in roads and crossings are more cost-effective than money spent on safety education drives. Safety posters, safety weeks and driver 'education' make money for the educators, advertisers and hoarding owners but do very little to save lives.

5 This new understanding is the outcome of a large number of ingenious studies in the best tradition of modern science. Policy and opinion makers in India have, however, turned a blind eye to this kind of information.

6 It is therefore not surprising that the two most important decisions in the area of transportation have guaranteed that more Indians are going to be killed, maimed and paralysed in the years to come. These two decisions are—increasing the availability of fast motor cycles and scooters in ever increasing numbers, and selecting one of the most unsafe cars for manufacture in India.

7 Our obsession with the motor car and the motor cycle has blinded us to concerns about other forms of transport. No one seems to be concerned about the more comfortable and safer bus transport. Scores of articles have appeared about the lack of innovation in Indian cars, but there has been no such clamour over the lack of innovation in bus design.

8 Few know that buses in India are still being made on chassis designs which are over 40 years old. One feature of this design is that the entry and exit steps of buses are very high making it most inconvenient for everyone except the athlete. This inconvenient design also makes sure that people take a much longer time to get on and off. This further annoys the driver, who has to make his trip in a given period of time. And because enough investment is not made on public transport, buses are often overcrowded and people have to hang out of

(*contd.*)

doors in desperation. A study conducted by the Indian Institute of Technology, Delhi, reveals that of the 39 bus passengers killed in one year, 82 per cent were people who fell off footboards or got crushed while riding on them.

9 Some drivers maintained that they could not see the passenger hanging so far out of the bus. This is not surprising. The rear view mirrors fixed on Indian buses are about the smallest one can find in the world.

10 Admitted, that for many years India may not be in a position to expand the bus fleet to prevent overcrowding. However, in principle, it may be possible to design buses to carry 100 persons safely instead of the present 55 and design them in such a way that people can buy tickets and move through the bus much faster than they do now. Some good designers and operations research experts should be able to come up with a novel design within a period of two or three years if given the proper encouragement.

11 But we should not stop here. We should also aim at a bus design which has a less rigid front surface. A pedestrian or a two-wheeler rider would have a better chance of surviving if hit by this more 'humane' bus. This is not a wild idea. Our present knowledge of biomechanics makes such design possible. However, these designs will not come from the West. Buses hitting pedestrians and cyclists is not their problem.

12 If we start now we should have an ingenious bus design by the end of the decade. Meanwhile, our existing buses could be fitted with speed governors, better rear-view mirrors and more comfortable steps. Route timings should be rationalized to give enough time for stops and only then can drivers be policed more seriously and effectively. Commuters' associations could be formed to put pressure on drivers and conductors to do their jobs efficiently and politely.

13 Similarly, a serious effort should be made through proper legislation as well as community pressure to prevent commuters from hanging on footboards.

14 We have not given serious attention to such concerns over the past 40 years. And there are no signs that the authorities are taking them seriously even now. That is why my friend lost his father. He was a victim of criminal neglect almost amounting to conspiracy. How many more victims do we need?

(Adapted from the *Times of India*, New Delhi, 9 July 1987)

Exercise 1 Look at the picture on page 173 and suggest another title for this text. One possible title can be: 'Overcrowded Buses'.

....

Exercise 2 Answer the following:

(*a*) In which paragraph is it mentioned that 'accidents' don't just happen?

....

(*b*) Human error is not the sole cause of an accident. In which paragraph, do you find this information?

....

(*c*) Two recent important decisions in India have contributed a lot to the increase in accidents. In which paragraph, do you come across this information?

....

(*d*) What percentage of motor-accident deaths in a year have occurred because of the faulty design of buses. (para 8)

....

(*e*) Is it possible to carry 100 passengers safely in a bus instead of the present 55? (para 10) Justify your answer.

....

....

(*f*) If we start working on a safe bus design today, how many years might it take for formulating a workable design? (para 12)

....

....

Exercise 3 Find words/phrases from the text with the following meanings:

(*a*) think out a plan/scheme (para 1) ....

(*b*) boards for displaying advertisements (para 4) ....

(*c*) introduction of new things (para 7) ....

(*d*) a fixed/false idea that occupies one's mind (para 7) ....

(*e*) base-frame of a bus/car/truck on which the body is built (para 8) ....

(*f*) tender/kind-hearted (para 11) ....

Exercise 4 Observe the following words which appear in the text: 'unsafe' and 'insensitive'. Words conveying opposite meanings can be formed by adding 'un-' or 'in-' as prefixes to the root words.

Now add 'un-' or 'in-' to the following words to form their opposites:

(*a*) just	....	(*f*) finite	....
(*b*) eligible	....	(*g*) fortunate	....
(*c*) believable	....	(*h*) efficient	....
(*d*) kind	....	(*i*) justice	....
(*e*) convenient	....	(*j*) popular	....

Exercise 5 Match the words in List A with their meanings given in List B:

List A	*List B*
commuters	something new that is introduced
conspiracy	failure to take proper care or precaution
innovation	persons who travel regularly by bus/train from house to place of work
ingenious	unresponsive to the feelings of others
negligence	a secret plan or plot
insensitive	skilfully made

Exercise 6 Discuss and then write a paragraph using the following hints:

(*a*) Last week I
(*b*) an urgent piece of work
(*c*) in a hurry

(*d*) a large number of passengers at the bus-stop
(*e*) an overcrowded bus
(*f*) hung on to the footboard
(*g*) fell off before the next stop
(*h*) a few bruises and minor injuries
(*i*) resolved never to travel on the footboard

Pre-reading exercises

1 Given below are some words and expressions used in a news report. Write down in your notebook what you think is the subject of the news item:

students	leopard	hides	playing hide-and-seek
search	pug-marks	police	fire brigade

2 Discuss with your partner(s) and list as many associations as you can think of for each of these words and expressions.

3 What questions arise in your mind when you read the following headline:

A LEOPARD HIDES ITSELF IN A COLLEGE BUILDING

Take down these questions in your notebook.

Read the news report given below in fifteen minutes. Do not stop at words and expressions you do not understand. Of the two titles given, which one do you think is appropriate to the news report and why?

LEOPARD PLAYS HIDE-AND-SEEK

LEOPARD 'BLOWN' TO DEATH

1 *The Hindustan Times*, New Delhi, 18 February. A leopard has been playing hide-and-seek with the students of a tool-training institute in Ashok Vihar since yesterday. As if playing solo to the tune *Catch me if You Can*, composed by the great pugilist Muhammad Ali, the leopard has managed to avoid the searchers.

2 The leopard was sighted yesterday by some students near the air-conditioning plant of the Tool Room and Training Centre of the Delhi Administration. Some tell-tale signs were also found on the lawns of the centre. The students ventured to search for the animal and even the Fire Brigade was called. The search was given up as the leopard failed to reappear.

3 However, this morning again, fresh pug-marks on the lawns and impressions on the walls and possible inlets leading to the air-conditioning plant, were found. The students once again launched a hunt for their visitor. The wild creature was spotted by several students while it was attempting to come out of the plant.

4 The Police and the Fire Brigade were summoned again. At first, nobody dared to come close to the building housing the plant. Some daredevil students subsequently got hold of a ladder and peeped into the plant from a ventilator. Since there was no lighting arrangement inside the plant, a search light was hastily arranged to have a look inside. There was no sign of the animal.

5 The Fire Brigade men approached the plant from all possible entry and exit points but nobody dared to enter lest the leopard attack him in panic. Even gun-toting policemen remained helpless spectators while all types of sugges-

(*contd.*)

tions were floated to catch the leopard.

6 A squad from the municipality came to the spot armed with lathis and ropes. Two men, who normally catch stray dogs, climbed on to the ventilator and one of them had a glimpse of the animal but before he could take any action, it had again disappeared.

7 At their wit's end, the Fire Brigade men finally poured water into the plant to force the animal out, but to no avail. The municipal squad even caught hold of a bitch to use her as a bait for the leopard. A rope was tied around her neck and the confused animal pushed into the plant. The hiding leopard did not take the bait. Several other tricks were employed but the animal didn't come out of its air-conditioned comfort.

8 UNI adds: A spokesperson for the National Zoological Park here said an expert armed with a tranquillizer gun has been sent to the spot. 'Our aim is to capture the animal alive', the spokesperson added.

(From the *Hindustan Times*, New Delhi, 19 Feb 1987)

1 Read through the news report once again and answer the following:

(*a*) Name the institute where the leopard has hidden itself.
(*b*) Name the locality where the institute is located.
(*c*) Who noticed the animal first?
(*d*) Name all the parties that joined in trying to catch the animal.

2 In which paragraph do you find the following information:

(*a*) The animal is seen inside the plant.
(*b*) No one dares to go inside the plant.
(*c*) A ladder is brought.

3 Various parties join in trying to catch the animal and they use different methods to bring out the animal from the air-conditioning plant. Complete the following table on the basis of this report:

Name of the search party	*Means used to bring out the leopard*	*Results achieved*

Post-reading exercises

1 Check if the various associations you thought of for the words in the first Pre-reading Exercise were correct. Make changes, if any, in your prediction.

2 You had listed some questions in the third Pre-reading Exercise. Have you got answers to all these questions? Write down the answers to as many questions as you can. If there are any questions which still remain unanswered, discuss these with your partner(s) and try to arrive at possible answers.

3 (*a*) Find at least one example of synonym in the text. Compare your answer with that of others in the group.
(*b*) In paragraph 5 find the equivalent of 'to have the courage'.
(*c*) The opposite of 'hide' is 'seek' (para 1). In paragraph 5 find two words which are opposite to each other in meaning.

(*d*) Guess the meanings of 'pugilist', 'at their wit's end' and 'daredevil'. Look up the dictionary to check your guess.

4 Look up in the dictionary the following:

(*a*) the pronunciation of 'leopard', 'policemen', 'lawn' and 'creature'.
(*b*) the stress in 'avoid', 'again', 'police' and 'compose'.
(*c*) the different meanings of 'hide', 'plant' and 'spot'.

5 Make a list of all the words and phrases used for 'leopard' in the news report. Compare your list with that of others in the group. Discuss with your partner(s) why the reporter does not use the same word everytime he refers to the animal.

6 What is the reporter's attitude towards the whole incident? Discuss your viewpoint with others in the group.

7 (*a*) What method would you have suggested to bring out the leopard from the air-conditioning plant? Discuss with others in the group to arrive at a decision. Then write a letter to the Police Commissioner offering your suggestion(s).

(*b*) Make a list of the steps you would take as the warden of your hostel if one morning you find that a wild animal has hidden itself in the hostel building. Discuss your list with your partner(s) to revise it, if necessary.

The priest and the mulberry tree

T L PEACOCK

Did you hear of the Curate who mounted his mare,
And merrily trotted along to the fair?
Of creature more tractable none ever heard,
In the height of her speed she would stop at a word;
But again with a word, when the Curate said, Hey,
She put forth her mettle and galloped away.

As near to the gates of the city he rode,
While the sun of September all brilliantly glowed,
The good priest discovered, with eyes of desire,
A mulberry tree in a hedge of wild briar;
On boughs long and lofty, in many a green shoot,
Hung large, black and glossy, the beautiful fruit.

The curate was hungry and thirsty to boot;
He shrank from the thorns, though he longed for the fruit;
With a word he arrested his courser's keen speed,
And he stood up erect on the back of his steed;
On the saddle he stood while his creature stood still,
And he gathered the fruit till he took his good fill.

'Sure never' he thought, 'was a creature so rare,
So docile, so true, as my excellent mare;
Lo, here now I stand,' and he gazed all around,
'As safe and as steady as if on the ground;
Yet how had it been, if some traveller this way,
Had, dreaming no mischief but chanced to cry, Hey?'

(*contd.*)

He stood with his head in the mulberry tree,
And he spoke out aloud in his fond reverie;
At the sound of the word the good mare made a push,
And down went the priest in the wild briar bush.
He remembered too late, on his thorny green bed,
Much that well may be thought cannot wisely be said.

Exercise 1 Circle all the words/phrases used to refer to the 'mare'.

Exercise 2 Guess the meaning of the word 'tractable' (line 3). Which line(s) help you in guessing its meaning? Then consult your dictionary.

Exercise 3 What is the subject of the following verbs:

(*a*) glowed (line 8) ....

(*b*) hung (line 12) ....

(*c*) chanced (line 24) ....

(*d*) went (line 28) ....

Exercise 4 Rewrite the sentences (*a*) to (*f*) given below in normal English prose following the pattern: Subject + Verb + Object/Complement/Adverb:

Example: 'Of creature more tractable none ever heard' (line 3) could be rewritten as 'No one ever heard of a more tractable creature than his mare.'

(*a*) As near to the gates of the city he rode,
(*b*) On boughs long and lofty, in many a green shoot,
Hung large, black and glossy, the beautiful fruit.
(*c*) With a word he arrested his courser's keen speed,
(*d*) On the saddle he stood
(*e*) At the sound of the word the good mare made a push
(*f*) And down went the priest in the wild briar bush.

Exercise 5 What rhyme scheme does this poem follow? How do we know?

....

Exercise 6 In this poem a statement of fact is made in line 3; this statement is followed by an explication in lines 4–6; next we are told what happened to the priest while he was riding to the fair; and finally in the last two lines a moral is given.

Follow this outline and narrate the story in your own words. You can start like this:

There was a priest. He had a wonderful mare. . . .

The atheist and the acorn

ANNE, COUNTESS OF WINCHILSEA

'Me thinks this world is oddly made,
And everything's amiss,'
A dull presuming Atheist said,
As stretched he lay beneath a shade,
And instanced in this:

(*contd.*)

'Behold,' quoth he, 'that mighty thing,
A pumpkin, large and round,
Is held but by a little string,
Which upward cannot make it spring,
Or bear it from the ground;

'Whilst on this oak, a fruit so small,
So disproportioned, grows;
That, who with sense surveys this All,
This universal casual ball,
Its ill contrivance knows.

'My better judgment would have hung
That weight upon a tree,
And left this mast, thus slightly strung,
'Mongst things which on the surface sprung,
And small and feeble be.'

No more the caviller could say,
No farther faults descry,
For, as he upward gazing lay,
An acorn loosened from the stay
Fell down upon his eye.

The offended part with tears ran o'er,
As punished for the sin;
Fool! had that bough a pumpkin bore,
Thy whimsies must have worked no more,
Nor skull had kept them in.

Exercise 1 Guess the meaning of the word 'Atheist' (line 3).

Exercise 2 Expand the following contracted forms:

(*a*) everything's (line 2) ....

(*b*) 'Mongst (line 19) ....

Exercise 3 What do the following refer to:

(*a*) he (line 4) ....

(*b*) which (line 9) ....

(*c*) it (lines 9 and 10) ....

(*d*) that weight (line 17) ....

Exercise 4 Rewrite in prose form: Subject + Verb + Object/Complement/Adverb:

(*a*) lines 1-4 ....

....

....

....

(*b*) line 21 ....

(*c*) line 26 ....

Exercise 5 Does this poem have any rhyme scheme? What is it?

....

Exercise 6 In writing we omit certain parts in a sentence to avoid repetition, e.g.

I carried the bag and my friend the suitcase.

This sentence actually means:

I carried the bag and my friend *carried* the suitcase.

Can you restore the omitted parts (ellipses) in the following sentences:

(*a*) Neither do I want to sing nor dance at present.

....

(*b*) The camera belongs to him and the film to me.

....

(*c*) He held the ladder and I the fan.

....

(*d*) It rains more in Shimla than in Solan.

....

(*e*) I value your friendship more than his wealth.

....

Do you find elliptical sentences in the poem? Indicate the ellipses in these sentences by means of caret signs (^).

Exercise 7 In this poem the Atheist makes an assertion in lines 1–2 in which he expresses an opinion about how this world is made. This assertion is followed by justification in lines 6–20 wherein he gives an instance to justify his assertion. Does the poet agree with the Atheist? Illustrate your answer.

Exercise 8 Narrate the story of this poem in your own words.

The arrow and the song

HENRY W LONGFELLOW

I shot an arrow into the air,
It fell to earth, I knew not where;
For, so swiftly it flew, the sight
Could not follow it in its flight.

I breathed a song into the air,
It fell to earth, I knew not where;
For who has sight so keen and strong,
That it can follow the flight of song?

Long, long afterward, in an oak
I found the arrow, still unbroke.
And the song, from beginning to end,
I found again in the heart of a friend.

Exercise 1 In what ways are the arrow and the song similar?

Exercise 2 In what ways are they different?

Exercise 3 Explain the difference in meaning between the following pairs of words:

(*a*) earth, world
(*b*) sight, vision
(*c*) keen, strong
(*d*) heart, soul

If necessary, consult your dictionary.

Exercise 4 Why does the poet say that the arrow was 'still unbroke'? (line 10)

Exercise 5 In stanza 2 in what sense does the poet use the word 'breathed'? Give another word for it, i.e. a synonym.

Grammar

UNIT 1 QUESTIONS, NEGATIVES AND QUESTION TAGS

1 Fill in the blanks with a question word, i.e. what, where, when, who, whom, why, which, how. In some sentences more than one choice is possible. The first blank has been filled in for you.

(*a*) *Who* is your principal?

(*b*) .... does he live?

(*c*) .... did you meet him?

(*d*) .... did he say?

(*e*) .... are his academic qualifications?

(*f*) .... is his office?

(*g*) .... did you greet him?

(*h*) .... room is he in?

(*i*) .... did you give the application to?

(*j*) .... is he on leave today?

2 Form questions from the statements given below, using the question words given in brackets. Do not forget to put the question mark. The first question has been done for you.

(*a*) This novel was written in 1946. (when)
Question: *When was this novel written?*

(*b*) The briefcase was stolen at the station. (where)
Question: ....

(*c*) The auditorium was constructed last year. (when)
Question: ....

(*d*) The money was collected by students. (by whom)
Question: ....

(*e*) I have bought six plants for my garden. (how many)
Question: ....

(*f*) His house was destroyed by fire. (how)
Question: ....

(*g*) The servant let out the secret. (who)
Question: ....

(*h*) The interview letters were sent out yesterday. (when)
Question: ....

(*i*) You have selected this book. (which)
Question: ....

(*j*) A hundred guests have been invited. (how many)

Question: ....

(*k*) The taxi driver turned up very late. (who)

Question: ....

(*l*) It is his fault. (whose)

Question: ....

3 Find in List B the answers to the questions in List A.

	List A		*List B*
(*a*)	Who was Ali Baba?	(*i*)	Early in the morning he heard the sound of horses' hooves.
(*b*)	When did he hear the sound of horses' hooves?	(*ii*)	He climbed up a high tree and hid himself.
(*c*)	Where did he hide himself?	(*iii*)	Ali Baba was a poor woodcutter.
(*d*)	How did he remain unseen?	(*iv*)	The Captain of the thieves cried 'Open sesame.'
(*e*)	What did he see?	(*v*)	He confided in his wife.
(*f*)	Why did he shake with fear?	(*vi*)	The branches let him remain unseen.
(*g*)	Which of the thieves cried 'Open sesame'?	(*vii*)	Seeing forty thieves at a time made him shake with fear.
(*h*)	Whom did he confide in?	(*viii*)	He saw forty thieves on horseback.

4 Form questions based on the following statements:

(*a*) She is a foreigner. *Is she a foreigner?*

Raman is afraid of dogs. ....

He was a good student. ....

They are happy. ....

He is going to Australia. ....

His passport is to be renewed. ....

(*b*) Radha likes sweets. *Does Radha like sweets?*

Naresh hates milk. ....

She loves singing. ....

He drives carefully. ....

It needs oiling. ....

(*c*) They love playing games. *Do they love playing games?*

They cheat customers. ....

Supriya and Shyam work for the same company. ....

Her children fall ill frequently. ....

They practice for six hours every day. ....

5 Complete the right-hand column.

Student A wants to find out from Student B if he:	Student A asks:
(*a*) has got any relations in Delhi.	*Have you got any relations in Delhi?*
(*b*) is studying hard.	....
(*c*) is good at football.	....
(*d*) was born in Delhi.	....
(*e*) has joined the hostel.	....
(*f*) belongs to a village or a town.	....
(*g*) would like to stand for election.	....
(*h*) knows typing.	....
(*i*) has a cycle.	....
(*j*) misses his family.	....

6 Answer the following questions both in the negative and affirmative:

(*a*) Do you like visiting relatives?	*Yes, I do.*
	No, I don't.
(*b*) Do you like drinking tea?	Yes, ...
	No, ...
(*c*) Does he like reading magazines?	Yes, ...
	No, ...
(*d*) Does she like dancing?	Yes, ...
	No, ...
(*e*) Do they like watching football?	Yes, ...
	No, ...
(*f*) Do they go to bed early?	Yes, ...
	No, ...
(*g*) Does he work seriously?	Yes, ...
	No, ...
(*h*) Is this a good book?	Yes, ...
	No, ...
(*i*) Are his neighbours nice to him?	Yes, ...
	No, ...
(*j*) Has he made a mistake?	Yes, ...
	No, ...
(*k*) Have they built a boundary wall?	Yes, ...
	No, ...
(*l*) Will he be forced to resign?	Yes, ...
	No, ...

(*m*) Was he a good student? Yes, ...
No, ...

(*n*) Were they singing patriotic songs? Yes, ...
No, ...

(*o*) Did they provide blankets? Yes, ...
No, ...

(*p*) Did he file a complaint? Yes, ...
No, ...

Question tags

It is quite common in conversation to make a statement and ask for confirmation. For example, in the following two samples:

(*a*) You won't forget, will you?
(*b*) You will be careful, won't you?

'will you' and 'won't you' are *question tags*. It must be noted that when the statement is positive, the question tag that goes with it is negative. However, if the statement is negative the question tag that goes with it is positive.

Exercise 1 Match each expression in List A with a question tag from List B.

	List A		*List B*
(*a*)	You won't forget,	(*i*)	aren't they?
(*b*)	Our train leaves at 10 a.m.,	(*ii*)	shall we?
(*c*)	The students are having fun,	(*iii*)	aren't you?
(*d*)	Mohan is also leaving soon,	(*iv*)	will you?
(*e*)	I'll see you again,	(*v*)	won't I?
(*f*)	We shan't need tickets,	(*vi*)	won't you?
(*g*)	You will be careful,	(*vii*)	doesn't it?
(*h*)	Sheila isn't going along,	(*viii*)	isn't he?
(*i*)	You are about to leave,	(*x*)	will they?
(*j*)	Your parents won't mind,	(*xi*)	is she?

UNIT 2 SUBJECT–VERB AGREEMENT

Last year, I had an opportunity to visit Mauritius by sea. We travelled in a big ship. There were other smaller ships going alongside. The whole fleet(1) was in formation. The captain and pilot(2) of our ship was very efficient. The journey was very comfortable. Bread and butter(3) was given to us at breakfast. Each one of us(4) was served food in plenty. I formed a useful friendship with one of the fellow passengers. We enjoyed the journey very much. Neither he nor I(5) was in a hurry to reach Mauritius. In the evening we sat on the deck with other passengers. We had a lot of conversation on politics, mathematics, love and marriage. Someone said: 'Politics(6) is a dirty game'. Another said: 'Mathematics(6) is fascinating'. Time passed pleasantly and we reached our destination. The captain, with all his crew members,(7) has earned a permanent place in our memory.

Explanation 1 Observe the underlined words in the above passage. These illustrate the agreement of the verb with the subject. For instance, 'fleet' (a group of ships), though plural, takes a singular verb because it is a collective noun. Similarly, we can write: 'The Tenth Lok Sabha has chosen its speaker'. If, however, a collective noun is not thought of as one unit, but as the items which compose it, then it takes a plural verb. Thus, we write: 'The jury were divided in their opinion'.

Exercise 1 In the following sentences, supply the correct form of the verb from within the brackets so as to make it agree with the subject:

A number of candidates .... late for the interview. (was/were)

The committee .... agreed on the main point. (was/were)

The public .... requested not to walk on the grass. (is/are)

The crew of the pirate ship .... taken prisoner. (was/were)

The crowd .... dispersed by the police. (was/were)

A few suggestions .... been made for the Staff Association to consider. (has/have)

Explanation 2 The second underlined phrase 'The captain and pilot' in the passage above takes a singular verb because the two nouns 'The captain' and 'pilot' refer to the same person. Similarly, we can write: 'The poet and dramatist of Bengal <u>is</u> dead'. If, however, the subject in such cases is made up of two nouns, both being used with 'the', it will take a plural verb. Thus: '<u>The</u> poet and <u>the</u> dramatist *are* dead'.

Exercise 2 In the following sentences, choose the correct alternative from within the brackets:

The accountant and the cashier of this firm .... run away. (has/have)

I am happy that my friend and benefactor .... come. (has/have)

Alas! The great philosopher and statesman of our country .... no more. (is/are)

The secretary and the treasurer of our society .... yet to be elected. (has/have)

The storyteller and poet of our state .... honoured recently. (was/were)

Explanation 3 The third underlined phrase 'Bread and butter' takes a singular verb because the two nouns express a single idea. Similarly, we can say: 'The horse and carriage *is* at the door'.

Exercise 3 In the following sentences, use a verb in agreement with the subject:

Slow and steady .... the race.

After his recent illness, bread and milk .... his only food.

Time and tide .... for no man.

The rise and fall of the tide .... due to the effect of the moon.

The long and the short of the matter .... that you must go to Bombay tomorrow.

Explanation 4 The fourth underlined phrase 'Each one of us' takes a singular verb because the subject is made singular by the use of 'each one of .... '. Similarly, we can say: 'Each one of the pupils has paid the fee'. The use of 'every' or 'none' with a plural noun also makes the subject singular. Thus: 'None of the boys <u>was</u> present in my class yesterday'.

Exercise 4 In the following sentences, use a verb in agreement with the subject:

Everyone of the boys and girls .... ready for the picnic.

None of the girls .... more than five feet tall.

Each one of the students .... given a prize.

When the plane exploded in mid-air, every man, woman, and child .... lost.

Each one of the suspected persons .... arrested by the police.

Explanation 5 The fifth underlined phrase 'Neither he nor I' takes a singular verb because the subject here is singular with the use of 'neither nor'. Similarly, with 'either or' a singular verb is used. Thus we say: Either Ravi or Naeem <u>is</u> at fault in this matter.

Exercise 5 Make corrections, if any, in the use of the verb in the following sentences and rewrite them:

Either an officer or an assistant are needed soon.

....

Neither the judge nor the lawyer have arrived at the court yet.

....

Either Abdul or Hanif has stolen Zoya's watch.

....

Neither food nor water were to be found in the deserted village.

....

Neither the president nor the secretary were present at the meeting.

....

Explanation 6 The sixth underlined words 'Politics/Mathematics', take a singular verb because these two nouns, although apparently plural in form, are singular in meaning. Similarly, we can say: 'Economics <u>is</u> a popular subject'.

Exercise 6 Write five similar sentences of your own:

....

....

....

....

Explanation 7 The seventh underlined phrase 'The captain, with all his crew members' takes a singular verb because the real subject in this underlined phrase is 'The captain' (which is singular) and 'with all his crew members' is only additional information about the subject. Similarly, when a singular subject is joined by 'together with' or 'as well as', a singular verb is used.

Examples : (*a*) The governor, together with his security guards, has arrived for the function.

(*b*) Shalini, as well as her friends, is interested in going for a picnic.

Exercise 7 Write correct/incorrect against each of the following sentences. Rewrite the incorrect sentences after making necessary corrections:

(*a*) The tribal chief, with all his followers, were present at the function. ....

....

(*b*) Smoking, as well as drinking, is bad for health. ....

....

(*c*) The plane, with all the passengers, was lost in a storm. ....

....

(*d*) Kindness, as well as justice, are the hallmark of a judge. ....

....

(*e*) The cow, as well as the horse, eats grass. ....

....

(*f*) The Prime Minister, with all his ministers, were present in the Parliament House. ....

....

(*g*) Sunil Gavaskar, as well as Kapil Dev, deserves praise for playing bright cricket. ....

....

(*h*) The box, with all its valuable contents, was lost. ....

....

(*i*) My wife, as well as my children, like hot curry. ....

....

(*j*) Wholesome food, with fruits, are necessary for good health. ....

....

UNIT 3 TENSES

Simple present and present continuous

Underline the verbs in the following paragraphs:

(*a*) This is Mr Ashok Srivastav. He works in a college. Mr Srivastav teaches English. He is very kind and helpful. He works hard and prepares his lesson well before going to the college. He pays special attention to weak students and holds extra classes for them. The students admire and love him.

(*b*) In this picture, you are looking

at Mr Srivastav. He is sitting in his study. He is typing a letter to one of his old students.

Points for discussion

The verbs in paragraph (*a*) are in the simple present form. Those in paragraph (*b*) are in the present continuous tense.

Can you say when we should use the simple present and when the present continuous form of the verb? Discuss with others in the group.

Can you think of other situations when these two verb forms are used? Make a list and compare it with that of others in the group.

Explanation The simple present tense usually shows that an action is habitual or happens regularly, e.g. 'The puppy *plays* with the ball every morning'. The present continuous form usually shows that the action is going on at the actual moment of speaking or writing, e.g. 'The boy is *running* to school'.

Note: There are certain verbs of perception/cognition which are not normally used in the continuous form. Some of these are:

abhor, agree, contain, deserve, love, like, know

Some other uses of the two tenses

Simple present	*Present continuous*
It is used in clauses of time and condition, e.g. 'I will leave the office when he *comes* back.' 'If it *rains* I'll not go to college.' It must be used with those verbs (verbs of perception, etc.) which cannot be used in the continuous form, e.g. 'I *see* an aeroplane coming towards us.' It can be used for dramatic narrative, description of people and places, etc., planned future action(s), and TV/radio commentary.	This form of the verb is also used: (*a*) to denote repeated action that occurs over a specified period of time, e,g. 'I am learning French this semester.' In such sentences the adverbial of time specifying the period of occurrence is often used; (*b*) for a planned action in the near future, e.g. 'I am going to meet him tomorrow afternoon.' (*c*) for a repeated action, often one which seems unreasonable to the speaker, e.g. 'Ravi is always eating out at weekends.'

Exercise 1 Fill in the blanks with the simple present or present continuous form of the verb given in brackets:

(*a*) He usually .... his letters in English, but today he is .... in Hindi. (write)

(*b*) Shiela often .... her homework as soon as she is back from school. (do)

(*c*) The train .... at 9.00 p.m. but it is late today and .... at 9.30 p.m. (leave)

(d) Bikash .... in the mornings but this month he .... in the afternoons. (lecture)

(e) He .... only one novel this year though he usually .... three novels in a year. (write)

Exercise 2 Fill in the blanks with the simple present or the present continuous form of the verb given in brackets:

We .... (see) two persons in this picture. They .... (be) Mr Reddy and Mr Kaul. Mr Reddy .... (sit) in the chair and Mr Kaul .... (stand) in front of him. Probably, Mr Reddy .... (consult) Mr Kaul on the arrangements for the school fete next week.

As in the past, the school .... (hold) its annual fete this year, too, and Mr Kaul .... (look after) the arrangements. Students usually .... (put up) about fifty stalls and .... (raise) a tidy sum. This time they .... (put up) about a hundred stalls. At the moment, the student union .... (hold) its meeting for a decision on this point.

Exercise 3 Supply in the following pairs of sentences either the simple present or the present continuous form of the verb given in brackets:

(a) The moon .... in the sky now. (shine)
The moon .... in the sky at night. (shine)

(b) I .... my scooter on Sundays. (wash)
I .... my scooter with detergent and water. (wash)

(c) She .... the windows when they are dirty. (dust)
She .... the windows because they are dirty. (dust)

(d) They .... students from the college for this offence. (expel)
They .... five students from the college for this offence. (expel)

(e) My sister .... how to swim. (learn)
My sister .... how to swim. (know)

Simple past, present perfect and past perfect

Underline the verbs in the following paragraph:

Mr Ashis Gupta has just finished writing a story. He wrote three stories last year. He started writing stories when he was still in school. By the time he was 21, he had written twenty stories. He has written thirty stories by now.

Points for discussion

Both the *simple past* and the *present perfect* are used for an activity which happened in the past. What then is the difference between the two tenses?

Explanation 1 *Simple past tense* indicates that the action occurred in the past. It can be a single or a repeated action, e.g.

I bathed at six this morning.
I always bathed at six when I was a boy.

It focuses our attention on the action and may also indicate when it happened. It is obligatory to use this form of the tense if an adverbial of fixed past time is used, e.g.

I bought this book yesterday.

It may also be used with the adverbials of immediate past time, e.g.

I bought this book just now.

Explanation 2 The *present perfect tense* expresses the completion of an action NOW. It focuses our attention on the present relevance of a past activity and not on the activity or the time of the activity, e.g.

I have read the book (i.e. I now know what there is in it, etc.).

The present relevance of this past activity will depend on the shared knowledge of the two interlocutors.

The present perfect is not normally used with the adverbs of definite past time. We can say

I have seen him.

but it would be wrong to say

I have seen him yesterday.

But it can be used with adverbs of present time, i.e. time which is not yet over at the moment of speaking or writing, e.g.

I have seen him twice today (the day is not yet over).

It can also be used with the adverbs of indefinite past time, e.g.

I have never seen your principal.

In fact, it is often found with 'already', 'never', 'recently', etc.

Explanation 3 The *past perfect tense* is a sort of 'double past', or 'past before past'. It shows that two events happened in the past and stresses the sequence of their happening, e.g.

The train had left when we reached the station.
(i.e. first the train left and then we reached the station)

Notice that when two actions are completed in the past, the action which happens first is expressed in the past perfect and the other is written in the simple past.

The past perfect is also used to express an action completed by a certain time in the past, e.g.

He had completed the job by six o'clock.

The past perfect is also used

(*a*) in a conditional clause, e.g.
If I had worked hard, I would have passed.

(*b*) to express an unfulfilled wish, e.g.
I wish I had worked harder!

(*c*) to make a grammatical change while rewriting in indirect narration a reported speech which is in the simple past or present perfect, e.g.
The woman told us that she had worked hard all her life.

Exercise 1 Fill in the blanks with the correct tense forms (simple past or present perfect) of the verbs given in brackets:

(*a*) Mr Anand now owns a house in Delhi. He .... it in 1989. (build)

(*b*) This party .... the election a second time. It first .... the election three years ago. (win)

(*c*) Shiela .... (buy) the novel a year ago but she .... it yet. (not read)

(*d*) Mr Singh .... (not see) our principal although the principal .... the college last month. (join)

(*e*) Mr Gupta
first novel when he was only 21. (publish)

Exercise 2 Fill in the blanks with appropriate tense forms (simple past or past perfect) of the verbs given in brackets:

(*a*) Mr Hussain .... (post) the letter before Arif .... (arrive) here.

(*b*) The woman immediately .... (recognize) the thief because she .... (see) him before.

(*c*) The woman said, 'I wish I .... (hit) the thief on the head when he .... (come) through the window.'

(*d*) If the police .... (arrive) in time, they would have caught the thieves.

(*e*) My sister told me that she .... (visit) the library in the morning.

The present perfect continuous

The *present perfect continuous* tense usually shows that the action began at a certain time in the past and that it is still going on at the present moment; or that it has been taking place for a certain length of time and is still doing so at the moment of speaking or writing, e.g.

I have been reading *Julius Caesar* for a week.

Note that we use 'for' or 'since' with this tense.

Points for discussion

Discuss with your group the distinction between the *continuous* and the *perfect continuous* tenses. How would you explain the distinction between:

I have been reading *Julius Caesar* for a week.

and

I am reading *Julius Caesar.*

Do you know that we use 'for' and 'since' in the present perfect and the perfect continuous tenses? Do you also know when we use 'for' and when we use 'since'? Discuss with the others in the group and check with the teacher.

Exercise 1 Select the correct form of the verb given in brackets in each of the following sentence:

(*a*) I (am/have been) waiting for him since morning.
(*b*) The commission (is/has been) submitting its report for action.
(*c*) We (are/have been) training teachers for four years.
(*d*) Malini (has been/is) acting in films since the age of twelve.
(*e*) Tomorrow morning Roshni (has been/is) painting a special card for the exhibition.

Exercise 2 Fill in the blanks with the correct form of the verb 'write' using only:

(*a*)	write	Simple present tense
(*b*)	am writing	Present continuous tense
(*c*)	have written	Present perfect tense
(*d*)	have been writing	Present perfect continuous tense

I .... regularly for a women's magazine. I .... every morning for about four hours. I .... ten short stories so far. I .... a novel now. Unfortunately, I .... very slowly. Although I .... since the age of ten, I .... not more than a few short stories till now because of this shortcoming.

Exercise 3 Fill in the blanks with the correct form of the verb 'play' using only:

(*a*)	played	Simple past tense
(*b*)	was playing	Past continuous tense
(*c*)	had played	Past perfect tense
(*d*)	had been playing	Past perfect continuous tense

I .... tennis yesterday afternoon with my neighbour. We .... one set only when I became very tired. He .... a very fast game because, as he told me, he .... regularly every afternoon for the last six months. I .... after a gap of six months so naturally I could not keep up with him.

Exercise 4 Select the correct form of the verb given in brackets in each of the following sentences:

(*a*) He (went/has gone) to Bombay yesterday.
(*b*) I (am/have been) waiting for two hours.

(*c*) They will serve you lunch if you (attend/will attend).
(*d*) They had left when he (arrived/had arrived).
(*e*) The bus (left/has left) an hour ago.
(*f*) Had I known you were coming I (would have waited/would wait) for you.
(*g*) I (did not write/have not written) the essay yet.
(*h*) She (lived/has lived) in Jaipur since 1947.
(*i*) I (am not hearing/have not heard) from her for a year.
(*j*) A new TV serial (has been started/was started) last Monday.

UNIT 4 ACTIVE AND PASSIVE VOICE

Look at the following sentences:

1 Ram kicks the ball.
2 The ball is kicked by Ram.

In the first sentence the subject 'Ram' is the doer of the action. The object 'ball' is being acted upon. This kind of sentence is said to be in the *active voice*.

In the second sentence the subject of the sentence 'ball' is being acted upon. It is passive in nature and receives an action. Such a sentence is said to be in the *passive voice*.

Both sentences convey the same information but there is a shift in focus. This in turn means a shift in emphasis. Now study the following sentences:

1 The minister has postponed the meeting.
2 The meeting has been postponed.

The first sentence is in the active voice. Here the doer of the action, i.e. the 'minister' is made prominent or is in focus.

The second sentence is in the passive voice. Here the emphasis is on what has been done about the meeting, i.e. postponement. The action becomes so prominent that the doer of the action is not even mentioned.

Some ideas are expressed more neatiy in the passive voice when we omit the agent or doer. This is done when the doer of the action can be classified under one of the following categories·

1 unknown
2 vague
3 self-evident
4 of little importance

Given below are some sentences to illustrate the categories listed above. In the space provided indicate the category of the agent(s):

1 My suitcase was stolen. ....
2 The diagnosis has been confirmed. ....
3 Ashok was given an affectionate farewell when he retired. ....
4 Ticketless travellers will be fined. ....
5 Students falling short of attendance will be detained. ....
6 He was charged with murder. ....
7 The match was televised. ....

8 Good news is expected soon. ....

9 He was fined a hundred rupees. ....

10 He was elected leader. ....

Use of the active and the passive voice

In certain situations the active voice is used more frequently than the passive voice. There are two reasons for this:

1 Some sentences cannot be changed from active to passive.
2 The passive seems unnatural and forced.

Now look at the sentences given below:

1 I saw a boy who was stealing mangoes. (active)
2 A boy who was stealing mangoes was seen by me. (passive)
3 Honey tastes sweet. (active)

In sentence 2 the passive construction is awkward and so the active form is preferred, while sentence 3 cannot be changed into the passive.

Rules for change of voice

The passive of an active tense is formed by putting the verb *to be* in the same tense as the active verb and adding the past participle of the active verb. The position of the subject and object is interchanged.

1 We *keep* our jewellery in the bank. (active)
2 Our jewellery *is kept* in the bank. (passive)

It should be noted that transformation from active voice to passive voice is possible only if the verb in the active voice is used transitively.

Transitive and intransitive use of verbs

When a verb is used transitively the action denoted by it *passes over* from the subject to the object in the sentence, e.g.

1 Gavaskar hit the ball for a six. (active)
2 The ball was hit for a six by Gavaskar. (passive)

In the active voice the action denoted by 'hit' *passes over* from the doer (Gavaskar) to the object (ball). Thus, the verb 'hit' is used transitively and change of voice is possible.

Now look at the sentence given below:

Amrita *screamed* loudly.

Here the action denoted by the verb 'screamed' does not *pass over* to an object. Thus, the verb is used intransitively and change of voice is not possible.

In general when a verb is used intransitively it denotes an action which does not *pass over* to an object. It expresses a *state* or *being*. A few examples are given below:

1 He *seems* to be clever.
2 The child *sleeps*.
3 There *is* a defect in the machine.
4 The bus *stopped* suddenly.
5 The plane *landed* smoothly.
6 Vikram *goes* to school.

Every verb has three forms. Very often the second and third form of a verb can be formed by adding 'ed' to the first form of a verb, e.g.

talk, talked, talked

However, there are some verbs whose second and third forms cannot be formed by adding 'ed' to the first form, e.g.

sing, sang, sung
fly, flew, flown

Such verbs are called irregular verbs and we have simply to learn their various forms. A list of irregular verbs is given at the back of most good dictionaries, e.g. *Oxford Advanced Learner's Dictionary of Current English.*

At this stage it would be useful to go through a table of active tenses and their passive equivalents. The active and passive form of the verb 'sing' is given below as an illustration:

Tense/Verb form	*Active voice*	*Passive voice*
Simple present	sing/sings	is sung
Present continuous	is singing	is being sung
Simple past	sang	was sung
Past continuous	was singing	was being sung
Present perfect	have/has sung	has been sung
Past perfect	had sung	had been sung
Future	will sing	will be sung
Conditional	would sing	would be sung
Present infinitive	to sing	to be sung
Perfect infinitive	to have sung	to have been sung
Present participle/gerund	singing	being sung
Perfect participle	having sung	having been sung

Use of prepositions in the passive voice

It should be noted that when the agent or doer is mentioned in the passive voice it is normally preceded by the preposition 'by', e.g.

Raman's father donated this shield to the college. (active)
This shield was donated to the college by Raman's father. (passive)

Conversion of interrogative sentences into the passive voice also requires the use of the preposition 'by':

Who wrote it? (active)
1 Who was it written by? (passive)
Or
2 By whom was it written? (passive)

The first alternative is preferred in speech.

Similarly, two constructions in the passive voice are possible for the following sentence:

What caused this defect? (active)
1 What was this defect caused by? (passive)
Or
2 By what was this defect caused? (passive)

Here too the first alternative seems more natural in speech.

Use of 'with' in passive voice

Sometimes there are sentences in which the preposition 'with' is used instead of 'by' in the passive voice:

1 Exhaust gases polluted the air. (active)
The air was polluted with exhaust gases. (passive)

2 Dew wet the grass. (active)
The grass was wet with dew. (passive)

3 Smoke filled the auditorium. (active)
The auditorium was filled with smoke. (passive)

4 Paint covered the keyhole. (active)
The keyhole was covered with paint. (passive)

It may be noted that in the sentences given above 'exhaust gases', 'dew', 'smoke' and 'paint' are materials, not agents.

If there is a verb + preposition + object combination, the preposition retains its place after the verb in the passive voice:

1 We must *write to* Ayub. (active)
Ayub must be *written to*. (passive)

2 You can *depend on* him. (active)
He can be *depended on*. (passive)

3 We can *dispense with* your services. (active)
Your services can be *dispensed with*. (passive)

4 Thieves *broke into* the house. (active)
The house was *broken into*. (passive)

Verb + preposition/adverb structures are dealt with in a similar manner:

1 They *sold off* the old furniture. (active)
The old furniture was *sold off*. (passive)

2 He *blew out* the candle. (active)
The candle was *blown out*. (passive)

3 She *looked after* the children well. (active)
The children were well *looked after*. (passive)

Passive voice in sentences with two objects

When there are two objects in a sentence, either object may become the subject of the verb in the passive tense, but it is usual for the indirect object, which usually denotes a person, to be made the subject of the passive sentence:

1 I gave the *child* a toy. (active)
The *child* was given a toy. (passive)

2 They offered *me* a job. (active)
I was offered a job. (passive)

3 They gave *him* a watch. (active)
He was given a watch. (passive)

Change of voice: examples and exercises

Simple present

Study the following sentences:

1 Most children like sweets. (active)
Sweets are liked by most children. (passive)

2 He suffers from vanity. (active)
(Change of voice not possible)

3 Do the employees like him? (active)
Is he liked by the employees? (passive)

4 Does he maintain discipline in the school? (active)
Is discipline maintained in the school? (passive)

5 When does he do his work? (active)
When is his work done? (passive)

Exercise Change the voice in the following sentences from active to passive mentioning the agent only, if necessary:

1 He sends money for his children every month.

....

2 They inspect the factory every week.

....

3 The security man checks every visitor at the gate.

....

4 Droughts upset the economy of the country.

....

5 We use room coolers to lower the temperature.

....

6 Do you sell medicines?

....

7 Why do they ignore the poor people?

....

8 Doesn't religion give her relief?

....

9 Where can I find honest men?

....

10 We cannot forget our childhood.

....

Simple past

Study the following sentences:

1 They held the Annual Day function at Mavlankar Hall. (active)
The Annual Day function was held at Mavlankar Hall. (passive)

2 Did he reject the sample? (active)
Was the sample rejected? (passive)

3 How did you catch the thief? (active)
How was the thief caught? (passive)

4 They completed the bridge in ten months. (active)
The bridge was completed in ten months. (passive)

5 Our cricket team won most of the matches. (active)
Most of the matches were won by our cricket team. (passive)

6 He posted the letter yesterday. (active)
The letter was posted yesterday. (passive)

Exercise Change the voice in the following sentences from active to passive mentioning the agent only, if necessary:

1 Someone left this bag here yesterday.

....

2 They wasted a lot of time waiting for the bus.

....

3 The postman delivered the letter today.

....

4 He gave a prize to the winner.

....

5 How did you get this confidential information?

....

6 Did the government allow these items to be imported?

....

7 Who issued the order?

....

8 People criticized the actor for his poor performance.

....

9 He injured his arm in an accident.

....

10 When did you send the letter?

....

Simple future

Study the following sentences:

1 The government will set up a cement plant. (active)
A cement plant will be set up by the government. (passive)

2 Will you finish your work in time? (active)
Will your work be finished in time? (passive)

3 We shall follow your instructions. (active)
Your instructions shall be followed. (passive)

Exercise Change the voice in the following sentences from active to passive mentioning the agent only, if necessary:

1 They will serve coffee and tea.

....

2 Will they declare Friday a holiday?

....

3 It will create problems.

....

4 How will you arrange the chairs?

....

5 The architect will submit a plan of the house.

....

6 When will they hold the next meeting?

....

7 We shall shoulder the responsibility.

....

8 They will consi der it a weakness on our part.

....

9 They will not spare us.

....

10 The bad weather will not stop us.

....

Present continuous

Study the following sentences:

1 They are demolishing unauthorized buildings. (active)
Unauthorized buildings are being demolished. (passive)

2 Are they criticizing you? (active)
Are you being criticized? (passive)

3 Who is performing the operation? (active)
By whom is the operation being performed? (passive)

Exercise Change the voice in the following sentences from active to passive mentioning the agent only, if necessary:

1 He is polishing the car.

....

2 They are doing good work.

....

3 They are clearing the roads of snow.

....

4 He is making a lot of money.

....

5 Are they avoiding me?

....

6 He is spraying the plants with insecticide.

....

7 The police are digging up the grave.

....

8 Are they observing the rules?

....

Past continuous

Study the following sentences:

1 They were doing good work. (active)
Good work was being done. (passive)

2 He was frying an egg. (active)
An egg was being fried. (passive)

3 Where were they playing the football match? (active)
Where was the football match being played? (passive)

Exercise Change the voice in the following sentences from active to passive mentioning the agent only, if necessary:

1 The secretary was typing the letter.

....

2 We were cheering our team.

....

3 The monkeys were eating bananas.

....

4 The officer was not maintaining discipline.

....

5 The artists were demanding higher wages.

....

6 The police was arresting drunken drivers.

....

7 Wasn't he driving the truck rashly?

....

8 Weren't you scolding the child unnecessarily?

....

Present perfect

Study the following sentences:

1 He has completed his assignment. (active)
His assignment has been completed. (passive)

2 The government has appointed many doctors recently. (active)
Many doctors have been appointed recently. (passive)

3 Have you solved the problem? (active)
Has the problem been solved? (passive)

Exercise Change the voice in the following sentences from active to passive mentioning the agent only, if necessary:

1 His wife has taught him household work.

....

2 His behaviour has shocked his parents.

....

3 Finance companies have cheated many investors.

....

4 The magistrate has warned him.

....

5 Has your brother won the race?

....

6 Who has broken this window-pane?

....

7 Have you given the details?

....

8 Have you found your passport?

....

9 Has he picked your pocket?

....

10 Have you given him permission?

....

Past perfect

Study the following sentences:

1 He had completed six years of service before his death. (active)
Six years of service had been completed by him before his death. (passive)

2 He had advised them not to indulge in violence. (active)
They had been advised not to indulge in violence. (passive)

3 Had you warned him not to drive? (active)
Had he been warned not to drive? (passive)

Exercise Change the voice in the following sentences from active to passive mentioning the agent only, if necessary:

1 He had made his plans well in advance.

....

2 Somebody had struck him on the head with a blunt weapon.

....

3 The dacoits had tortured him to death.

....

4 They had taken precautions to prevent his escape.

....

5 He had displeased his superiors.

....

Future perfect

Study the following sentences:

1 We will have crossed the border by tomorrow. (active)
The border will have been crossed by tomorrow. (passive)

2 They will have declared the results by the time you reach there. (active)
The results will have been declared by the time you reach there. (passive)

3 Will they have closed the shops before we get there? (active)
Will the shops have been closed before we get there? (passive)

Exercise Change the voice in the following sentences from active to passive mentioning the agent only, if necessary:

1 This batsman will have completed six thousand runs by the end of the season.

....

2 By the year AD 2000 we will have made a lot of progress in computerization.

....

Imperative sentences

Given below are some examples illustrating change of voice for imperative sentences:

1 Open the windows. (active)
Let the windows be opened. (passive)

2 Reveal the secret. (active)
Let the secret be revealed. (passive)

3 Sell this old house. (active)
Let this old house be sold. (passive)

Sentences beginning with 'Let'

When sentences begin with 'Let', they are changed into the passive voice as shown below:

1 Let him buy a radio. (active)
Let a radio be bought by him. (passive)

2 Let us forget the past. (active)
Let the past be forgotten. (passive)

Exercises Change the voice in the following sentences from active to passive mentioning the agent only, if necessary:

1 Do not trouble your parents.

....

2 Bring some vegetables from the market.

....

3 Do not give up hope.

....

4 Let him try this question.

....

5 Give him these medicines every day.

....

6 Let us send him a telegram.

....

7 Bring the food.

....

8 Send him to prison.

....

9 Release the prisoner.

....

Change of voice in sentences with auxiliary verbs

Study the sentences given below containing the following auxiliary verbs:

can, could, may, might, should, would, must, ought

1 *Can* we forget the past? (active)
Can the past be forgotten? (passive)

2 You *could* have sent a telegram. (active)
A telegram *could* have been sent. (passive)

3 They *may* not accept the proposal. (active)
The proposal *may* not be accepted. (passive)

4 Someone *might* have poisoned the food. (active)
The food *might* have been poisoned. (passive)

5 They *should* release the prisoners. (active)
The prisoners *should* be released. (passive)

6 They *would* prefer the new scheme. (active)
The new scheme *would* be preferred. (passive)

7 You *must* vacate the house by September. (active)
The house *must* be vacated by September. (passive)

8 You *ought* to inform the police immediately. (active)
The police *ought* to be informed immediately. (passive)

Change the following sentences from active to passive mentioning the agent only, if necessary:

1 They should dismiss inefficient workers.

....

2 The government will hike petrol prices every year.

....

3 You can write an article on this subject.

....

4 He must mention this in the report.

....

5 I can fix an appointment.

....

6 We could use this story for our television serial.

....

7 The authorities might not like this move.

....

8 Floods may destroy the crops this year.

....

9 They ought to punish corrupt officials.

....

UNIT 5 MODALS AND THEIR MEANINGS

Study the sentences given below:

1 I *could* have complained about it.
2 I *could* run very fast when I was young.
3 *Could* I use your pen for a while?

The helping verb 'could' imparts different meanings to these sentences. Thus, it expresses 'possibility', 'ability' and 'polite request' in the first, second and third sentences, respectively.

Helping verbs that express a wide variety of meanings are called *modals*. A list of modals is given below:

can, could, shall, should, will, would, may, might, must, ought

'Can' expresses ability or capacity, permission, request and possibility.

I can speak English fluently. (ability)
You can leave the office an hour earlier today. (permission)
It can happen to anybody. (possibility)
He can study for six hours at a stretch. (capacity)

'Shall' expresses willingness or intention, suggestion and insistence.

Shall we drop the idea? (suggestion)
I shall do my best. (willingness/intention)
I shall not give up my seat. (insistence)

'Should' expresses obligation, advice, necessity and expectation.

You should bring your textbook to class. (obligation)
We should take all aspects into consideration. (advice)
You should attend your classes regularly. (necessity)
A clever boy like you should not find this difficult (expectation)

'Will' expresses willingness or intention, prediction and insistence in questions.

You will fail in the examination. (prediction)
Do you think he will accept our offer? (willingness/intention)
He will check the lock thrice, even though there is nothing worth stealing. (insistence)
Will you close the door, please? (request)

'Would' expresses willingness, habitual action in the past, polite request, probability, wishes and desire.

Would they be at home now? (probability)
He would welcome this opportunity. (willingness)
Whenever he was nervous he would chew his nails. (habitual action)
Would you close the door, please? (polite request)
I would like to have coffee. (desire)

'May' expresses permission, possibility, wishes, purpose and concession.

She may or may not come. (possibility)
May I see this play? (permission)
Since you are not feeling well you may leave the office an hour earlier today. (concession)
May God bless you! (wish)
He should inform us of his new address so that we may contact him when the need arises. (purpose)

'Might' expresses permission, possibility, concession and reproach.

He wrote to ask if he might extend his leave by a few days. (permission)
Disappointment in love might have led to his suicide. (possibility)
He might be dull but he is hard-working. (concession)
You might have told me before to enable me to make alternative arrangements. (reproach)

'Must' expresses necessity, prohibition, compulsion, obligation, deduction, certainty and prohibition.

You must practise for six hours every day to become a champion. (necessity)
Children must obey their parents. (obligation)
You must not drive unless you hold a licence. (prohibition)
It must have happened like this. (deduction)
You must finish your homework before going out to play. (compulsion)
Parents must take care of the needs of their children. (obligation)
He must have been selected. (certainty)

'Ought to' is similar in meaning to 'should' but is, as a rule, more *emphatic*. This is illustrated in the pairs of sentences given below:

1 The building should have been completed long ago.
The building ought to have been completed long ago.

2 You should bring your textbook to class.
You ought to bring your textbook to class.

3 You should not offend your employer.
You ought not to offend your employer.

Exercise 1 Choose the correct alternatives given in brackets in the following passage:

Doctors (should/can/will) remember to treat their patients with kindness. They (must/would) explain how medicines are to be taken. While in hospital patients (ought to/can) cooperate with the nurses. Patients (may/could/would) be encouraged to be frank with their doctors. However, at times doctors (would/might) not reveal their diagnosis to the patients.

Exercise 2 In the sentences given below fill in the blanks with the correct alternative provided in brackets:

(*a*) A good teacher .... ignore any pupil in her class. (should not/might not)

(*b*) The principal insists that teachers .... be late for class. (would not/must not)

(*c*) .... students take their practicals seriously? (should not/may not)

(*d*) Students .... respect their teachers. (can/should)

(*e*) Students .... be allowed to talk during the examinations. (should not/would not)

Exercise 3 Fill in 'can', 'cannot,' 'could' or 'could not' in the blanks in the sentences given below:

(*a*) I .... meet him now; he will have to wait.

(*b*) I told him that he .... complain if he wanted to.

(*c*) I will buy a house as soon as I .... save enough money.

(*d*) Without your help I .... have got such good marks.

(*e*) It .... be 7 o'clock already! My children will miss the schoolbus.

Exercise 4 Fill in 'will', 'must', 'would' or 'could' in the blanks in the sentences given below:

(*a*) I hope it is not necessary but he .... demand your resignation.

(*b*) If you had not come to my rescue, I .... have had to plead for mercy.

(*c*) Savitri's husband has been posted abroad; now she .... have to manage on her own.

(*d*) You .... shout into his ear; he is quite hard of hearing.

(*e*) Arshad was a very naughty child; his mother .... give in to every wish of his.

Exercise 5 Fill in 'must' or 'can't' in the blanks in the sentences given below:

(*a*) He isn't serious, is he? He .... be joking!

(*b*) It .... be Kapil, he plays better shots.

(*c*) He is not very young; he .... be in his late thirties.

(*d*) Of course it is true! It .... be otherwise.

(*e*) Did you see that cycle go by? It .... have been travelling at more than 50 kmph!

Exercise 6 Fill in 'may' or 'can' in the blanks in the sentences given below:

(*a*) .... you tell me the time, please?

(*b*) Who .... be outside?

(*c*) You are refused permission; you .... not go out today.

(*d*) Please do not come tomorrow; we .... not be at home.

(*e*) He says he .... run a mile in less than four minutes.

(*f*) He .... look like a saint but is a rogue in reality.

(*g*) No one .... avoid death.

(*h*) He .... listen to my advice but he seldom acts upon it.

(*i*) .... you put up the list of candidates by tomorrow?

(*j*) Many parents believe that their children .... do no wrong.

UNIT 6 ARTICLES

Read the following paragraphs carefully paying special attention to the italicized words:

Australia is *a* land of contrasts. It is geologically one of *the* oldest of land masses, yet it ranks as one of *the* youngest of nations. It is half *a* world away from Europe, but its people are largely of European descent and they follow *a* Western lifestyle. One of *the* most sparsely populated of nations, it is also one of *the* most highly urbanized with 85 per cent of its people living in cities.

Australia is *a* land of great distances, covering *an* area of 7,682,303 sq km, almost twice *the* combined area of India and Pakistan. *The* flattest of all continents, Australia has *an* average elevation of less than 300 m, compared with *the* world's mean of 700 m. *The* highest point in Australia, Mount Kosciusko, has *an* elevation of only 2228 m.

Points for discussion

(*a*) Can you guess when we use 'a'/'an'?
(*b*) Can you say when we use 'a' and when 'an'?
(*c*) Can you specify the important uses of 'the'?

Explanation

1 'A'/'an', and 'the' are articles. 'A'/'an' are *indefinite articles* and 'the' is a *definite article.*

2 Articles in English are not merely ornaments used to decorate the language. They are meaningful. Compare the following sentences:

(*a*) I have a black and white dog.
(*b*) I have a black and a white dog.

The indefinite article The indefinite article is used before a word denoting a non-proper singular noun when it is mentioned for the first time but only if the noun is a countable noun. Things we cannot count take no indefinite article and usually no plural.

The indefinite article can also be placed before 'Mr/Mrs/Miss/Ms' followed by the surname, e.g. 'A Mr Smith' meaning 'A man called Smith' and implies that he is a stranger to the speaker.

'An' is used with words whose pronunciation begins with a vowel sound and 'a' is used with words whose pronunciation begins with a consonant sound. What matters is the initial sound and not the initial letter of the alphabet, e.g. *a* hair, *an* heir, an hour, an honourable man, a university, a union, a European, an uncle, an MP.

The definite article 'The' is used before nouns to represent a class of objects and also to denote a definite person or a thing. The noun may become definite when (*a*) it is mentioned for the second time, (*b*) a clause/phrase is added to define it, and (*c*) it is the only one of its kind and conveys the sense, 'you know which one I mean'.

Hence, 'the' is used before the names of seas, rivers, chains of mountains, groups of islands (but *not* before a single mountain or single island), sacred/well-known books, buildings, names of ships, newspapers, nations, communities, descriptive geographical names, and in such phrases as 'the better of the two', etc.

Exercise 1 Fill in the blanks with 'the', 'a' or 'an':

.... girl in .... blue sari is .... good friend of mine. I still remember .... time I first met her. She was reading .... book in .... university library. .... book had .... unusual title. .... couple of my friends were with me in .... library. I soon found out that she was .... history student like me. We both shared .... interest in hunting out .... most uncommon books from .... shelves.

Exercise 2 Fill in the blanks the indefinite article 'a' or 'an', where necessary:

My mother is .... good cook. .... accomplished cook can make .... cake in .... hour. I spend .... enormous amount of time just collecting .... ingredients.

Exercise 3 Fill in the blanks with the definite article 'the', where necessary:

.... winter season is .... best season in .... Delhi. .... sky is blue and it is sunny most of .... time. I spend a lot of time in .... garden.

.... weather is always .... best in .... October..................... garden is .... place where I like to spend all .... day.

.... winter is .... best time to enjoy growing .... flowers. .... best flower is .... rose.

Exercise 4 Unnecessary use of articles as illustrated below must be avoided. Rewrite the following sentences after making corrections:

(*a*) I advise you to keep him at *an* arm's length.

....

(*b*) The principal asked us to take *an* action on it.

....

(*c*) He likes *an* egg but I like *a* fish.

....

(*d*) This is not *a* child's play.

....

(*e*) Lalita has finally obtained *an* employment with a company in Bombay.

....

(*f*) The publicity campaign is *an* eyewash.

....

(*g*) What *a* fun we had!

....

(*h*) *An* information has been received that the wedding has been cancelled.

....

(*i*) These days one finds it difficult to make both *the* ends meet.

....

(*j*) No news is *a* good news.

....

UNIT 7 PREPOSITIONS

Underline the prepositions in the following passages:

On Christmas Day, in the year 1642, Isaac Newton was born at the small village of Woolsthorpe, in England. Little did his mother think when she saw her new-born babe that he would one day discover and understand many matters which had been a mystery ever since the creation of the world.

Isaac's father being dead, Mrs Newton was married again to a clergyman, and went to live in North Witham. Her son was left in the care of his good old grandmother. She was very kind to him and sent him to school. In his early years Isaac did not appear to be very intelligent but was chiefly remarkable for his skill in all mechanical occupations. He had a set of little tools and saws of various sizes which he had made himself. With the aid of these Isaac contrived to make many curious articles, at which he worked with so much skill that he seemed to have been born with a saw or chisel in hand.

(From 'Sir Isaac Newton' by Nathaniel Hawthorne)

Points for discussion

1 Discuss the use of 'to' in the following two sentences:

(*a*) Isaac contrived *to* make many curious articles.
(*b*) Isaac was sent *to* school.

2 What type of word(s) follow the prepositions?

3 List as many prepositions as you can. Compare your list with that of others in your group.

Explanation Prepositions occur before nouns, noun phrases or pronouns. They show the link between these and another word or element in the sentence. Some prepositions may also occur at the end of a sentence.

Prepositions may also be used as adverbs without a following noun or noun phrase or pronoun.

There are prepositions which consist of only one word but there are others which may consist of two or more words or a phrase.

Many verbs get strongly associated with certain prepositions in one of the following two ways:

1 with verb and prepositions keeping their basic meanings, e.g. 'He kept *looking out of* the window for hours together.'

2 as a compound having an idiomatic meaning, i.e. when we cannot guess the meaning from the two parts e.g. '*Look out* Peter, that step is not safe!'

Every good dictionary lists compounds made with prepositions or adverbial particles under the verb. *Oxford Dictionary of Current Idiomatic English* (Vol. 1) is particularly useful, as it is exclusively devoted to this area.

Exercise 1 Look at the pictures and complete the sentences given below:

(*a*) (*b*) (*c*)

(*a*) The dog jumped .... A .... B.

(*b*) The dog is jumping .... A .... B.

(*c*) You can see the arrow pass .... the ball.

Exercise 2 Here is a series of drawings showing a girl participating in an obstacle race. Study the illustrations and fill in the blanks in the sentences given below using the following prepositions:

over, across, under, on, onto, off, near, away from

(*a*) The girl is running .... the starting block.

(*b*) The girl is climbing .... the wall.

(*c*) The girl is jumping .... the ground.

(*d*) The girl is running .... the wall.

(*e*) The girl is swimming .... the pond.

(*f*) The girl is crawling .... the net.

(*g*) The girl is .... the finishing line.

(*h*) The girl is standing .... the victory stand.

Exercise 3 Look at pictures (*a*) to (*e*) and fill in the blanks in the following sentences using 'between', 'out of', 'into', 'in front of' and 'behind'

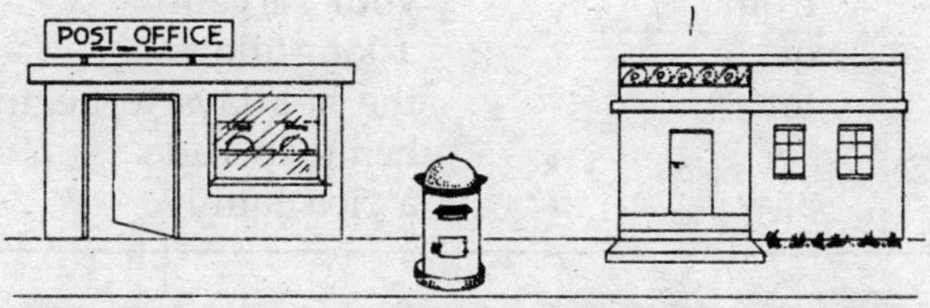

(*a*)

(*b*)

(*c*)

(*d*)

(*e*)

(*a*) The letter-box is .... the post office and Mr Wagle's house.

(*b*) Mr Wagle is going .... his house.

(*c*) Mr Wagle is coming .... the post office.

(*d*) Mr Wagle is .... the letter-box.

(*e*) Mr Wagle is .... his house.

Exercise 4 Fill in the blanks in the following sentences using suitable prepositions:

(*a*) What did you do .... your birthday?

(*b*) It is cool .... night.

(*c*) It will be ready .... Thursday.

(*d*) How do you go .... college?

(*e*) Keep .... the grass.

(*f*) You are .... time.

(*g*) The cup fell .... the shelf.

(*h*) He is .... serious trouble.

(*i*) I'll meet you .... the New Delhi Railway Station.

Exercise 5 First underline the verb in List A. Next choose the appropriate preposition from List B which goes with this verb and then complete the sentence choosing an appropriate phrase from List C:

Example: I *borrowed* some money *from* the bank.

	List A	*List B*	*List C*
(*a*)	When did you get rid	against	authority.
(*b*)	He has just recovered	to	voting.
(*c*)	The students can hardly wait	from	your servant?
(*d*)	She has to apologize	of	a long illness.
(*e*)	No student should abstain	for	the holidays to begin.
(*f*)	Deepak belongs		being so rude.
(*g*)	Young people rebel	at	a rich family.

Exercise 6 First underline the adjective in List A. Next choose the appropriate preposition from List B which goes with this adjective and then complete the sentence choosing an appropriate phrase from List C:

Example: The *first few* rows *of* the cinema hall were full.

	List A	*List B*	*List C*
(*a*)	It is different	of	school.
(*b*)	My beliefs are contrary	for	the company's products are good.
(*c*)	Few	to	what I had expected.
(*d*)	Vedant was late		the beliefs of others.
(*e*)	It was a bad decision		scented soap.
(*f*)	I am allergic	from	boycott the elections.
(*g*)	All the students absent	on	the list was my friend's name.
(*h*)	They were aware		all the rules of the game.
(*i*)	And last		that day were fined.

Exercise 7 Fill in the blanks in the following sentences using suitable prepositions:

(*a*) This woman has been charged .... the murder of her husband.

(*b*) The Prime Minister was accompanied .... his wife.

(*c*) We expect to come back .... a week.

(*d*) I bought this pen .... two rupees.

(*e*) At the age of 60, my mother still takes a bath .... cold water.

(*f*) I go to my college .... foot.

(*g*) She prefers coffee .... tea.

(*h*) Applicants for this post must have a good command .... English.

(*i*) The Seminar on Rural Development will commence .... Monday.

(*j*) The Minister showed concern .... the rising incidents of violence in the city.

(*k*) All those present were fascinated .... her new hair style.

(*l*) I shall get .... at the next bus-stop.

(*m*) My friend is very good .... writing radio plays.

(*n*) Please do inform me .... the details of the training course.

(*o*) John's marriage .... his first wife did not last long.

Exercise 8 Unnecessary use of prepositions as illustrated below *must be noted and avoided.* Rewrite the following sentences after making corrections:

(*a*) Just before elections you will find people discussing *about* politics.

....

(*b*) The candidates should contact *on* our office between 9 and 11 a.m.

....

(*c*) She has already approached *to* the bank for a loan.

....

(*d*) Priya was awarded *with* a prize for the best essay.

....

(*e*) The police decided to investigate *into* the crime.

....

(*f*) My house is opposite *to* the post office.

....

(*g*) Science has greatly benefited *to* mankind.

....

(*h*) She said she would not bow *down* to their demands.

....

(*i*) The principal is going to call *for* a meeting of the staff to discuss *about* this matter.

....

(*j*) Students should contact *with* the class teacher for further instructions.

....

(*k*) The course comprises *of* seven study areas.

....

(*l*) The car hit *against* the tree.

....

(*m*) In this poem the poet describes *about* his experience of nature.

....

(*n*) We were really surprised when he entered *into* the room.

....

(*o*) Can you find *out* some job for me?

....

(*p*) Please follow *after* me.

....

(*q*) We have already ordered *for* four cups of tea.

....

(*r*) Please list *down* the main points for discussion.

....

(*s*) He has come to meet *with* the principal.

....

(*t*) The students are making too much *of* noise.

....

(*u*) Why do you pick *up* a quarrel with everyone?

....

(*v*) We will not reach *at* the station in time.

....

(*w*) He resembles *with* his father.

....

(*x*) After retirement, he intends to settle *down* in Shimla.

....

(*y*) She stitched *up* that dress.

....

(*z*) He was wearing a torn *out* shirt.

....

UNIT 8 CONJUNCTIONS

Unless/until

Mr Sood told his students one day, 'It will not be possible for me to teach you unless you bring your books with you to the classroom.(1) If you do not have your books in front of you, you cannot follow the lesson.(2) Therefore, I shall not meet your class until each one of you brings along the book.'(3)

Explanation 1 Look at the above passage. It illustrates the use of 'unless' and 'until'. In the first sentence it can be seen that 'unless you bring your books with you to the classroom' is the condition. Similarly, in the third sentence, 'until each one of you brings along the book' is the condition. The first part of these two sentences is in the future tense. Such sentences are known as *future conditionals,* and 'unless' and 'until' do the job of joining or linking the two parts of such sentences. 'Unless' has the meaning of 'if not' as can be seen in sentence 2 in the passage above. 'Until' has the meaning of 'till such time' as can be seen in sentence 3 in the passage above.

Exercise 1 Fill in the blanks in the following sentences using 'unless' or 'until' according to the meanings given above:

(*a*) You must wait .... the traffic light changes to green.

(*b*) Do not get off a DTC bus .... it stops.

(*c*) You will not pass .... you work hard.

(*d*) Let us wait .... the rain stops.

(*e*) .... bad weather stops me, I go for a walk everyday.

Explanation 2 Note that all the three sentences in the given passage have future tense in the principal clause and present tense in the conditional clause. Thus, 'It *will not be*... unless you *bring* your books...' and 'I *shall not meet*... until each one of you *brings* along...'.

Exercise 2 In the following sentences, put the verbs in brackets into the correct tense:

(*a*) I (stay) here until he answers me.

....

(*b*) You will have to wait until he (come).

....

(c) I (not move) from here until he changes his mind.

....

(*d*) He will not go to the door unless he (hear) the bell.

....

(*e*) I (not write) to him unless he writes to me.

....

Exercise 3 Match clauses in List A with clauses in List B to make complete sentences:

List A	*List B*
(*a*) You will not catch the train	until he comes.
(*b*) Unless you are careful on the road	we will not have good crops.
(*c*) We shall wait here	until I call him.
(*d*) Unless it rains	you will not be safe.
(*e*) He will not come in	unless you go early.

UNIT 9 ADJECTIVES

Little/few

Last week, I went to the market. I had *a little* money with me and I wanted to buy *a few* articles. I was, however, surprised to discover that the price of almost everything had gone up. The result was that I could buy *few* things and when I had finished I had very *little* money left, not even enough to take the bus back home.

Explanation Observe the use of 'a few', 'a little', 'few' and 'little' in the above passage. These are usually used incorrectly and often confused. Here it can be seen that these words have the following meanings:

few/little = not many/hardly any/not much
a few = a small number/some but not many (as opposed to none)

a little = some but not much/a small quantity of/a certain though small amount (as opposed to none)

Note: While 'few' or 'little' have negative meanings, 'a few' and 'a little' have positive meanings.

Another thing to be noticed is that 'a few'/'few' is used before plural countable nouns (number), whereas 'a little'/'little' before uncountable nouns (quantity). Thus, we can say, 'a few books', 'a few boys', etc., but we cannot say 'a little books' or 'a little boys'. Similarly, we can say a 'a little milk', 'a little sugar', but we cannot say 'a few milk' or 'a few sugar'.

Exercise 1 Fill in the blanks in the following sentences using the correct alternative given in brackets:

(*a*) There is .... milk left in the bottle. (few/little)
(*b*) .... towns have such splendid market places as Delhi. (Few/Little)
(*c*) We had .... time for amusement. (few/little)
(*d*) There are .... things we have to talk about. (a little/a few)
(*e*) I think you would like to have .... rest. (a little/a few)
(*f*) There is .... hope of his recovery because the doctors think that his disease is incurable. (a little/little)
(*g*) He has not read much literature. He has .... appreciation of good poetry. (little/a little)
(*h*) .... people live to be a hundred. (A few/Few)
(*i*) .... words should be added to this paragrah. (A few/Few)
(*j*) .... care would have saved the situation. (Little/A little)

Exercise 2 Rewrite the sentences given below substituting the italicized words with 'little'/'a little'/'few'/'a few':

(*a*) We prepared a lot of food for the party, but *hardly any* of it was eaten.
....

(*b*) In modern politics, there are *not many* people who can be trusted.
....

(*c*) I have *practically no* reason to be angry with her.
....

(*d*) There are *some* points to be discussed before we finalize our agreement.
....

(*e*) Will you please give me *a small amount of* sugar?
....

(*f*) He is not a specialist, but he knows *something* about medicine.
....

(*g*) There were *hardly any* people at the theatre last night.
....

(*h*) *Three or four* days in the village can be a refreshing change from city-life.

....

(*i*) A lot of people have tried to find a cure for cancer, but *almost none of* them has succeeded.

....

(*j*) *Hardly anything* could be seen on account of the dense fog.

....